THE BATTLE FOR NORWAY
1940–1942

DESPATCHES FROM THE FRONT
The Commanding Officers' Reports From the Field and At Sea.

THE BATTLE FOR NORWAY 1940–1942

Introduced and compiled by
Martin Mace and John Grehan
With additional research by
Sara Mitchell

Pen & Sword
MILITARY

First published in Great Britain in 2015 by
Pen & Sword Military
an imprint of
Pen & Sword Books Ltd
47 Church Street
Barnsley
South Yorkshire
S70 2AS

ISBN 978 1 78346 2 322

Printed and bound in England
By CPI Group (UK) Ltd, Croydon, CR0 4YY

Pen & Sword Books Ltd incorporates the Imprints of
Pen & Sword Aviation, Pen & Sword Family History,
Pen & Sword Maritime, Pen & Sword Military, Pen & Sword Discovery, Pen &
Sword Politics, Pen & Sword Atlas, Pen & Sword Archaeology, Wharncliffe Local
History, Wharncliffe True Crime, Wharncliffe Transport, Pen & Sword Select, Pen &
Sword Military Classics, Leo Cooper,
The Praetorian Press, Claymore Press, Remember When,
Seaforth Publishing and Frontline Publishing.

For a complete list of Pen & Sword titles please contact:
PEN & SWORD BOOKS LIMITED
47 Church Street, Barnsley, South Yorkshire, S70 2AS, England
E-mail: enquiries@pen-and-sword.co.uk

Website: www.pen-and-sword.co.uk

CONTENTS

INTRODUCTION

The Germans invaded Norway on 9 April 1940, pre-empting Allied plans to prevent Germany access to the iron ore mines at Gällivare in the north of the country. Consequently, by the time that Lieutenant General H.R.S. Massy was appointed Commander-in-Chief, North West Expeditionary Force on 19 April, German forces were already well established in Norway. However, as the Germans had not penetrated far into the north in great strength, there was still a chance of stopping them before they had achieved complete control of the country.

Trondheim was seen as the gateway to the north and had been seized by the Germans. Massy was instructed to take it. In his despatch submitted to the War Office, Massy declared that as a first step his intention was to stop the German advance from Oslo, before then planning a deliberate combined operation for the capture of Trondheim itself.

He informed the Chiefs of Staff that any possibility of landing further troops or of maintaining the troops that had already been landed depended entirely on achieving air superiority. With control of the air, Massy believed that his forces could indeed hold back the Germans. Without it he was certain that further operations would be impossible and that the British forces would be compelled to withdraw from southern and central Norway. He would, of course, be proven correct.

The first problem that Massy had to deal with was the precarious situation which Major-General Carton de Wiart faced at Namsos to the north of Trondheim. His combined Anglo-French force was already under heavy aerial and artillery bombardment and, according to de Wiart, could not hold out for much longer.

Attempts at landing Gloster Gladiator fighters on the frozen Lake Lesjaskog failed, as did a further effort at landing them at a shore-based aerodrome. This meant that the Allied troops had no protection from the *Luftwaffe*. The entire Norwegian operation was doomed to failure.

As the campaign in Norway was a brief affair Massy was able to provide a detailed account of the fighting and, what became the most crucial aspect of the operation, the withdrawal of the Allied forces. That this was achieved with any degree of success was due in no small measure to the arrival of aircraft carriers in theatre. "The Germans would not face our Fleet Air Arm fighters," Massy wrote, "which were handled with a boldness that was an inspiration to the troops who watched their manoeuvres from the ground."

Apart from the efforts of the Fleet Air Arm, the Royal Navy also engaged the *Kriegsmarine* on 10 April, the day following the German invasion, at Narvik, in the

Ofotfjord to the far north of Norway, within the Arctic Circle. A report on the battles there on the 10 and then on 13 April, are the subject of the second despatch in this volume.

German naval forces were spotted in Ofotfjord by the commander of the Royal Navy's 2nd Destroyer Flotilla, Captain Bernard Warburton-Lee. "Norwegians report Germans holding Narvik in force also 6 destroyers and 1 submarine are there and channel is possibly mined." Warburton-Lee informed the Admiralty, and in true Nelsonian style, concluded his brief signal with the simple sentence, "Intend attacking at dawn, high water". No permission to attack was asked or further instructions were sought and at dawn he launched his attack.

Warburton-Lee did not survive the battle and his award of the Victoria Cross was the first to be gazetted in the Second World War. The despatch on the First Battle of Narvik was compiled by the senior surviving officer, Commander H.F. Layman, and Lieutenant-Commander R.E. Courage.

The second battle at Narvik, fought on 13 April 1940, is described by Vice-Admiral W.J. Whitworth. This was an entirely different affair with a much stronger force being deployed, including the battleship HMS *Warspite* and the aircraft carrier HMS *Furious*. In his report Whitworth claimed that all eight German destroyers and the submarine present at Narvik had either been sunk or scuttled, though at the time Whitworth did not know that there was a second submarine in the port which survived the engagement.

In his despatch Whitworth made the following observation: "I am convinced that Narvik can be taken by direct assault now without fear of meeting serious opposition on landing." As a result of this information it was decided to quickly attempt to land troops and seize Narvik before the Germans could reinforce their units in that area.

A plan to capture Narvik had already been put in motion but following the receipt of Whitworth's report, it was decided to move against Narvik as soon as possible. Consequently, William Henry Dudley Boyle, Admiral of the Fleet the Earl of Cork and Orrery, who was to lead the expedition, was instructed to attack Narvik without delay.

The small German garrison in Narvik was supplemented by the sailors from the ships that had been destroyed, bringing the total force up to around 5,000 men. French, Norwegian and Polish troops were sent to strengthen the British contingent until there were in excess of 24,000 men deployed.

Despite their numerical disadvantage the Germans held out until the second week of May. The sudden German attack upon France and the Low Countries on 10 May changed the strategic situation completely and attention was diverted away from Norway to the Battle of France.

Events moved very rapidly over the course of the next few days and as the British Expeditionary Force in Belgium retreated towards the Channel ports, the following signal was sent to Admiral Boyle: "His Majesty's Government has decided your forces are to evacuate Northern Norway at earliest moment. Reason for this is that the troops, ships, guns and certain equipment are urgently required for defence of United Kingdom. We understand from military point of view, evacuation operations will be facilitated if enemy forces are largely destroyed or captured. Moreover, destruction of railways and Narvik port facilities make its capture highly desirable. Nevertheless, speed of evacuations once begun should be of primary consideration in order to limit duration maximum naval efforts."

With the troops in direct contact with the enemy and subject to repeated air attacks, the evacuation was not going to be straightforward. Nevertheless, over the course of five nights the evacuation was accomplished successfully.

Included within Admiral Boyle's despatch are reports from Major-General P.J. Mackesy, who commanded the land forces up to 13 May when he was superseded by Lieutenant-General C.J.E. Auchinleck. The latter's report also forms part of this despatch.

The withdrawal of the troops from Norway in 1940 did not stop naval operations continuing in that theatre and on 30 July 1941 an attack was delivered by aircraft of the Fleet Air Arm against German and Finish merchant ships in the ports of Kirkenes and Petsamo. The raid was a disaster. It was undertaken in broad daylight from the carriers HMS *Victorious* and HMS *Furious* and resulted in sixteen aircraft being lost, though one cargo ship and a small steamer were sunk.

As Admiral Sir John C. Tovey wrote in his despatch, "Attacks by low performance aircraft in broad daylight where fighter opposition is present can only hope to achieve results commensurate with their losses if complete surprise is obtained". Unfortunately the crew of a German Heinkel He 111 bomber spotted the carriers just before the thirty-eight Albacores and Swordfish of the torpedo strike force took to the air. When the Fleet Air Arm aircraft reached their targets the Germans were waiting.

Tovey believed that the chances of catching the enemy unawares would have been greater if the raid had taken place at night. Whilst in those high northern regions it is light throughout the night during the summer, there was still a greater possibility of avoiding detection than in the early afternoon. "There is no doubt that some of the survivors felt that an attack on such poor targets against heavy opposition was not justified," Tovey wrote, "and their morale was rather shaken".

The next two despatches, also from Tovey, are quite different in that they describe successful attacks upon the Lofoten Islands and Vaagso Island. These were comparatively small-scale commando operations.

The main objectives of the attack on the Lofoten Islands (Operation *Claymore*) was defined by the commander of Special Service Brigade, Brigadier J.C. Haydon, as being: "To destroy the facilities for producing herring and cod oil in the Ports of Stamsund, Henningsvaer, Svolvaer and Brettesnes, all of which are situated in the Lofoten Islands; to arrest local supporters of the Quisling party; to capture any enemy personnel found in the ports, and to enlist recruits for the Free Norwegian Forces." At the same time any German ships found there, or Norwegian ships in German employ, were to be sunk.

Success was complete with the shore facilities being destroyed and ten ships sunk. Just one soldier was wounded.

Operation *Archery*, defined by Tovey as "a raid on military and economic objectives in the vicinity of Vaagso Island with the object of harassing the coastal defences of S.W. Norway and diverting the attention of the enemy Naval and Air Forces from Operation 'Anklet' [a second attack upon the Lofoten Islands]". Once again ten ships were sunk and considerable damage was done to the factories and stores at the main town and port of Måløy.

*

The objective of this book is to reproduce the despatches from Whitworth, Boyle, Auchinleck *et al*, as they first appeared to the general public some seventy years ago. They have not been modified, edited or interpreted in any way and are therefore the original and unique words of the commanding officers as they saw things at the time they were written.

The only change is the manner in which the footnotes are presented, in that they are shown at the end of each despatch rather than at the bottom of the relevant page as they appear in the original despatch. Any grammatical or spelling errors have been left uncorrected to retain the authenticity of the documents.

Martin Mace and John Grehan
Storrington, 2015

LIST OF ILLUSTRATIONS

from Sergeant A. James' Hudson with literally just seconds to go until disaster struck – a disaster in which the aircraft nearest the camera was shot down by the guns of HMS *Curacoa*. (Historic Military Press)

11   The crew of 224 Squadron's Hudson Mk.I N7264 pictured together at RAF Wick following their safe return from operations over Norway on 23 April 1940. The damage was caused by the guns of HMS *Curacoa*. (Historic Military Press)

12   British prisoners of war being processed by their captors in the Norwegian port of Drontheim, April 1940. (Bundesarchiv, Bild 183-L03926/CC-BY-SA)

13   A contemporary artist's depiction of the action during the First Battle of Narvik for which Captain Bernard Armitage Warburton Warburton-Lee was awarded the Victoria Cross. On 10 April 1940, in Ofotfjord, Warburton-Lee, of HMS *Hardy*, commanded the British 2nd Destroyer Flotilla in a surprise attack on German warships and merchant ships in a blinding snowstorm. This was successful, but was almost immediately followed by an engagement with more German destroyers during which Captain Warburton-Lee was mortally wounded by a shell. (Historic Military Press)

14   British commandos in action during the attack on the island of Vaagso, Operation *Archery*, on 27 December 1941. (Historic Military Press)

15   A Messerschmitt Bf 109 attempts to take off from the Norwegian airfield of Herdla during a raid by Bristol Blenheim Mk.IVs of 114 Squadron which were operating in support of the Combined Operations attack on Vaagso, 27 December 1941. Note how bombs can be seen exploding. (Historic Military Press)

16   A survivor of the Norwegian campaign – the remains of a 263 Squadron Gloster Gladiator, Mk.II N5628, which can be seen at the RAF Museum at Hendon. This aircraft was one of those flown off from HMS *Glorious* on 24 April 1940, landing at the airstrip on the frozen Lake Lesjaskogsvatnet. Damaged during the German air raids the following day, N5628 eventually sank through the melting ice. (Courtesy of Michael Matthews)

1

LIEUTENANT GENERAL H.R.S. MASSY'S DESPATCH ON OPERATIONS IN CENTRAL NORWAY 1940

WEDNESDAY, 29 MAY, 1946

OPERATIONS IN CENTRAL NORWAY, 1940.
PREFACE BY THE WAR OFFICE.

Of the two expeditions which the United Kingdom and France sent to Norway in April, 1940, one to Northern Norway and one to Central Norway, the following despatch covers the latter from the beginning of operations.

In Central Norway two main landings were made, one in the Namsos area by a force under the command of Major-General A. Carton de Wiart, V.C., C.B., C.M.G., D.S.O., and one in the Åndalsnes area by a force under the command, first of Brigadier H. de R. Morgan, D.S.O., and later of Major-General B.C.T. Paget, D.S.O., M.C. On 19th April, 1940, Lieutenant-General H.R.S. Massy, D.S.O., M.C., was instructed to assume the appointment of Commander-in-Chief of the forces operating in Central Norway. He exercised this command from his Headquarters in the United Kingdom as the course of events did not permit the opening of a Headquarters in Norway.

When the decision to withdraw from Central Norway was taken on 27th April, 1940, it was agreed to press on with operations against Narvik, and the force in Northern Norway comprising British, French and Polish troops succeeded in capturing the town of Narvik before it, in turn, had to be withdrawn at the beginning of June, 1940.

The following despatch was submitted to the Secretary of State for War on 13th May, 1940 by Lieutenant-General H.R.S. MASSY, D.S.O., M.C., Commander-in-Chief, North Western Expeditionary Force.

I have the honour to submit my report on the operations in Central Norway, up to and including 3rd May. This report is divided into four Parts as under:-

PART I. – General Summary of Events.
PART II. – Operations in the Namsos area.
PART III. – Operations in the Åndalsnes area.
PART IV. – Conclusions and lessons.

I am indebted for Part II of this report to Major-General Carton de Wiart and for Part III to Major-General B.C.T. Paget and Brigadier H. de R. Morgan, who have provided me with the necessary material for them.

PART I.
GENERAL SUMMARY OF EVENTS.

I. When the original plan for operations in Southern Norway was made, the landings at Åndalsnes and Namsos were intended as diversions to a main attack to be made on Trondheim. When the landings at Åndalsnes and Namsos were effected without loss, and our troops advanced inland from these bases, it was decided that Trondheim might be captured by a converging movement instead of by a hazardous direct attack from seaward.

It was hoped too that sufficient troops could be put into Åndalsnes to stiffen Norwegian resistance in the South, and thus put a limit to the German advance from Oslo.

It was against this background that I was instructed on 19th April to assume the appointment of Commander of the North-Western Expeditionary Force and to form my Headquarters with a view to taking command as soon as possible of the operations in progress North and South of Trondheim.

My instructions, as I understood them, were to capture Trondheim, and I decided that the first step towards this end must be to stop the German advance from Oslo, and then to plan a deliberate combined operation for the capture of Trondheim itself.

I record below a narrative of the operations which took place and the various decisions arrived at as the turn of events required. I have purposely kept this report as short as possible, fuller details on subjects which may require consideration will be forwarded separately to the War Office.

2. In accordance with my instructions I assumed direct control of operations on 22nd April. In view of the fact that my Headquarters were still in the process of forming and were not in a position to operate as such, orders were issued by my Staff in collaboration with the Staff of the War Office. This unusual and difficult position was made workable by the co-operation and assistance not only of the Military

Operations Directorate but also of the numerous War Office branches which were necessarily consulted and whose aid was invoked during the period of operations.

Briefly, the situation in Southern Norway when I assumed command was as follows:-

In the area South of Trondheim Brigadier H. de R. Morgan with the 148th Infantry Brigade (I/5 Leicesters and 8 Foresters) was in the Lillehammer area South of Dombås in touch with Norwegian troops. The ship carrying Brigadier Morgan's first-line transport had been sunk. He was therefore bereft of essential fighting equipment, including anti-tank guns. In the Namsos area, North of Trondheim Major-General Carton de Wiart had under his command Brigadier C.G. Phillips' 146th Infantry Brigade (4 Lincolns, I/4 K.O.Y.L.I., and Hallams) and one demi-brigade of Chasseurs Alpins commanded by General Audet. The 146th Infantry Brigade was in contact with German forces near Verdalen, 45 miles North-East of Trondheim. The Chasseurs Alpins were in the vicinity of Namsos.

Major-General B.C.T. Paget had been selected to command the British forces operating South of Trondheim, and on this day he was handed my instructions, a copy of which is attached to this report at Appendix "A." Accompanying him to assume control of the Base Area of Åndalsnes and to make a plan for its development as a base were Brigadier D. McA. Hogg, D.A. and Q.M.G. of Force Headquarters, and Brigadier D.J.R. Richards as Air Defence Commander to plan the air defence of the Base Area.

During this day news was received that the 146th Infantry Brigade had been attacked on the previous day, the 21st April, by enemy landed from a cruiser and destroyers, and that Steinkjer had been heavily bombed. The base at Namsos was now being regularly bombed and General Carton de Wiart reported that the maintenance of his force in this area was becoming difficult and that, unless some respite from the enemy bombing could be gained, it might well become impossible. Bombing of Åndalsnes was also taking place and considerable damage had been done. Arrangements were then made with the Royal Air Force to land Gladiators on a frozen lake at Lesjaskog, between Åndalsnes and Dombås, as soon as the necessary maintenance personnel could be landed. The support provided by the Royal Navy consisted of fighters from H.M.S. "Ark Royal" and "Glorious," which were to operate over the ports, and torpedo bombers, which were to attack the enemy aerodromes in the neighbourhood of Trondheim and his ships in that harbour. Anti-aircraft cruisers and sloops were also allotted to give protection to the Base Areas.

3. On the 23rd, General Paget and his staff with Brigadier Hogg and Brigadier Richards left for Norway. During this day news was received from General Carton de Wiart that Brigadier Phillips had succeeded in extricating the 146th Infantry Brigade which, supported by the French, was occupying a position covering Namsos and Bangsund.

On this day too British troops on the Southern Sector had withdrawn as the result of heavy enemy attacks to hold a line South of Tretten, and behind them an effort was being made to re-organise Norwegian troops in the sector. During the whole of this day and the next both Base Areas were continually bombed, as were forward troops and the communications between them and the Base.

4. On the evening of the 24th, the 263rd Fighter Squadron, R.A.F. (I8 Gladiators) was flown ashore on Lake Lesjaskog. It was however immediately spotted by the enemy who commenced bombing next morning and continued it throughout the day. It is understood that, in spite of valiant efforts by the pilots and ground staff, but few of them were able to take off, and were quite insufficient to hold off the innumerable enemy bombers who attacked the aerodrome continuously.

5. On the 25th April, I was directed by the Chiefs of Staff to submit an appreciation on the situation in Norway. As it appeared to me then, the possibility of landing further troops or of maintaining the troops then ashore depended entirely on our being able to obtain control of the situation in the air. In my appreciation I stated this fact and gave it as my opinion that should adequate air support be available I had no reason to suppose that we could not hold our existing positions against the Germans, and at a later date eject them from Trondheim. Without it I had little doubt that any further operations would become impossible and that we should be compelled to evacuate our forces from Southern and Central Norway. I further stated that should evacuation be decided upon it would have to be done at short notice and that all necessary plans for this operation must therefore be made without delay. I requested that the Inter-Service Planning Staffs should be directed to make the necessary preparations forthwith. I was not aware when this appreciation was written that the attempt to establish the Gladiators ashore had failed.

During this day, the I48th Infantry Brigade was withdrawn to Otta and it became evident that the I5th Infantry Brigade, which had sailed under General Paget's orders, part on 22nd and part on 24th April, would be required to hold Dombås and Opdal if the process of putting further troops ashore in the Åndalsnes area was to be contemplated. Instructions to this effect were sent to General Paget in amplification of his original instructions in Appendix "A". The situation at Namsos did not materially alter during this or the following day, though bombing of this port and Åndalsnes continued. Both towns had been completely destroyed, and as the nights were getting shorter, the amount of unloading which could be undertaken was becoming progressively less.

6. During 26th April the situation at Namsos did not materially alter. From reports received from the South however it became increasingly obvious that in the face of artillery and mortar fire and incessant bombing, to none of which the Allied troops could effectively reply, the German advance could not be stopped. General Paget stated it as his opinion that his troops could not endure for more than four days unless adequate air support was forthcoming. During the whole of this day the bombing of Åndalsnes and Namsos continued and the possibility of these ports being rendered inoperative as bases had to be faced. During the afternoon I became aware of the previous day's failure of the Gladiators to operate from a shorebased aerodrome, and it then became evident to me that the chances of our getting any air support which would enable us in any way to compete with the German air menace had practically

vanished. I was convinced that evacuation would therefore be necessary. I reported my views verbally to the C.I.G.S. who informed me that the Chiefs of Staff had that morning been considering the possibility of re-instituting a modified operation for the direct attack on Trondheim, and had come to the conclusion that it would take some ten days to mount. I understood from him that, in view of the situation, the Chiefs of Staff were not prepared to recommend this course to the Government as they doubted, as I did, whether the forces in Southern Norway could hold on long enough to enable the operation to be put into effect.

7. Accordingly next morning, 27th April, I wrote an appreciation of the situation which convinced me that evacuation was necessary and that there were two main ways of doing it. In the first case, as we had few stores and little heavy equipment ashore we might, by means of a rapid evacuation of personnel only, cut our losses to the lowest level. In the second, by continuing to send anti-aircraft guns and artillery, and possibly subsequently further infantry, we might be able to hold the position for some time longer. This however would undoubtedly involve the loss of large quantities of valuable material and certainly heavy casualties in personnel. The period could not be sufficient to allow of any direct attack on Trondheim being planned and mounted. In my opinion the correct solution was a rapid withdrawal with the object of reducing our losses to the lowest possible figure.

That evening I was sent for to report to the Military Co-ordinating Committee. My report was in terms similar to those I have stated above and the Committee agreed that the evacuation was to take place and approved instructions (App. "B") given to me for the purpose. To relieve the pressure on General Paget's force the Air Ministry were requested to attack with bombers the Germans in the Gudbrandsdal valley and their communications, but this was found impossible.

8. During the 28th, plans for the evacuation were concerted with Admiralty representatives and orders were issued to both General Carton de Wiart and General Paget as to how the evacuation was to be carried out. The evacuation of the French was commenced on the night of the 28th/29th and arrangements were made for the evacuation of the remaining troops from Namsos to be completed on the nights of the Ist/2nd and 2nd/3rd May. Plans for the evacuation of Åndalsnes were for the evacuation to be carried out on two nights, Ist/2nd, and 2nd/3rd May, but the plan was made sufficiently elastic so that if necessary the process of evacuation from this latter port could be put forward 24 hours. It had been planned when the force was evacuated from Namsos that a rearguard should fall back by land to Mosjoen retiring in the face of the enemy, and that in the meantime a party should be sent by sea to ensure holding the latter port against enemy troops landed by parachute from the air, and orders to this effect were issued. General Carton de Wiart opposed this plan on the grounds that owing to lack of petrol and transport and more important still, the fact that the road during the thaw was practically impassable, the operation would be likely to end in disaster.

Subsequent telegrams did not induce him to alter his view and even the passage by the land route of a small party of French Chasseurs was by him deemed impossible. My final wire on this subject was to the effect that if in the opinion of

General Audet the retirement of a small rearguard of French Chasseurs by the land route was impossible, this operation was not to take place. It was evident that, if French Chasseurs could not retire along this route, the Germans could not advance along it. In the event no withdrawal by land did take place, though this was an error as the Germans have since made full use of this route, and have advanced so rapidly along it that our troops in Mosjoen have not had time to get properly established and it is more than likely that we shall not be able to hold the place.

9. During the 29th the situation on the Namsos front did not alter. Forces operating to the southward were withdrawn to a position 3 miles south of Dombås which position General Paget proposed to hold until the night of the 30th/Ist to cover the evacuation. On this day owing to urgent representations from Åndalsnes it was decided to make the dates of evacuation from this port the nights of 30th/Ist and Ist/2nd and the necessary arrangements for shipping were made accordingly. Further requests that long range bombers should be directed against the enemy troops and his Lines of Communication were made to the Air Ministry who were, however, as far as I am aware, unable to comply with them. During the day however Blenheim fighters were despatched to the area and their presence resulted in the immediate disappearance of enemy bombers for the period during which the Blenheims were able to remain over the area.

I0. In the early hours of the 30th April a party of 340 personnel, mostly wounded, were embarked on H.M.S. Fleetwood from Åndalsnes and at I900 hours H.M.S. Janus embarked I00 men and two Bofors guns at Namsos and conveyed them during the night to Mosjoen, where they arrived on 2nd May having been delayed by dense fog. During the nights 30th/Ist and Ist/2nd evacuation was successfully carried out from Åndalsnes. On 1st May thick fog off Namsos prevented the ships entering the harbour. The whole evacuation of Namsos was however successfully carried out on the night of the 2nd/3rd, the last ship leaving at 0220 hours, and a total of 5,400 having been embarked during that night, an operation for which the greatest credit is due to the Naval forces employed.

II. During the whole of the 3rd the convoy was continually bombed on its passage across the North Sea. It has been reported to me that one German aeroplane continually shadowed it whilst relays of bombers came up, presumably directed by the shadowing aeroplane. That the losses were not heavier than they were is evidence of remarkable luck. The presence of some long range fighters during the day would have been invaluable, but none were available owing to question of range.

PART II.
OPERATIONS AT NAMSOS.

I2. On I4th April Major-General Carton de Wiart was informed by the War Office that it had been decided to land an allied expedition in Central Norway, and that the operation was to be carried out independently of the landings already begun in the Narvik area.

13. Major-General Carton de Wiart was given written instructions (Appendix "C") on 14th April appointing him in command of the Allied forces being despatched to Central Norway, and his role was defined as "to secure the Trondheim area." He was informed that the Royal Navy were making preliminary landings in the Namsos area with landing parties about 300 strong in all, in order to seize and hold points at which disembarkation of Allied forces might subsequently take place.

The written instructions suggested the initial landing of army formations should be in the Namsos area and that this should be carried out by 146th and 148th Infantry Brigades and Chasseurs Alpins, after the Royal Navy had cleared the Trondheim fjord of German vessels.

It must be mentioned here that at the time these instructions were issued 146th Infantry Brigade was at sea with orders to land in the Narvik area; that 148th Infantry Brigade (less one battalion) was diverted to Åndalsnes; that 147th Infantry Brigade never sailed from the United Kingdom.

14. On the evening of 15th April General Carton de Wiart, with a junior staff officer, arrived at Namsos in a flying boat to confer with the naval landing parties who had already established a footing there. The flying boat and the destroyer "Somali" lying in the Namsen Fiord were repeatedly attacked by German aircraft with bombs and machine-gun fire, and General Carton de Wiart's staff officer was wounded. Meanwhile 146th Infantry Brigade had been ordered, while at sea, to go to Namsos instead of Narvik, but it was evident that the landing of these troops direct from transports was not a feasible operation at Namsos, and that they would, have to be transferred to destroyers at Lillesjone and then taken to Namsos on two successive days.

15. On 16th April the first battalion arrived and were disposed to cover Namsos and Bangsund, the remainder of 146th Infantry Brigade getting ashore during the 17th April. By the 19th April, this brigade having moved Southward from Namsos, was disposed as follows:-

Advanced Brigade Headquarters at Steinkjer.
One battalion – about Steinkjer.
One battalion – in the area South of Steinkjer including Verdal and Stiklestad.
One battalion – in the area North of Steinkjer including Bangsund.

These dispositions gave General Carton de Wiart control of the roads and railways leading Northwards from Trondheim, and placed him in a favourable position to co-operate with any direct attack on Trondheim which might be developed from seaward.

16. During the night of 19th/20th April the 5th Demi-Brigade of Chasseurs Alpins arrived in Namsos under General Audet, but with the indifferent port facilities there it was impossible to clear the two small jetties during the hours of darkness. Consequently on the following morning the large quantity of supplies, munitions and stores lying at the jetties was spotted by enemy aircraft, and for two hours the quay, station and western half of Namsos town were heavily bombed. The station and most of the town were destroyed, and one of the two jetties was badly damaged.

The French Demi-Brigade was put into billets and bivouacs close round Namsos, and, while they were settling in, General Carton de Wiart visited the headquarters of 146th Infantry Brigade at Steinkjer and met there the commander of the local Norwegian forces. So far no British troops had been in contact with German land forces.

17. At about 0600 hours on 21st April an enemy detachment of some 400 men landed at Kirkenesvaag and began to advance on Sandvollan and Strömmen. Other German landings were carried out at Hylla and Tronestangen, and an attack was directed on Verdal. The enemy land forces were supported by warships operating in the Trondheim fiord. These German landings presented a serious threat to the flank and rear of 146th Infantry Brigade who were severely hampered by having no artillery and by their inability to move anywhere off the roads on account of the deep snow.

During the afternoon of 21st April enemy aircraft were also active; Steinkjer was bombed and reduced to a flaming mass of ruins, and the roads from Steinkjer to Verdal and Stiklestad were machine-gunned and bombed.

18. In view of these events and the inability of the British infantry to operate off the roads, General Carton de Wiart decided to withdraw 146th Infantry Brigade into a position north of Steinkjer where its flanks could not be threatened, and issued orders to that effect.

During the withdrawal a German destroyer was very active with its gun fire, and enemy mortar and light artillery fire was directed upon the British battalions. In addition 4 Lincolns were attacked about Steinkjer by German ski troops and had somewhat heavy casualties. By 24th April the Brigade was established in its new position north of Steinkjer, having carried out the withdrawal in very trying conditions.

19. On 23rd April General Carton de Wiart sent a signal to the War Office that evacuation from Namsos might be advisable, since the scale of enemy air attack was heavy and he had received no further information about the proposed landing of an Allied force at Trondheim.

In reply General Carton de Wiart was instructed by Headquarters North Western Expeditionary Force to keep his force in being and to remain on the defensive in the Namsos area.

20. For the first time on 25th April British aircraft appeared over Namsos. These belonged to the Fleet Air Arm, but three were forced to land owing to lack of petrol. Their intervention, though temporary, had a beneficial effect on the air situation, but since their effect could not be sustained, enemy air activity was again unhampered during the next few days.

On account of the deep snow, which prevented movement off the roads, it was not until 26th April that a reconnaissance party of the R.A.F. started to search for landing grounds in the Namsos area.

21. On the following day the advanced party of General Carton de Wiart's staff arrived. Until now he had made use of the services of Captains Fleming and Lindsay (of the Military Intelligence Directorate) and of one General Staff Officer who had reported for duty on 23rd April at Namsos.

In the same ship as the advanced party of the staff there arrived a Royal Marine

Howitzer battery, a field ambulance, a dock labour company, representatives of the base sub-area organisation, rifles and ammunition for the Norwegians, and many other natures of stores, but owing to the fact that the quay side was already piled high with French stores and that a French ship was still alongside the one usable jetty unloading transport and equipment, only the party of headquarter staff, a portion of the howitzer battery (but no ammunition) and some dock labour could be got ashore.

22. Such was the situation at Namsos when on 28th April General Carton de Wiart received the message that the evacuation of Namsos had been decided on in principle.

At a meeting with Admiral Vivian (Flag Officer commanding 20 Cruiser Squadron), General Audet and Brigadier Phillips, he decided to plan for evacuation on two successive nights. In the meantime it was possible to send away one French battalion on the night 28th/29th April in an empty ship.

It was decided that the French contingent should re-embark before the British, but that the French would leave some ski troops to operate with the British rearguard. The probable dates for evacuation were the nights of Ist/2nd and 2nd/3rd May.

On the night 28th/29th April a battery of Bofors guns was landed at Namsos. These guns were unfortunately without predictors.

23. On the following day General Carton de Wiart received the message instructing him to send a detachment to Mosjoen by sea and to post a rearguard at Grong which would delay the enemy for as long as possible and then withdraw Northwards overland to Mosjoen.

At first he appears to have been in some doubt as to whether the rearguard at Grong was intended to comprise his whole force, and he referred the matter to this Headquarters. The reply made it clear that the strength of the rearguard to remain at Grong was left entirely to his discretion. I have referred in Part I to the abandonment of this operation.

On the 30th April, a party of I00 French Chasseurs and a British detachment with two Bofors guns was sent by destroyer to Mosjoen. Throughout that day, enemy aircraft were again active and sank H.M.S. "Bittern" and two trawlers.

24. On Ist May all arrangements were made to evacuate the French contingent, and by 2II5 hours all were ready on the quayside. But no transports or destroyers arrived owing to thick fog in the Namsen Fiord, and the evacuation had to be postponed for 24 hours.

25. On 2nd May General Carton de Wiart was asked to carry out the evacuation in one night if possible, instead of two, as the Admiralty were anxious to complete the task with all speed.

After consultation with Admiral Vivian it was agreed that all troops could be got away on the night 2nd/3rd May but that no stores or equipment could be saved.

26. By 0I50 hours on 3rd May all troops except a small rear party were re-embarked and the convoy sailed from Namsos.

At 0220 hours the destroyer "Afridi" took off the rear party.

At 0430 hours the usual German air reconnaissance came over Namsos and sighted the convoy which was now well out to sea.

Between 0800 hours and I530 hours wave after wave of enemy bombers attacked

H.M. Ships and the transports. No transport ship was hit, but the French destroyer "Bison" and H.M.S. "Afridi" were sunk fighting to the end. The losses might well have been far heavier, for there were no air forces supporting the convoy.

COMMENTS.

27. In view of the instructions issued to him and the size of the force which according to those instructions was eventually to be placed at his disposal, General Carton de Wiart's action in pushing straight ahead towards Trondheim was justified. Had he been aware of the limited forces which were actually to be placed at his disposal and of the fact that the direct attack on Trondheim was not to take place, his advance would undoubtedly have been a more methodical one, and his position at Steinkjer would have been consolidated before a further advance would have been considered. The position of the I46th Infantry Brigade, with its head at Verdalen and its right flank open to attack from the Fiord by sea-borne troops, was, as events proved, a somewhat dangerous one.

The withdrawal of this Brigade when attacked was cleverly planned and executed and reflects great credit on Brigadier Phillips and the troops under his command.

28. I have already commented in Part I, paragraph 8, on the decision not to dispatch a force by road to delay the enemy in his advance on Mosjoen after the final evacuation took place. The importance of this operation was strongly stressed in several telegrams from these headquarters, its feasibility could only be left to the judgment of the man on the spot. In this case an error of judgment was made.

PART III.
OPERATIONS IN THE ÅNDALSNES AREA.

29. The area of operations was confined to the Gudbrandsdal valley between the base at Åndalsnes and Lake Mjösa, a distance of some I40 miles. Except in the area of Lesjaskog, and at its Southern end, where there are roads on either side of Lake Mjösa, the valley is seldom more than a mile wide and in places narrows to a few hundred yards; along the whole length of the road, river and railway intertwine. The valley is flanked with mountains and hills which are covered in snow at the high levels. The side roads and tracks leading into the valley are for the most part impassable at this time of the year, except to ski troops, of whom the enemy were reported to have a considerable number. Scattered along the valley throughout its length are wooden farm buildings and occasional villages or small towns such as Åndalsnes, Lesja, Dombås, Otta, Ringebu, Öyer and Lillehammer.

30. It would be difficult to imagine a Line of Communication more exposed to air attack, to which it was continually subjected during the hours of daylight by means of heavy bombing and machine gun fire: and there were no means of protecting it nor of repairing the damage done to the roads and railway: for this latter work reliance

had to be placed entirely on the Norwegians, who did their best with very limited resources. The key point of Dombås was completely destroyed by bombing and Otta almost completely so. Large craters on the road made motor transport movement increasingly difficult; it was singularly fortunate that the railway was not more seriously damaged.

31. The 148th Infantry Brigade commanded by Brigadier H. de R. Morgan and consisting initially of I/5 Leicesters, less two companies, 8 Sherwood Foresters and one light Anti-Aircraft Battery, a total of 1,000 all ranks, landed from His Majesty's ships in the Åndalsnes area on the evening of 18th April. A force of Marines had landed previously to make preliminary arrangements. Brigadier Morgan's instructions were to land in the Åndalsnes area, secure Dombås and then operate Northwards and take offensive action against the Germans in the Trondheim area. His instructions also stated that his force was an independent command under the War Office until receipt of further orders. As a preliminary to carrying out his rôle Brigadier Morgan despatched a company to Dombås where it arrived at 0400 hours, 19th April.

32. On 19th April, the British Military Attaché, Lieutenant-Colonel King Salter, represented that the Norwegian Army was in urgent need of assistance, and stated that unless this was forthcoming immediately, the Army would abandon all further resistance. He further stated to Brigadier Morgan that the War Office had sanctioned the 148th Infantry Brigade coming under the command of the Commander-in-Chief, Norwegian Army. Owing to the urgency of the situation Brigadier Morgan decided to comply with the Norwegian request for assistance, at the same time sending a signal to the War Office for further instructions.

The Norwegian Commander-in-Chief's orders were that 148th Infantry Brigade should be sent at once to the Lillehammer area to replace the Norwegian troops who were tired out. He hoped that the arrival of the British troops would lend fresh heart to his force and consequently he required Brigadier Morgan to attach his troops under direct command of Norwegian formations. The force was moved by train to the Lillehammer area during 19th and 20th April, where it was placed under command 2nd Norwegian Division.

33. On 21st April, it was to move forward in three groups to take up previously reconnoitred positions south of Lillehammer and on either side of Mjösa Lake.

Owing to a German attack during the afternoon these groups never reached these positions and orders were issued for a withdrawal at 0100 hours, 22nd April, to the high ground between Fålberg and Lillehammer. During this withdrawal a party of 5 officers and 50 men, I/5 Leicesters, was cut off and lost.

34. On 22nd April our position was heavily attacked from the air and with 3.7 inch howitzers and 4 inch mortars. Shortly after mid-day the Germans succeeded in working round the Eastern flank and a daylight withdrawal became imperative if the whole force East of the river was not to be cut off.

The Norwegians had made no arrangements for the occupation of the position in rear, but the timely arrival of the remaining two companies of I/5 Leicesters at the base enabled them to be rushed forward by rail and bus to positions near Öyer.

The Germans made no serious efforts to follow up the withdrawal, being checked by fire and road blocks. Their aircraft were however very active and the force suffered heavy casualties from bombs and machine gun fire from the air.

The position at Öyer was reached by about 1800 hours, though battalions and companies were somewhat mixed. At this hour the force was some 12 miles in front of any formed body of Norwegians though three squadrons of the Dragoons, a motorised machine-gun unit, were placed under Brigadier Morgan's command, with orders to report to him at Tretten.

35. During the night 22nd/23rd April the British force fell back to a previously reconnoitred position just South of Tretten.

Owing to this continued withdrawal rations had been jettisoned in order to transport troops so there was a shortage of supplies. Also positions were not entrenched, as all tools had been left behind in the early stages of the withdrawal. Consequently the men were lying in the open exposed to full view of the enemy aircraft and to artillery fire.

36. During 23rd April the Germans brought up a section of 5.9 howitzers and at least two tanks. They again started working round our Eastern flank and a further withdrawal became essential. Owing to the difficulties of communications it is doubted whether the forward companies ever received any orders and they were cut off by the enemy getting round behind them.

The withdrawal of the remainder was followed up by tanks and aircraft and casualties were heavy, but the forward companies were still holding out and must have inflicted heavy losses on the enemy. The Norwegians had taken up a defensive position about Favang and the remainder of the force withdrew through them during the night 23rd/24th April.

By this time the I K.O.Y.L.I. from 15th Brigade had arrived from Åndalsnes and on 24th April reached Otta with orders to occupy a position behind the Norwegians about Kvam.

During the above period 148th Brigade suffered about 700 casualties, while only two combatant officers were left with the Leicesters and four with the Foresters.

37. In the instructions issued to Major-General Paget by Lieutenant-General Massy on 22nd April (Appendix A) he was given the task of co-operating with the Norwegian Army in preventing the Northward advance of the German Army based in Southern Norway, and at the same time in safeguarding his left and rear against attack by the German forces in Trondheim and parachute landed detachments on his Line of Communications of over 100 miles.

38. On arrival at Åndalsnes on the evening of 25th April, General Paget went forward by car to meet the Commander-in-Chief of the Norwegian Army, General Ruge, who, with a staff of about six officers, was then in a small farm house on the hillside 10 miles South of Dombås. General Paget had been told en route by the British Minister, whom he saw at the Park Royal, Åndalsnes, that General Ruge was the only man who could keep the Norwegian forces in the field, and this would certainly appear to have been the case. General Ruge was gravely concerned about the smallness of the British forces and the fact that he was not fully aware of our plans. He said, that his own troops were exhausted in trying to hold up the German advance

from the South pending the arrival of British reinforcements, and that they could fight no more until they had been thoroughly rested, re-organised and re-equipped.

General Paget came to the conclusion that this was right, and that he could look for very little support from these troops. He asked, however, that Norwegian ski detachments should be used to protect the flanks on the high ground as he had no means of doing this himself, and General Ruge promised that they would do so and would operate under British command. General Ruge then said, and later confirmed in writing, that General Paget was to be entirely responsible for the Gudbrandsdal valley, and also for the protection of the railway from Dombås as far North as Opdal (40 miles North of Dombås).

During the following day all other Norwegian troops were withdrawn from the area South of Dombås down the Gudbrandsdal valley towards Åndalsnes.

39. I K.O.Y.L.I. were thus the most forward Allied troops and were holding a position across the valley at Kvam with I Y. & L. in a supporting position some two miles in rear about Sjoa. I Green Howards moved up from Åndalsnes to Dombås by train joining the remnants of 148th Infantry Brigade in that place.

By 1600 hrs. it was obvious that I K.O.Y.L.I. could not maintain their front much longer. They had held the Kvam position for nearly 48 hours, in spite of repeated enemy attacks, and were constantly subjected to enemy artillery fire, air bombing and low flying machine gun fire. Brigadier Kent Lemon was therefore ordered to withdraw I K.O.Y.L.I. on the night of 26th/27th April by motor transport to Dombås through I Y. & L. This latter battalion was to remain in its present position, reinforced by one company Green Howards (sent up in motor transport from Dombås), and thus cover the preparation of a strong position just South of Otta.

The situation on the left flank was causing some anxiety, as the enemy were reported to have reached Alvdal in the Österdalen valley. There were only small detachments of Norwegian troops at Foldal and Hjerkinn. Hence it was possible for the enemy to develop a threat against the Lines of Communications by way of Foldal, Hjerkinn, Dombås. Brigadier Morgan was, therefore, placed in command of the troops in Dombås to organise the defence of the village with his own force (400 strong but short of officers and weapons) and one company of the Green Howards, who were given the task of blocking the Hjerkinn road.

The remainder of the Green Howards was then moved by train at night to Otta to occupy a position South of the village as a firm base in rear of I Y. & L.

During the withdrawal of I K.O.Y.L.I. several minor demolitions were successfully carried out.

40. General Paget's object at this stage was still to stop the enemy. He judged that he could not expect his forward troops to withstand the enemy for more than 48 hours in any one position without any form of artillery and air support. Planning was therefore directed to delaying the enemy as much as possible so as to give time for the arrival of artillery and air support. When this should arrive little difficulty was anticipated in stopping the enemy.

41. The withdrawal of I K.O.Y.L.I. was successfully carried out, and I Y. & L. held the Sjoa position throughout the day. The enemy had been slow in following up and

did not press his attack for the time being, contenting himself with air and ground bombardment.

I Green Howards organised the Otta position for defence, and the preparation of Dombås defences was continued. Owing to the rocky nature of the ground it was seldom possible to dig and concealment from air was essential.

During the morning a report from the French Military Attaché again indicated enemy action from the direction Foldal – Hjerkinn. General Ruge was confident in the ability of his detachment to hold off any such threats; but General Paget judged that a reconnaissance was desirable in case it became necessary to reinforce the Norwegian troops. Unfortunately a breakdown in motor transport limited this reconnaissance to the vicinity of Dombås.

42. Throughout the day the need for reconnaissance aircraft was acute, not only for normal tasks, but also to confirm or deny the many alarmist reports received.

At a conference with General Ruge earlier in the day it was agreed that the Otta position was a strong one, on which there should be a good chance of holding the enemy until the arrival of guns from the base. General Ruge requested that the Otta position should be held until a Norwegian detachment, which had been isolated in the hills West of Tretten, could be withdrawn by the roads leading into the Gudbrandsdal in the area Otta – Sel. To this General Paget replied that he would be prepared, with the situation as it was then, to hold the Otta position for two or three days, and that he would do his best to cover the Norwegian detachment's withdrawal. The Otta position required two battalions to hold it, and as the Y. and L. would have found difficulty in defending the Sjoa position they were ordered to withdraw on the night 27th/28th to reinforce the Green Howards on the Otta position.

This withdrawal was not as successful as on the previous night. The enemy had anticipated it, and made every effort to work round the flank. Parties of the enemy (dressed as Norwegian troops) succeeded in cutting off some of the forward companies, and eventually only some 12 officers and 300 men were available to assist the Green Howards on the Otta position. Many of I Y. and L. who had been thus cut off rejoined subsequently after an adventurous passage of the hills on the flanks of the valley.

43. At about 0500 hours the liaison officer who had taken up the motor transport for the withdrawal of I Y. and L. returned to General Paget's headquarters with the news of the difficulties experienced by this battalion. In his opinion the Y. and L. were not in a fit state to hold their sector of the Otta position, which would have to be held solely by the Green Howards.

This situation necessitated some precautionary measures. Movement of troops in the open or on the Lines of Communication by daylight could be justified only as a last resort; but there were still some two and a half hours left before the usual time of arrival of the German morning air reconnaissance. Throughout the operations the enemy was methodical in his air action, and his probable active hours could be forecast with accuracy.

44. The company of the Green Howards in Dombås was, therefore, ordered into a

concealment area some two miles to the South of Dombås, with motor transport immediately available for a further forward movement if necessary.

At the same time the K.O.Y.L.I. in Dombås were placed at one hour's notice to move.

While these adjustments were being made, the first news of the intended evacuation reached headquarters. The War Office telegram requested acceptance of a plan or a suggested alternative. General Paget considered he could not answer this without reference to General Ruge, as the evacuation was not possible without his co-operation.

He therefore went to his headquarters and told him frankly the situation, which at the first General Ruge was unable to accept. Finally, he did so, on General Paget's assurance that British troops would cover the withdrawal of the Norwegian Army and would not relinquish Dombås until this had been effected.

45. Meanwhile the situation of the Green Howards and Y. and L. was causing anxiety at the headquarters of the 15th Infantry Brigade. Y. and L. had not recovered from the severe handling they had received during the previous night's withdrawal, and though Green Howards were in good heart they were all too few to cover an extensive position. The enemy had gained contact at I030 hours, and quickly began a methodical bombardment of the forward troops with artillery and mortars. The bombing and the machine gun fire on the forward troops were the heaviest experienced up to that time. It was apparent that to hold the position until dark and then extricate the forward battalions might be a matter of considerable difficulty.

46. The time and space problem of the withdrawal had now to be considered. The major factors were:-

(*a*) The obligation to cover the withdrawal of all Norwegian troops in this area.

(*b*) The shipping available on the nights 29th/30th April, 30th April/Ist May, Ist/2nd May.

(*c*) The withdrawal would be dependent on one single railway line and one road over a distance of I00 miles.

(*d*) The physical endurance of the troops.

It was obvious from the start that demolition must play a large part in the plan. A vital point was the bridge over the Rostå gorge between Dovre and Otta. If this was successfully blown, the enemy would be unlikely to get tanks, guns or wheeled vehicles forward of the gorge for at least 48 hours.

One section of the 55 Field Company, R.E., was withdrawn at once from the forward area to prepare the Rostå demolitions, and the company of Green Howards, then in concealment South of Dombås, was sent to cover their preparations.

47. During the afternoon and early evening the Green Howards on the Otta position fought splendidly. One medium and two light tanks were destroyed by the 25 mm. Anti-Tank Company. Other targets included reconnaissance parties and groups of enemy in buildings. There is no doubt that the enemy suffered many casualties in this battle and his subsequent actions showed little desire or ability to press home an attack. It was, however, irritating in the extreme, owing to lack of artillery, to be

unable to deal with the German close support guns, which came into action in the open, outside the range of British light machine guns and 3 in. mortars.

At about 1800 hours the K.O.Y.L.I. were ordered to occupy the position South of Dombås, which had been reconnoitred in the morning.

48. The plan for the night withdrawal is worth considering in some detail, because it was the first of a series of precarious operations, where the balance between success and disaster was extremely slender.

Otta is some 25 miles from Dombås, where lay the next secure base occupied by the K.O.Y.L.I. The only means of transport available were the train and a very limited amount of motor transport, both of which had to be wheedled out of the Norwegians. The motor transport was allotted to the rear parties. The train was assembled at Dombås and the motor transport at Dovre, with a staff officer in charge of each. Both started about 2000 hours. The train ran forward to Rudi and the motor transport to Formo, both of which were close behind the front line. At about 2030 hours the fighting slackened on the whole front and the withdrawal started at 2300 hours, the troops falling steadily back on the train and motor transport column.

The train left Rudi about 0230 hours, and the troops detrained into assembly areas at Dombås between 0500 and 0600 hours, where they were covered by I K.O.Y.L.I, in position South of Dombås.

Demolitions at Rostå and Dovre were blown after the rear parties had crossed the bridges.

49. The breakaway was clean, and the fact that the enemy made no immediate attempt to follow it up was undoubtedly due to the reverse he had suffered during the afternoon.

The value of the Norwegian Ski Troops operating on the flanks should be mentioned. They were the only means of flank protection, and were of great value in guarding against surprise.

During the night 28th/29th April, many Norwegian troops were withdrawn from the Lines of Communication and there was a possibility of having no troops between Dombås and the base at Åndalsnes, some 60 miles away.

The obvious danger was that enemy parachute detachments might land on the Lines of Communication. Brigadier Morgan's force was therefore disposed in detachments at Lesja, Lesjaverk, Lesjaskog and Verma, with as much transport for each detachment as he could raise.

50. During the night 28th/29th April, General Paget's headquarters moved to Botheim. An early reconnaissance made of the Dombås position disclosed that the K.O.Y.L.I. was well established there, with the Green Howards and Y. and L. just assembling in the woods after their train withdrawal.

During the morning, General Ruge pointed out that he could not withdraw his Foldal detachment until the night 29th/30th April. There could thus be no question of the withdrawal of British troops from Dombås until night 30th April/Ist May. This meant the enemy had 48 hours to follow up from Otta, and that another battle might have to be fought on the Dombås position. General Ruge offered the support of a

Norwegian Field Battery of four guns, which was gratefully accepted. These guns were later to prove most useful.

The enemy was very active all day in the air, bombing and machine gunning all movement on the Lines of Communication. It was the habit of his bombers to fly direct to their objective, drop their bombs at the most convenient height, and then on their way home to carry out low flying machine gun attacks on the road traffic.

5I. About noon Lieut. Colonel Clarke arrived from England to say that shipping would be available as follows:-

Night 29th/30th April for I,000-I,500 personnel.
Night 30th April/Ist May for 2,200 personnel.
Night Ist/2nd May for the remainder if necessary.

The plan made as a result of this was to withdraw I Y. and L. from Dombås and send them with Base Details on the night 29th/30th April.
On night 30th April/Ist May:-

(*a*) I5th Infantry Brigade and all troops (less I Y. and L.) would withdraw from present positions through the Royal Marines (covering Åndalsnes) and embark.
(*b*) The following were approximate strengths:-

H.Q. Sickle Force	40
I K.O.Y.L.I.	500
I Green Howards	500
Anti-Tank Company	80
Section, 55 Field Company	I00
I68 Light A.A. Battery	65
H.Q. I5 Infantry Brigade	60
Signals, I5th Infantry Brigade	40
Morgan's Force	400
	I,775

(*c*) *Transport:*

This plan was communicated to Norwegian G.H.Q. and the necessary details arranged.

By Motor Transport.	
Leave Dombås 2030 hrs.	55 Field Company H.Q. I5th Infantry Bde. & Sig. Sec. Rear parties K.O.Y.L.I. and Green Howards.
By Train	
Leave Dombås 2I30 hrs.	I K.O.Y.L.I., I Green Howards (less rear parties) Anti-tank Coy. Details R.E. & R.A.

During night 29th/30th April the Norwegian detachments at Hjerkinn and Foldal withdrew through the British force at Dombås. These were the last Norwegian troops in the area for the covering of whose withdrawal General Paget was responsible.

52. The train conveying the Y. and L. to Åndalsnes on the night 29th/30th April only reached Lesjaskog, owing to a break in the line. There was no train available to take them on from the other side of the break to Åndalsnes, so they marched on.

Enemy reconnaissance aircraft and bombers were active, but no other special incident occurred during the day until 1530 hours when 15th Infantry Brigade reported that the enemy could be seen advancing up the valley from Dovre. The early reports were conflicting, one mentioned four battalions, another parachute troops, a third transport. The force was probably the usual reconnaissance detachment, possibly reinforced by machine gun and mortar detachments landed by parachutes. This contact, though not unexpected, was undesirably early. There were some five to six hours of daylight left and it seemed possible for the enemy to stage an attack on the K.O.Y.L.I. from which it might be difficult to extricate them.

53. The K.O.Y.L.I. were extremely well hidden; it is probable that the Germans were surprised to find them there at all, and they must have been even more surprised when the Norwegian guns opened fire on their forward positions. Lieutenant-Colonel Cass commanding I K.O.Y.L.I. had made a very wise decision earlier in the day to withdraw his right company across the river, as the water level had risen considerably, making the river un-fordable for the withdrawal. When later the Germans made contact, they were forced to use rubber boats to attempt the crossing. These were all destroyed and their crews knocked out.

The enemy's forward troops were supported by a close reconnaissance aircraft, which dropped bombs and flares on likely targets. Fortunately this aircraft was shot down by our troops early in the engagement and thus the Norwegian battery was able to shoot unmolested.

About 1800 hours Brigadier Kent Lemon sent a reassuring message to the effect that he was confident he could hold the enemy, and that he was adopting an aggressive attitude. The train was assembled in the Dombås tunnel, wherein it lay all day. This tunnel was indeed providential throughout the operations. It housed trains, rations, ammunition and stores, and was a secure refuge for the Norwegian station staff, without whose help the system could not have been maintained.

54. During the afternoon it was discovered that owing to a misunderstanding Brigadier Morgan had withdrawn his anti-parachute detachments at Lesja, Lesjaverk and Lesjaskog. This might have had serious results as all Norwegian troops had also been withdrawn from this area. The Anti-Tank Company was therefore sent back to occupy Lesja against parachute attack, and to meet a possible threat by German ski troops using the Vagamo – Lesja road.

Throughout the day there had been considerable doubt as to whether the line was clear to Åndalsnes; but by 1700 hours it was reported in working order, and the withdrawal started according to plan. The train started a little late, but both it and the rear parties in Motor Transport got away well and the road and railway demolitions

West of Dombås were blown. The train stopped at Lesja to pick up the Anti-Tank Company and 300 Norwegian Infantry – the last Norwegian troops to be withdrawn.

55. Headquarters moved back by motor transport and efforts were made en route by telephone to find out the progress of the train. These were unsuccessful until Verma (19 miles from Åndalsnes) was reached. There the unwelcome news was learned that there was a break in the line near Lesjaskog. The train had been wrecked by a bomb crater. Both engines had overturned, the front coach had telescoped and there were a good many casualties. This meant that the troops would have a 17 miles march to the nearest shelter which was in the tunnel at Verma.

A staff officer was sent to get Marines up from Romsdalshorn to cover the Verma Gorge and to get as much transport forward as he could to help the troops in their journey from Lesjaskog to Verma.

56. At 0100 hours the troops set out on their long march to Verma. It was, of course, too much to hope that they would gain the security of the Verma tunnel before the early enemy air patrols were active, but it was very desirable that as many as possible should have crossed the open Lesjaskog plateau and have reached the comparative safety of the Verma Gorge.

The Marines came up about 0530 hours and established a road block near the scene of the train wreck which they held till 1000 hrs., subsequently withdrawing to cover the first of a series of demolitions arranged in the Verma Gorge.

With the aid of some motor transport all the troops were in the tunnel by 0900 hours, but their destination had been spotted by the enemy aircraft and many of them had been subjected to low flying attacks on their way back.

The tunnel merits description. In it was a loaded ammunition train; the train which was the only means of reaching Åndalsnes, and 1,500 troops, who were packed like sardines and filled the tunnel completely. The tunnel itself ran through the side of a hill and was bomb proof.

57. Throughout the morning the men slept, disturbed occasionally by bombing and low flying machine gun attacks on the entrances to the tunnel. In the afternoon they began to recover and their spirits were remarkably good, giving proof once again of the high powers of endurance of the British soldier.

A conference was held at 1600 hours at which orders for the withdrawal to Åndalsnes were issued. The train was to start at 2230 hours and the rear parties by motor transport at 2300 hours.

At about 1730 the engine in the tunnel began to get up steam and the tunnel filled with dense smoke. It was necessary to get the men out of the tunnel and accept the risk of their detection. They behaved very steadily and went quickly outside to disperse.

58. At about 1800 hours a message came in reporting that the Marines at the head of the Gorge had broken and the enemy had made contact in some strength.

Both K.O.Y.L.I. and Green Howards deployed immediately and the former sent back one company some 2,000 yards up the Gorge to reinforce a platoon of Green Howards already in position.

The Norwegian station-master was asked to get the train ready as soon as possible.

He estimated that it would be ready by 2000 hours. Success or failure now depended on the loyalty and goodwill of the Norwegian railwaymen. As a precaution the engine driver was placed under an armed guard. There was no doubt that the troops, tired as they were, could hold off the enemy; but it was necessary that the withdrawal should not be interfered with as the train ran forward up the valley for about half a mile before turning North to Åndalsnes.

At 2030 hours the tram was ready and the troops started to entrain. They were very steady and the whole entraining was quickly carried out covered once more by rear parties whose motor transport was waiting on the road below.

59. The only remaining anxiety was the security of the 300 Norwegian Infantry who had entrained at Lesja. Transport had gone up to Lesjaskog to evacuate them early in the morning, but their subsequent return was not confirmed. The train journey was without further incident and the troops arrived on the quay at Åndalsnes about 2300 hours to embark. They were taken on board H.M S. "Birmingham," H.M.S. "Manchester," and H.M.S. "Calcutta," while H.M.S. "Auckland" remained for the rear parties who were all on board by 0200 hours.

Åndalsnes had been bombed earlier in the evening but the actual embarkation was carried out unmolested, and once again thanks are due to the Royal Navy for rescuing the Army from a precarious situation as they did twenty-five years ago.

COMMENTS.

60. Without being unduly wise after the event it is possible to make certain general comments. Brigadier Morgan's decision to exceed his instructions and move his forces forward to the support of the Norwegians was in the circumstances entirely justified.

Owing to a misunderstanding the Norwegian Commander-in-Chief was under the impression that Brigadier Morgan's force was under his orders. Brigadier Morgan cannot be in any way blamed therefore for deciding to place himself under the orders of the Norwegian C. in C., and once having done so for employing his force in accordance with those orders.

6I. Desire to carry out these orders may, however, have led him to adopt tactics which were not the best calculated to enable his force to provide the strongest support to the Norwegians or to give it the best chance of stopping the German advance. The Norwegian Army was withdrawing in the face of a rapid German advance. As our Manual on the subject teaches (Mil. Training Pamphlet No. 23, Part VI Withdrawal, Sec. 2) "the first step in the process of withdrawal will be the establishment of fresh troops on a position in the rear of those troops which are in contact with the enemy and through which the latter can retire. This position should be at such a distance that the troops occupying it will be given time to devise an effective defence before the position is reached by the enemy."

62. A more effective solution of the problem therefore would have been the establishment of the Brigade on a selected naturally strong position some distance in

rear of the Norwegians where they would have had time to dig in and organise a proper defence. Such a position might well have enabled the Brigade, ill equipped as it was, with the aid of proper demolitions, to obtain protection against the attacks of Armoured Fighting Vehicles and to get sufficient cover to withstand bombardment and to hold off infantry attacks for a prolonged period. Behind such a position the Norwegians would have had a better opportunity to reorganise than was in fact ever given them.

63. After the arrival of Major-General Paget, I have no detailed comments to make on these operations except to say that there is abundant evidence to show that they were conducted with great skill and energy on the part of General Paget. The fact that it was possible to withdraw this force over a distance of 100 miles under the conditions which have been described in this narrative, to fight five rearguard actions and finally to re-embark without enemy interference is in itself a magnificent tribute to the skilled and determined leadership not only of the Commander but also of the subordinate commanders, notably Brigadier Kent Lemon, commanding 15th Infantry Brigade and Lieut.-Colonel Robinson, commanding 1 Green Howards, and also to the endurance, discipline and fighting qualities of the troops engaged: also to the fine work of the Royal Engineers in the destruction of communications which successfully delayed the enemy for the required period.

PART IV.
CONCLUSIONS AND LESSONS.

64. I now proceed to set down what are, in my opinion, the salient lessons to be learned from the operations which have terminated with the evacuation of Central Norway.

65. *Co-operation with the Royal Navy.*

I am able to report with confidence that the co-operation between the Navy, including the Fleet Air Arm, and the Army has been of the highest standard possible.

Every officer to whom I have spoken is full of praises of the efficiency, the tireless devotion to duty and the complete disregard of personal safety of all ranks of the Navy with whom they came in contact.

The whole of the forces operating in Norway fully realise the deep debt of gratitude they owe to their sister service both for the support the latter gave them ashore and for the efficiency with which they were withdrawn at the end.

The arrival of the carriers of the Fleet Air Arm off the coast, and the operation of the Skuas and Rocs, gave a respite from bombing to the ports, especially Namsos, which was invaluable. The Germans would not face our Fleet Air Arm fighters which were handled with a boldness that was an inspiration to the troops who watched their manoeuvres from the ground.

Similarly the anti-aircraft cruisers and sloops, though continuously and heavily bombed themselves, kept station in the confined waters of the Fjords at the ports until their ammunition was exhausted and, by doing so, so affected the accuracy of the enemy bombing with their fire that the damage done whilst they were present was much reduced.

No words of mine can adequately express the gratitude and admiration I feel for the skill in planning and efficiency in execution of the tasks which the Navy have carried out in support of the forces in Norway.

66. *Armies and Air Support.*

The first outstanding lesson of these operations has been the vital need for air support for a modern army.

As in Poland, the Germans have used their air force in the closest co-operation with their military forces. They have been employed in three main ways:-

(*a*) In direct support of their forward troops.
(*b*) To attack H.Q. and communications.
(*c*) To attack Base areas and aerodromes.

In the case of (*a*) high level bombing has been employed, but in addition low level bombing with small bombs from as low as 400 feet and the machine gunning of individual posts has been undertaken continuously. Headquarters have been unceasingly bombed. It is not known whether the position of these was indicated by spies or German sympathisers who were working behind our lines, or by direction-finding of the wireless sets operating near these headquarters. The effect of this bombing on the conduct of operations is always serious and may easily be disastrous. The effect on the Lines of Communication was not serious. Craters were quickly filled and rails repaired. Such bombing is of a harassing value only. Unchecked bombing of communications will undoubtedly make supply and maintenance very difficult but it is infinitely less effective than direct attacks on troops using those communications.

The attack on the Bases was continuous and persistent. During the course of one day's bombing of Åndalsnes, which commenced at 0700 hours and ended at 2100 hours, some 400 heavy bombs up to 500 kg. were dropped in addition to countless numbers of incendiary bombs. The methods employed were high level bombing at between 10,000 and 15,000 feet and dive bombing from 8,000 to 2,000.

As a result the port became unusable by day, wooden quays were destroyed, and stone and concrete quays and their approaches were seriously damaged. In one day one Norwegian torpedo boat, three trawlers and two ferry steamers were sunk.

67. As has been recounted above, valiant efforts were made to operate Gladiators from the neighbourhood of Åndalsnes. These, however, failed because the enemy, having immediately noticed their arrival, bombed the airfield continuously throughout the day. Had they succeeded I have little doubt that a marked change would have come over the whole situation. As I have already reported when referring to the work of the Fleet Air Arm, the German bomber will not stand up to the boldly handled fighter, and there can be no question but that, had these Gladiators been able to keep the air until Hurricanes and subsequently Blenheims could have operated, the Allied troops would have had no difficulty in landing the guns and other supporting arms they needed and in entirely stopping the German advance.

68. It is easy to be wise after the event, but it is now quite obvious that the establishment of an aerodrome in the face of hostile aircraft is a combined operation requiring the most careful planning.

Looking back on this operation it is clear that there are several essentials:-

(*a*) Strong A.A. Defences must be established before the first aircraft arrives.

(*b*) All preparations must be made so that aircraft can operate in the shortest possible time after landing.

(*c*) During the period of first arrival, long range fighters or Fleet Air Arm fighters should be provided to cover the landing.

(*d*) Sufficient aircraft must be landed to provide continuous protection for the aerodrome and to provide protection for the establishment of at least a second aerodrome.

(*e*) Bombers should be flown on as soon as the aerodrome is secure.

69. I have already reported that several requests were made to the Air Ministry for Bombers to attack the German Forces moving up the Gudbrandsdal valley and the communications behind them.

This was found impossible, and I am not in a position to question the correctness of this decision.

I can, however, say that had it been possible to attack the German Army and its communications, a direct effect on the operations would have been achieved with a considerable saving certainly in material. The withdrawal and evacuation could not then have been closely followed up by the enemy, as in fact it was, and the process of evacuation need therefore not have been as hurried as it necessarily was under the existing conditions.

I have no hesitation in saying that it is essential that a degree of co-operation between the Army and the Air Force, comparable to that which is now the case with Germans, is essential if we are not to remain at a dangerous disadvantage. The direction of the two forces in any theatre of war must be the task of one commander in that theatre if results are to be obtained commensurate with the effort made.

70. *The Dangers of Improvisation.*

A further outstanding lesson of these operations is the grave handicap under which both the commanders and the troops suffer when force and formation headquarters are improvised and thrown together at the last moment.

For this campaign in Central Norway the expeditionary force headquarters was ordered to form after active operations, involving British troops, had begun, and I was charged with the conduct of those operations whilst my headquarters was still in the process of assembling. I cannot stress too strongly the dangers of such improvisation. It is clear that we were taken by surprise by the methods which the Germans employed to seize the key points in Norway, and consequently we were forced to resort to unorthodox methods of procedure.

Even if it is hoped that a landing will be unopposed, efforts to build up the Base and Lines of Communication organization must be continuous from the earliest possible moment. I realise that difficulties arose owing to a change of plan and shipping limitations, but, when evacuation was decided upon, the organization at Åndalsnes was very incomplete while that at Namsos had hardly started. As a result, no clear administrative picture was ever available as regards either force, the consequences of which might have been serious.

It is quite certain that the functions of 2nd Echelon cannot be carried out in the United Kingdom for a force operating under Norwegian conditions. 2nd Echelon for the forces based upon Åndalsnes and Namsos was located in Margate and, as a result of long and uncertain communications and of changes in plan, was never in touch with the situation.

7I. The least that can now be done is to ensure that this undesirable situation does not occur again, and that provision is made for a force headquarters and certain formations and units and a complete establishment of Base and Line of Communication units which can be held as reserve for use in any theatre to which the war may spread, including France if necessary.

I submit that the nucleus of such a force should be:-

A Corps Headquarters, modified to control an expeditionary force.
One regular division.
One territorial division.
A small armoured brigade.
Certain corps troops.
Base and Line of Communication units.
2nd Echelon for all the above.

If a reserve such as this is to be able to act swiftly and decisively at any point overseas, there are certain other requirements which must be met.

These are:-

(*a*) Time for training in amphibian operations.
(*b*) A suitable training area.
(*c*) An allotment of landing craft and ships fitted to carry them.
(*d*) Facilities for studying and practising air co-operation, particularly with a fighter and bomber component.

72. *The Provision and Loading of Ships.*

The provision of suitable shipping for an overseas expedition has always been difficult because our merchant shipping in peace is designed either for passengers or for cargo. Neither of these types is suitable for the carriage of the large number of motor vehicles now in use by the Army. The result, so far as the expedition to Southern Norway was concerned, was well nigh disastrous. Guns were landed without their detachments and with little or no ammunition; vehicles arrived without their drivers. Even the essential first line transport of infantry battalions was divorced from its units.

Again I realise that this was due to a certain extent to a change of plan which aggravated an already difficult shipping situation, but we cannot accept a situation which admits of no strategical and tactical elasticity.

I am convinced that, if troops are proceeding overseas to land at a point where they may go directly into action, units must be embarked complete with their weapons, ammunition and equipment, and accompanied in the same convoy by their M.T. with its drivers.

This object could be achieved in various ways:-

(*a*) By constructing new ships.

(*b*) By altering existing shipping.

(*c*) By loading available ships tactically.

I realise that it is uneconomical to keep shipping idle or available at short notice for a hypothetical operation, and that at present our resources are inadequate; but I am quite certain that we must find some way out of this difficulty. It will almost certainly be necessary to use existing ships with little alteration and in that case personnel may have to travel under conditions of extreme discomfort for short periods. We must be prepared to accept such conditions. To put our troops ashore under any other conditions is to court disaster if on arrival they are required to go straight into action.

73. I would further emphasize the grave consequences which may arise if a change of plan is made after troops and stores have been embarked. Even had the air situation in Southern Norway been favourable to us, the order of arrival of troops, weapons and vehicles at Åndalsnes and Namsos was based on plans prepared for an unopposed entry into the country.

In the event, the order was such that the force that arrived ashore was deficient of supporting arms and was in no condition to engage an enemy properly organised and equipped as was the German Army to which it was opposed.

74. *Military Doctrine.*

These operations have confirmed the correctness of the principles, laid down in our training manuals, which should guide us in the varying phases of warfare. The principles of war remain, though occasions have undoubtedly occurred where we have not been sufficiently quick to grasp their application to new and somewhat unexpected conditions.

75. *Morale and Discipline.*

Finally I desire to draw your attention to the generally excellent behaviour of the British troops and their leaders, especially their junior officers. Brigadier Morgan's 148th Infantry Brigade were young soldiers or Territorials to whom these operations were their first experience of war. These quite inexperienced troops were rushed into action in an effort to stem the German advance, when the Norwegian forces were already withdrawing. With their flanks turned owing to the fact that the exhausted Norwegian troops had been obliged to withdraw, and their centre pierced by armoured vehicles to which they had no adequate reply, owing to the loss of their anti-tank guns at sea, it is not surprising that their casualties in missing were heavy, and heavier than would have been the case with more experienced troops under more experienced regimental officers' leadership.

76. The behaviour of Brigadier Phillips' 146th Infantry Brigade has been reported as excellent. When this Brigade, quite unsupported as it was, was shelled and

practically cut off by superior enemy forces, it proved only too clearly that man for man the British soldier is far superior to his German counterpart. By skilful handling, good discipline and good fighting qualities the battalions of this Brigade extricated themselves from a position which might well have been conceived as disastrous. The only occasion when confusion and needless casualties were caused was one which was due to an error of judgment on the part of an inexperienced company commander. The fighting qualities displayed in both these Brigades was excellent. The great importance that these young troops should be given the advantage of the best leadership that we can provide cannot be over-stated. To ensure this a strong nucleus of regular officers in every unit is essential.

77. The 15th Infantry Brigade gave an account of itself which is in accordance with the highest traditions of the British Army. Though bombed, shelled and machine-gunned without the means of adequate reply, it repulsed a series of enemy attacks supported by tanks with heavy losses in men and tanks to the enemy, at the expense of comparatively few casualties to itself. In its final withdrawal it proved that it had nothing to learn in cohesion and marching power from its predecessors, the old contemptibles of 1914.

78. The Demi-Brigade of French Chasseurs under the command of General Audet who were landed at Namsos were only engaged in patrol combats with the enemy. I have received, however, the highest reports of their efficiency, their cheerfulness and generally excellent bearing, and their hardihood under conditions of extreme discomfort which might well have shaken the morale of less highly trained troops. I have no doubt but that they would have been, and indeed yet will be, far more than a match for the finest troops the Germans can bring against them.

79. I am not delaying this report to include in it the names of the many different officers and other ranks whose services I desire to bring to your notice and whose names I will forward at an early date. I do, however, desire to put on record now the services rendered by Major-General B.C.T. Paget, for the skill with which he conducted operations on the southern front from the time he took command until the final evacuation. Major-General A. Carton de Wiart proved that he still possesses the energy and dash for which he has always been famous. Brigadier C.G. Phillips proved by his handling of his Brigade during the difficult days of Steinkjer, that he is a commander of marked ability. Brigadier Morgan gave abundant evidence of the capacity for making decisions which is so essential in a commander. Brigadier Kent Lemon proved himself a skilful and determined leader.

APPENDIX A.

Headquarters, 5th Corps,
22nd April, 1940.

EXPEDITIONARY FORCE INSTRUCTION No. I.

To:-
Major-General B.C.T. Paget,
D.S.O., M.C.
SICKLE FORCE.

I (*a*) A German Army of about one Corps, based on Southern Norway, is operating against the Norwegian Army, which is believed to be fighting a delaying action on the approximate line Hamar – Elverum.

(*b*) The Germans have also landed about 3,000 men at Bergen; at Stavanger, where they have occupied the aerodrome; and at Trondheim, where they have between 3,500 and 5,000 men and at least two destroyers. The aerodrome at Vaernes, near Trondheim, is also in their hands.

(*c*) The German force in the Trondheim area is believed to be disposed as under, but the numbers may be increased by airborne reinforcements.

    (i) I,500 in the area Levanger – Verdalen facing the British force based on Namsos.

    (ii) 500 protecting the coast defences at the entrance to the Trondheim Fjord about Agdenes.

    (iii) 200 at Stören (25 miles South of Trondheim) operating in a Southerly direction.

    (iv) 300 operating on the Trondheim – Östersund railway to the East of Trondheim.

2. Allied forces, consisting of I46 Infantry Brigade and a demi-brigade of Chasseurs Alpins, both under command of Major-General Carton de Wiart, are based on Namsos. If possible these forces are to be kept in being in order to maintain pressure against Trondheim from the North.

You have been informed separately of the composition of the British forces now operating South of Dombås and of the forces to accompany you.

3. A force of Gladiators will, it is hoped, be ashore by the 25th April. In the meantime a Carrier with fighter aircraft will be off your base at Åndalsnes. Contact with these should be arranged through Brigadier Hogg at the Base.

4. An advanced skeleton Corps H.Q., under the orders of Brigadier Hogg (D.A. & Q.M.G.) is travelling with you and will be responsible for:-

(*a*) Organising the Base at Åndalsnes and organising the anti-aircraft defence of that Base.

(*b*) Reconnoitring a subsidiary base at Geiranger and arranging for its anti-aircraft defence and for the requisitioning of transport for employment on the road L. of C. from Geiranger to your forces South of Dombås.

(*c*) Making similar arrangements at Sundalen.

(*a*), (*b*) and (*c*) above are in order of priority. Brigadier Hogg will be operationally under your orders.

5. On arrival in Norway you will assume command of all British troops in the Country, other than those operating under the orders of Major General Carton De Wiart based on Namsos and those in the Narvik area.

6. Your task will be to co-operate with the Norwegian Army in preventing the Northward advance of the German army based on Southern Norway.

7. It will be necessary for you to safeguard your left and rear against attack by the German forces in Trondheim and parachute-landed detachments on your L. of C.

8. You should make the earliest possible contact with the Commander-in-Chief, Norwegian Army, with a view to obtaining close co-operation towards the fulfilment of your task and the safeguarding of your forces and your communications.

You will not be under the orders of the Commander-in-Chief, Norwegian Army.

9. You should report your situation and your requirements at frequent intervals and all information that you are able to obtain.

Your channels of communication are laid down in the Outline Plan and first Maintenance project (G.S. (P) No. 650).

> (Sgd.) H.R.S. MASSY,
> Lieutenant General,
> Commander, 5th Corps.

APPENDIX B.

INSTRUCTIONS FOR LIEUTENANT-GENERAL H.R.S. MASSY, D.S.O., M.C.

1. His Majesty's Government have placed you in command of all British and French troops operating in Central Scandinavia, excluding any which may be operating in the Narvik area or based on Narvik. These latter will continue to be commanded by Major-General Mackesy under the orders of Lord Cork and Orrery.

2. The policy of His Majesty's Government is ultimately to evacuate Central Norway.

3. Your object, therefore, will be to evacuate your troops from Central Norway.

His Majesty's Government do not wish to impose any delay upon your operations which would be inconsistent with the military security of your force. They hope, however, that it will be militarily possible to postpone evacuation until after the capture of Narvik.

4. The final decision as to when the evacuation ought to take place rests with you. The final withdrawal and re-embarkation, however, is a joint operation, for which Admiral.........is appointed Naval Commander and Air Marshal...........Air Commander. The actual dates, times and places are the joint responsibility of yourself, the Naval Commander and the Air Commander.

5. You are authorised, in conjunction with the Naval and Air Commanders, to plan and carry out any combined operation which you jointly consider necessary for the achievement of your object.

6. A list of the Allied forces which are already operating in Central Norway is given in Annexure I.

You are already familiar with the roles of these forces.

7. A list of reinforcements which have not yet been despatched from the U.K. but which are at your disposal, is attached.[1] In addition, His Majesty's Government are prepared to withdraw from France the remainder of the 5th Division, should you require it.

8. You will act in co-operation with, but not under the command of, the Commander-in-Chief, Norwegian forces.

Should the Norwegian Commander-in-Chief wish to evacuate any part of the Norwegian forces in conjunction with your force, you should include their evacuation in your plan. You are at liberty, however, to insist that a condition of such evacuation should be that the Norwegian Commander-in-Chief should place any force to be withdrawn under your command.

9. Should you become a casualty or otherwise be prevented from exercising command of your force, command will pass to the next senior British Officer, who will exercise command and, in the event of a French General Officer being with the force, assume the acting rank of Lieutenant-General until another British Officer can be appointed.

10. In order to ensure secrecy, you will restrict knowledge of your object to those officers who must know it for the proper execution of your plan.

(Sd.) J.G. DILL, General,
for S. of S.

War Office,
27th April, 1940.

ANNEXURE I.
DETAIL OF THE ALLIED FORCES WHICH ARE ALREADY OPERATING IN OR EN ROUTE TO CENTRAL NORWAY.

MAURICE. – Commander Lt.-Gen. Carton de Wiart.

Unit	*Remarks*
Force Headquarters	Due to arrive 27/28.
	Adv. H.Q. arrived.
H.Q. 146 Inf. Bde. – Brig. Phillips.	Arrived.
4th Lincolns	Arrived.
1/4th K.O.Y.L.I	Arrived.
Hallams	Arrived.

Artillery.

193 A.A. Battery (of 82 A.A. Regt. 3.7"). (vehicles sail 27th).	Due 29th
166 Lt. A.A. Battery (vehicles of 166 Lt. A.A. Bty.)	Due 27th (personnel arrived) Sail 27th Due about 1st May.

Engineers.

H.Q. R.E. 61 Division	Not yet started.
Section 55 Field Coy.	Arrived.

Medical.

I58 Field Ambulance (I6 motor ambulances).	Due about Ist May.
I47 Field Ambulance	Due from Narvik for I46 Inf. Bde.

French Contingent.

5th Demi Brigade Chasseurs Alpins (Three Battalions).	Arrived.
I0I3th and I0I4th Light A.A. Batteries. (I2 guns).	Arrived.
One Section Engineers	Arrived.

SICKLE – Commander Maj.-Gen. Paget.

Force Headquarters	Arrived.
H.Q. I5 Inf. Bde.	Arrived.
I Green Howards	Arrived.
I K.O.Y.L.I.	Arrived.
I Y. & L.	Arrived.
I5 Inf. Bde. Anti-Tk. Coy.	Arrived.
H.Q. I48 Inf. Bde.	Arrived.
I/5 Leicesters	Arrived. Reduced to a composite battalion.
8 Foresters	Arrived. Reduced to a Composite battalion.

Artillery.

5I Field Regt. Less I Bty.	Due to arrive 28/29.
7I Field Regiment	Not yet embarked.
H.Q. 56 Lt. A.A. Regiment	Ready to embark 6th May.
I67 Light A.A. Battery	Ready to embark 6th May.
I68 Light A.A. Batter	Arrival complete 25/26.
260 A.A. Battery (3″)	Arrived.
82 A.A. Regiment (less I Bty.).	Ready to embark 28th.
One Bty., 58 Anti-Tk. Regt.	Due to arrive 27/28

Engineers.

55 Field Coy. (less I section)	Arrived.

Medical.

I46 Field Ambulance	Arrived.
I89 Field Ambulance	Due 28/29.
Drivers of I89 Field Amb.	Due 28/29.

L. of C. Troops.

687 Artizan Works Coy. R.E.	Not yet started.

COPY.

ADDENDUM No. I TO INSTRUCTIONS FOR LT. GENERAL H.R S. MASSY, D.S.O., M.C.

I. Certain independent companies are being formed, and will come under your orders. It is the intention that they should operate in the area between exclusive Mosjoen and inclusive Bodö.

2. In addition, arrangements should be made to withdraw part of the French detachment in Maurice Force along the road and railway to Mosjoen.

3. The role of the above detachments will, be:-

(*a*) To prevent the enemy seizing key positions with parachute troops.

(*b*) To delay the enemy's advance by land by every means, particularly demolitions.

4. These detachments should be self-contained for as long as possible. You should make arrangements for their subsequent maintenance by sea.

APPENDIX C.

INSTRUCTION TO MAJOR-GENERAL CARTON DE WIART COMMANDING FORCES SCHEDULED FOR "MAURICE" OPERATION.

I. His Majesty's Government and the Government of the French Republic have decided to land an expedition in Central Norway with the object of

(*a*) Providing encouragement for the Norwegian Government.

(*b*) Forming a rallying point for the Norwegian Government and armed forces.

(*c*) Securing a base for any subsequent operations in Scandinavia.

This operation will be carried out concurrently with but independent of the operations already initiated in Northern Norway.

2. You are appointed to command the Allied forces which are being despatched to Central Norway.

3. Your role will be to secure the Trondheim Area.

Subsequently you should take such steps as are possible to secure the use to the Allies of the road and rail communications leading from Trondheim, especially to the east.

4. *Points of Landing.*

(i) It is suggested, but of this you, together with the S.N.O., must be the final judges, that the initial landing should be in the Namsos area, and should be carried out by Morgan's and Phillips' Brigades.

(ii) A second landing should be carried out about Trondheim preferably to the east of the town, and after the Navy has cleared the Fjord of German vessels, by I47th Inf. Bde. and Chasseurs Alpins.

(iii) Administrative facilities should initially be developed about Namsos until Trondheim has been secured.

5. A forecast of the dates of arrival in the Trondheim – Namsos area of the elements of your force is as follows:-

(*a*) I46th Inf. Bde., Brigadier Phillips, available on I5th April.

(*b*) One infantry brigade (less one battalion), under Brigadier Morgan, should be available about dawn I7th April.

(*c*) I47th Inf. Bde., with artillery and ancillary troops, should be available on 20th or 2Ist April.

(*d*) Two battalions Chasseurs Alpins available (in same area) I8th April.

6. Should you become a casualty or otherwise be prevented from exercising command of the force, command will pass to the next senior British officer, who will exercise command, and in the event of a French General Officer being with the force, assume the acting rank of Major-General until another British officer can be appointed.

7. As soon as you are established ashore you will get in touch with any Norwegian forces in your vicinity, inform them of the impending arrival of further Allied forces and secure their co-operation in action against any German forces.

8. The Royal Navy are making preliminary landings in the Namsos area with landing parties about 300 strong in all and it is their intention to seize and hold any point in the Namsos area at which your disembarkation might take place.

9. Your force is not organised for a landing in face of opposition, and it is not intended that you should undertake such an operation.

I0. During the voyage and during landing operations, the senior naval officer will be in command, and he will decide, in co-operation with you, where and when to land.

II. A note as to the strength of the Norwegian forces in the area, and of the strength of any German forces operating in the vicinity is being given to you separately.

I2. Your force will constitute an independent command directly under the War Office. You will keep a constant communication with the War Office and report as regularly as is practicable as to the situation.

(sd.) EDMUND IRONSIDE,
C.I.G.S.

The War Office,
14th April, 1940.

Footnote
I This appendix was not received.

2

REAR ADMIRAL R.H.C. HALIFAX'S DESPATCH ON THE FIRST AND SECOND BATTLES OF NARVIK, 1940

10 AND 13 APRIL 1940

The following Despatch was submitted on the 25th April, 1940, to the Lords Commissioners of the Admiralty by Rear Admiral R.H.C. Halifax, Rear Admiral (D), Home Fleet.

> *Rear Admiral (D), Home Fleet,*
> H.M.S. *Woolwich.*
> *25th April, 1940.*

Be pleased to lay before the Board a narrative of the First Battle of Narvik, which has been prepared by the Commanding Officer, H.M.S. HOTSPUR, the senior surviving officer, and the report of the C.O. H.M.S. HAVOCK.

> (Sgd.) R.H.C. HALIFAX,
> *Rear Admiral.*

> H.M.S. *HOTSPUR.*
> *25th April, 1940.*

Sir,

I have the honour to forward herewith reports from H.M. Ships HOTSPUR and HOSTILE on the destroyer raid on Narvik on 10th April, 1940. As senior surviving officer of this raid, I feel I should also attempt to give some co-ordinated account. In doing so, I am using information obtained from H.M. Ships HOTSPUR, HOSTILE and surviving officers from H.M.S. HARDY. No report has yet been received from H.M.S. HAVOCK and of course, nothing is available from H.M.S. HUNTER.

2. HARDY (Captain B.A.W. Warburton-Lee[1]), HUNTER (Lieutenant-Commander L. de Villiers), HOTSPUR (Commander H.F.H. Layman) and HAVOCK (Lieutenant-Commander R.E. Courage), left Sullom Voe[2] at dawn on 7th April, in company with the Twentieth Destroyer Flotilla and joined RENOWN north of the Shetlands. The whole force proceeded in company towards Vest Fiord, destroyers being eventually detached to lay the minefield off Eggeloysa at dawn, 8th April, 1940.

3. After guarding the minefield for a few hours reports of 2 enemy destroyers were received from GLOWWORM and ships of the Second Destroyer Flotilla joined RENOWN southwest of the Lofoten Islands before dark.

4. At daylight on 9th April, 1940, the RENOWN encountered SCHARNHORST and HIPPER. The Second Destroyer Flotilla, stationed astern of RENOWN carried out a divisional concentration on HIPPER but the range was probably too great. All destroyers were soon left behind in the heavy seas, but not before both HARDY and HUNTER had narrowly escaped being hit.

5. The Second Destroyer Flotilla was then detached to patrol east of the Lofoten Islands. After about two hours this patrol was broken off on receipt of orders to go to Narvik. Just before leaving her patrol position HOTSPUR made visual contact with REPULSE.

6. Available reports tended to show that Narvik was only lightly held so the flotilla was stopped off Tranoy at about 1600 to obtain information and HOSTILE (Commander J.P. Wright) joined. It was then learnt that the enemy held the place in force.

7. The following "Most Immediate" message was sent by Captain (D), Second Destroyer Flotilla, to Admiralty, Commander-in-Chief, Home Fleet and Vice Admiral Commanding Battle Cruiser Squadron.

"Norwegians report Germans holding Narvik in force also 6 destroyers and I submarine are there and channel is possibly mined.

Intend attacking at dawn, high water."

T.O.O.[3] 1751/9/4/40.

No permission to attack was asked or further instructions sought. I submit that this message, made by the late Captain Warburton-Lee, should be given a place in our historical records.

8. The Admiralty replied as follows in message 0136/10 to Captain (D), Second Destroyer Flotilla, repeated Vice Admiral Commanding Battle Cruiser Squadron, and Commander-in- Chief, Home Fleet.

"Norwegian coast defence ships EIDSVOLD and NORGE may be in German hands. You alone can judge whether in these circumstances attack should be made. We shall support whatever decision you take."

9. The plan for the attack was given by Captain (D) Second Destroyer Flotilla in the following messages to the flotilla:-

1430/9 as amended by 1955/9, with a final addition in message 2040/9. The gist of these messages was briefly as follows. Ships were to be at action stations from 0030/10 as enemy batteries were reported on both sides of Ofot Fiord near Ramsundet. On approaching Narvik, HARDY, HUNTER and HAVOCK were to attack ships in the inner harbour. HOTSPUR and HAVOCK were to engage batteries reported on Framnesodden and any ships seen to the northwest. These two ships were also to cover the retirement of those in the inner harbour, with smoke. All ships were to be ready to send a small landing party in the event of opposition proving light.

10. The 50 mile passage from Tranoy to Narvik was made in continuous snowstorms with visibility seldom greater than 2 cables. Ships were twice separated owing to merchant vessels passing through the line and on the one occasion that land was seen the whole flotilla almost ran aground. The safe arrival of ships off Narvik at 0415 on 10th April, 1940, is a tribute to the skill of the navigating officer of HARDY (Lieutenant-Commander R.C. Gordon-Smith) and to the handling of the ships in rear.

11. HARDY immediately entered the harbour at Narvik. After backing and filling among the merchant ships at anchor she fired torpedoes, 3 at a warship and 4 more into the north-eastern corner of the harbour. One torpedo must have hit the warship, as there was a violent explosion and sparks came out of her. HARDY then used her guns on another warship seen at anchor and then withdrew.

12. Surprise had been complete and the enemy had not yet opened fire. HUNTER and HAVOCK now entered the harbour. HUNTER fired 4 torpedoes at a destroyer and 4 more at some other target but the result is not known. HAVOCK fired 5 torpedoes and secured hits on a destroyer with gunfire.

13. By this time the enemy destroyers and shore batteries inside the harbour had opened fire. The shore guns all used tracer ammunition, which appeared to be smaller than 4 in. and the shooting was not accurate.

14. HOTSPUR and HOSTILE saw nothing to the northward of Narvik though low visibility prevented a proper examination of Rombaks and Herjangs Fiords. These two ships covered the retirement of the other three from the inner harbour by putting up a smoke screen, which seemed very effective. HOTSPUR then fired 4 torpedoes into the harbour and hit two merchant ships, which sank. At least six torpedoes were fired by the enemy out of the harbour but all missed or ran under without exploding.

15. All five ships then approached the harbour entrance again and engaged any suitable targets they could see. This time a fairly intense fire was encountered from shore batteries and enemy destroyers but the flotilla was able to withdraw, practically undamaged, to a position off Skjomnes.

16. On board HARDY the position was then summed up as follows. The Flotilla had been off an enemy harbour for over an hour and were undamaged. A surprise attack had been made and 24 torpedoes had been fired into the harbour. HOSTILE still had her full outfit of torpedoes whilst HOTSPUR had 4, HAVOCK 3 and HARDY 1 torpedo remaining. There was no sign of enemy warships outside the harbour and those inside must have been either sunk or damaged. It was estimated that 3 or 4 enemy warships had been inside the harbour and that probably only 2 were

somewhere outside and could be dealt with if met. Captain (D), Second Destroyer Flotilla, therefore, decided to make one more attack on the harbour.

I7. At about 0520 HARDY led the Flotilla into the final attack on the harbour, ships forming astern of her in the order HAVOCK, HUNTER, HOTSPUR and HOSTILE. A speed of I5 knots was not exceeded and the line was snaked to keep guns bearing on the harbour entrance, now shrouded in mist. As each ship turned to port off the harbour entrance, shore batteries or any other targets visible were engaged. Whilst turning, HOSTILE fired 4 torpedoes into the harbour and one enemy torpedo passed harmlessly underneath her. She was also hit by a shell just abaft her starboard anchor but this did little damage.

I8. Just after turning to port HARDY sighted enemy ships north of Narvik and Captain (D), Second Destroyer Flotilla, made an enemy report "I enemy cruiser and 3 enemy destroyers off Narvik. Am withdrawing to the westward." T.O.O. 055I/I0. At the same time he ordered the Flotilla to withdraw at 30 knots.

I9. Whilst turning to port and withdrawing to the west, the Flotilla engaged these enemy ships at ranges between 6,000 and 8,000 yards. The enemy replied but did no damage.

20. When about half way along the Ofot Fiord HARDY sighted 2 more warships about 3 miles ahead crossing from port to starboard. At first she hoped they might be our own cruisers and made the challenge; but it was answered by a salvo. Captain (D), Second Destroyer Flotilla, soon identified the 2 ships as large German destroyers (Leberecht Maas Class) and engaged them.

2I. Captain (D), Second Destroyer Flotilla, then made to the Flotilla "Keep on engaging enemy." T.O.O. 0555/I0. This was the last signal he made as shortly afterwards a shell burst on HARDY'S bridge and he was mortally wounded. Everyone on HARDY'S bridge and in the wheelhouse was now either killed or wounded. The ship, not under control and on fire forward, was making at high speed for the south shore of the fiord. The Captain's Secretary (Paymaster Lieutenant G.H. Stanning) was wounded, but struggled down from the bridge to find an empty wheelhouse. He took the wheel himself for a short time but on relief by an Able Seaman returned to the bridge. By this time the ship had practically lost steam and the Captain's Secretary directed her to be beached. The torpedo officer (Lieutenant G.R. Heppel), thinking that bridge steering was out of action, had gone aft to connect tiller flat steering but finding the bridge still controlling had returned there in time to agree to the beaching of the ship. The action taken at a critical time by Paymaster Lieutenant Stanning may well have resulted in saving many lives. Whether it was right or wrong, he showed great initiative in an unaccustomed role.

22. Shortly after HARDY had been hit, HUNTER was seen to be on fire and her forward torpedo tubes were missing, indicating some explosion. She was seen to lose steam just ahead of HOTSPUR at the same moment the latter's steering and all bridge communications were put out of action. Whilst not under control HOTSPUR collided with the damaged HUNTER and these two ships, locked together drew all the enemy's fire. By means of verbal orders to engine room and tiller flat, given from "X" gun deck, HOTSPUR was able to extricate herself from this predicament but the

combined effects of the collision and the damage done by the enemy caused HUNTER to sink.

23. The enemy, however, must have received considerable punishment. One destroyer appeared to have been struck by a torpedo and seemed to be aground whilst others had been hit by gunfire. HOTSPUR and HOSTILE had fired torpedoes at the enemy who had replied with four, which passed close down HOTSPUR'S starboard side.

24. When withdrawing after her collision HOTSPUR was still under fire from at least 4 enemy ships. HOSTILE and HAVOCK had got clear to the westward practically undamaged. Quickly taking in the situation, they immediately turned back into the Fiord and covered HOTSPUR'S retirement. This was a bold move, skilfully executed in narrow waters and it probably persuaded the enemy from following up his advantage.

25. As HOTSPUR was being conned from aft and had no signalling arrangements HOSTILE took charge and escorted her to Skjel Fiord. When about 18 miles west of Narvik, the German ammunition ship RAUENFELS was seen steaming up the fiord. Mistaking us for German destroyers she continued her course and was then stopped and blown up by HAVOCK.

26. HARDY had last been seen aground and on fire with men clambering over the side. One gun was still firing and it seemed likely that the enemy would close and finish her off. In the event, however, the enemy held off and 160 men got ashore. The epic story of how most of these men reached the village of Ballangen and were rescued by IVANHOE 3 days later, has been told elsewhere.

27. About an hour after landing, HARDY's torpedo officer made his way back on board and with a 9 lb. T.N.T. charge from the detonator tank blew up the steel chests in the Captain's Cabin. He was also able to rescue the Navigating Officer, who had been too badly wounded to abandon ship. The action of Lieutenant G.R. Heppel in returning to the ship, which was still on fire forward, is most creditable.

28. The results of the raid are difficult to assess and time alone will show the full effect. It is probable that 2 or 3 enemy destroyers were put out of action and 7 or 8 merchant ships sunk. One ammunition ship was blown up. Some damage was done to wharves and jetties by gunfire. On our side, HUNTER was sunk, HARDY put out of action and HOTSPUR severely damaged. The appearance of the flotilla in a snowstorm must have given a shock to the Germans on the day after their occupation. Any plans which the enemy had for blocking the approaches must have been interfered with and the way was paved for our subsequent attacks. Some encouragement must have been given to the Norwegians by the prompt appearance of our warships in their occupied waters.

29. Finally, on behalf of those who took part in the raid, I would like to pay a tribute to the initiative and fine fighting spirit shown by our leader, Captain B.A.W. Warburton-Lee, whose conduct was an example to us all.

I have the honour to be,

Sir,

Your obedient Servant,

(Sgd.) H.F. LAYMAN,
Commander.
The Rear Admiral Commanding
Home Fleet Destroyers.

H.M.S. *HAVOCK,*
27th April, 1940.

H.M.S. HAVOCK was in company with Captain D.2 in HARDY, HOTSPUR, HOSTILE and HUNTER during the night of April 9th-10th and was the fourth ship in the line during the passage up the Otfiord.

2. The weather was overcast, with frequent squalls of snow and the visibility varied between 5 and 2 cables.

3. The passage up the fiord was without incident except that touch was lost once due to a sudden alteration of course.

4. At 0426 the snowstorm cleared and the south side of the harbour of Narvik and some merchant ships were disclosed.

5. Captain D. entered the harbour between the British S.S. NORTH CORNWALL and the remainder of the merchant ships, and opened fire with guns and torpedoes. HUNTER followed and as soon as she was clear HAVOCK followed her. Fire was opened with the guns at a destroyer alongside a merchant ship whose gun-flashes could be seen, and with torpedoes at merchant ships and a destroyer at anchor. Three torpedoes only were fired as HUNTER appeared to have hit all the merchant ships in sight, and a second destroyer was not seen until the sights were past. All torpedoes were heard to hit and the destroyer vanished. As the enemy gun-fire was getting hot and they had the advantage of the light I increased speed and cleared out.

6. Just before entering the harbour two columns of water were seen ascending just inshore of the HUNTER, and it is thought that they were caused by badly aimed torpedoes from an enemy destroyer.

7. While leaving the harbour I passed close to NORTH CORNWALL, and one of the guards there fired on the bridge with a revolver. He was silenced by a Lewis gun.

8. Firing now increased from the harbour and HAVOCK was straddled but not hit. Fire was returned by the after group and an explosion seen in an enemy ship, while the foremost group bombarded the shore with H.E. shell, from which quarter a hot fire from rifles and machine guns was arriving.

9. Once clear of the harbour HAVOCK passed backwards and forwards across the entrance engaging ships inside with gunfire at 3,000 to 4,000 yards. Spotting was almost impossible owing to smoke but blind ladders were used and success hoped for.

10. At 0507 a number of torpedoes were seen approaching from the harbour and were avoided by going full speed ahead or astern. One torpedo appeared to pass underneath the ship, and if it was fitted with a magnetic pistol the degaussing circuit undoubtedly saved the ship. I then withdrew out of torpedo range and as ships were

interfering with each others fire formed astern of Captain D. who made a signal "Follow Round" at 0514. By this time we were 6,000 yards from the harbour.

II. At 0535 we passed the harbour for a second time but were not fired at and then HARDY led towards Rombaks Fjord.

I2. At 0540 three German destroyers were sighted bearing 350 degrees apparently coming from Herjangs Fjord. Captain D. ordered 30 knots and withdraw to the westwards at the same time opening fire on the second ship. I turned to follow him and engaged the leading ship at I0,000 yards. HARDY made an enemy report of a cruiser and two destroyers and in the bad light this looked possible. The enemy however appeared to turn away under our fire.

I3. At 0558 two more enemy destroyers appeared ahead and opened fire. HAVOCK was slightly to port of HARDY and I engaged the left hand ship but as soon as I saw that the leader was not fired at shifted to her. The range was about 3,000 yards, and fire soon took effect, the third salvo hitting aft and caused a violent explosion. She ceased fire with her main armament but continued to fire machine guns, an incendiary bullet from which set fire to a ready-use cordite locker at A gun.

I4. As we passed her I ordered the remaining torpedoes to be fired but they unfortunately passed astern due to an underestimation of the enemy speed.

I5. Just before HAVOCK fired torpedoes enemy torpedoes were seen approaching on the surface and easily avoided by combing the tracks. HARDY however who was steering more to port appeared to be hit by one as there was a high column of smoke from her after boiler room and much flame from the funnel. Actually from accounts afterwards this was a salvo of shell, and she rapidly lost way and passed astern.

I6. As I was now at the head of the line and no enemy appeared to be to the westward of us, I turned to starboard I80 degrees and closed the enemy astern, opening fire at I0,000 yards.

I7. During this run I passed HUNTER who was on fire and losing speed and HOTSPUR whose steering gear seemed to be out of action.

I8. Unfortunately the order to open fire could not be complied with as both foremost guns were out of action, and having no torpedoes I decided that it would be folly to close the range any further, and turned to starboard passing close astern of HOSTILE who was making smoke.

I9. At this moment the two leading enemy appeared to be unhit and were firing well placed salvos, while two in rear were very ragged. HAVOCK was again straddled but not hit except by splinters. While withdrawing the after group continued the engagement, until the enemy was lost in smoke.

20. While running to the west HOTSPUR was observed to collide with HUNTER who appeared to be in a bad way, but the former got clear.

2I. Once clear of the smoke I drew up alongside HOSTILE and both foremost guns being reported again in use, followed her back into the action to relieve the pressure on HOTSPUR. Fire was opened at I0,000 yards and continued until HOTSPUR was out of range when all ships withdrew. The leading enemy appeared to be still untouched and were straddling effectively while we were turning. They made no attempt however to close the range, after we had slowed to HOTSPUR'S speed.

22. On the way down the fjord a merchant ship was sighted which proved to be the German S.S. RAUENFELS, and HOSTILE stopped her with a shot and ordered me to examine her. I fired another round into her bow and she stopped and her crew hurriedly abandoned ship. I stopped and picked them up while the ship slowly drifted to the beach. I sent an armed boat over but she was burning furiously and I was uncertain as to whether she had used her W/T to call her friends, I decided not to risk the loss of my party and ordered their return. When the boat was hoisted I fired two H.E. into her to hasten the fire and went ahead. The result was certainly startling, as the German literally erupted and a column of flame and debris rose to over 3,000 feet as testified both by HOSTILE and HARDY'S survivors to the west who saw it over the mountains that height. Fortunately no casualties were sustained in HAVOCK but some damage to the hull was done. Judging from the fragments picked up she contained all the reserve ammunition and torpedoes for the destroyer flotilla, and also the Narvik minefield.

23. HAVOCK then joined HOSTILE off Tranoy Light.

24. From the evidence of the crew of the NORTH CORNWALL there were four destroyers in Narvik harbour when the attack commenced, two alongside the oiler, one alongside the one pier and one at anchor. Two of these were hit by torpedoes from HARDY, HUNTER or HAVOCK and sank immediately. The other two were hit by gunfire and set on fire. They never left the harbour. One of the five met outside was driven ashore and two more damaged. The former were seen ashore by HARDY survivors. The number of merchant ships sunk cannot be stated.

(Sgd.) R.E. COURAGE,
Lieutenant-Commander.

The following Despatch by Vice-Admiral W.J. Whitworth, C.B., D.S.O., Vice-Admiral Commanding, Battle Cruiser Squadron, was submitted on the 27th April, 1940, to the Lords Commissioners of the Admiralty by the Commander-in-Chief, Home Fleet.

H.M.S. *WARSPITE.*
25th April, 1940.

SIR,

I have the honour to forward the following report of the attack on the enemy Naval Forces and Shore Defences at Narvik on Saturday, 13th April, 1940.

2. Force "B" which was placed under my orders for this operation, was composed of the following of His Majesty's Ships:-

WARSPITE. – Captain V.A.C. Crutchley, V.C., D.S.C. (Flying the flag of Vice-Admiral Commanding, Battle Cruiser Squadron).

BEDOUIN. – Commander J.A. McCoy.

COSSACK. – Commander R. St.V. Sherbrooke.

ESKIMO. – Commander St. J.A. Micklethwait, D.S.O.

PUNJABI. – Commander J.T. Lean.

HERO. – Commander H.W. Biggs.

ICARUS. – Lieutenant-Commander C.D. Maud.

KIMBERLEY. – Lieutenant-Commander R.G. K. Knowling.

FORESTER. – Lieutenant-Commander E.B. Tancock, D.S.C.

FOXHOUND. – Lieutenant-Commander G.H. Peters.

3. The following instructions for the conduct of the operation were received from you.

"Operation D.W. will take place Saturday 13th April.

   (i)   Object destruction of German warships, Merchant ships and defences in Narvik area.

   (ii) Ships of Force "B" are to rendezvous with WARSPITE flying the flag of the Vice-Admiral Commanding, Battle Cruiser Squadron, in position 67° 44' North 13° 22' East at 0730.

   (iii) HOSTILE and HAVOCK to protect Skjel Fiord.

   (iv) Remaining destroyers are to rendezvous with Commander-in-Chief, Home Fleet, in position 68° 00' North 11° 20' East at 1030.

   (v)   After arrival of other Destroyers, HERO, FOXHOUND and FORESTER will be detached to get out T.S.D.S. Destroyer of the 20th Destroyer Flotilla is to get out Bow Protection gear[4] and is to form ahead of leading T.S.D.S.[5] Destroyer when latter is in station on WARSPITE. The four destroyers working their Asdics as far as practicable. Other destroyers form Anti-submarine screen as ordered by the Vice-Admiral Commanding, Battle Cruiser Squadron. The force will proceed up Vest Fiord in this formation and it is suggested a destroyer should be detailed on each side to throw a depth charge in any likely inlet that could harbour a submarine.

   (vi) On reaching Baroy Island which is the suspected Minefield area, the A/S[6] screen should as far as practicable swing into the swept waters until past the Island.

   (vii) The force will proceed into Ofot Fiord engaging shore defences in passing, making full use of short range weapons as well as heavier guns. Non-T.S.D.S. destroyers and WARSPITE covering advance of sweeping destroyers with gunfire. It is specially important that destroyers sighted should be engaged before they can fire torpedoes at WARSPITE.

   (viii) T.S.D.S. sweeping is to be continued up to longitude 16° 55' East. Sweeping destroyers are then to haul clear of WARSPITE recover or cut their sweeps and assist the non-T.S.D.S. destroyers. Failing other targets they may drop back and destroy shore defence guns on Baroy Island or elsewhere. WARSPITE will proceed to a position 5 miles from Narvik depending on circumstances and from there cover the advance of the destroyers into the harbour and adjacent waters where enemy ships may be located.

(ix) Destroyers are normally to make smoke if required by Vice-Admiral Commanding, Battle Cruiser Squadron.

(x) The force will withdraw as ordered by the Vice-Admiral Commanding, Battle Cruiser Squadron.

(xi) FURIOUS is to arrange Air Attacks on the following enemy positions. All forces to synchronise with WARSPITE'S approach.

Attack (a) Baroy Island defences about 1215.

(b) Romness Point, longitude 16° 31' East and opposite shore about 1300.

(c) Warships in Ballangen, longitude 17° 00' East, and Narvik harbour and Herjangs and batteries at Narvik about 1345. Vice-Admiral Commanding, Battle Cruiser Squadron, will signal exact times at which these attacks are to commence.

(xii) FURIOUS is to provide Anti-submarine patrol for WARSPITE from 0830 vide paragraph (ii).

Time of origin 1909/1201 April.

4. The following information in regard to the Operation was contained in your signal 1547/12th April:-

(i) Minefield reported 68° 24' North 15° 59' East.

(ii) U-Boat in Vest Fiord area.

(iii) Five or six LEBERECHT MAAS class some damaged and six Merchantmen sunk inside harbour.

(iv) HARDY beached 68° 23' North 17° 06' East.

(v) Baroy Island 68° 21' North 16° 07' East has Military Defences including possibly magnetic Torpedo tubes.

(vi) Three 12 or 18 pounder guns on hill North of Ore Quay, Chart Number 3753, facing North-west. Four inch calibre guns both sides of fiord near entrance to Ranchet 68° 26' 30" North 16° 29' 30" East and 68° 24' 30" North 16° 29' 30" East.

(vii) One or two unidentified aircraft were sighted in Vest Fiord on 12th April.

(viii) Two friendly Norwegian submarines are in vicinity of Sommersoct 68° 27' North 15° 29' East.

5. At 0200 on 13th April, 1940, having with considerable difficulty, owing to heavy swell, completed the transfer of my flag to H.M.S. WARSPITE at sea, I proceeded with H.M. Ships COSSACK, HERO, FOXHOUND and FORESTER to the rendezvous in position 67° 44' North 13° 22' East, where H.M. Ships BEDOUIN,

PUNJABI, KIMBERLEY and ICARUS joined my flag. H.M.S. ESKIMO was at this time on patrol in the vicinity of Tranoy Light.

6. Force "B" proceeded up Vest Fiord. The weather was overcast, heavy melting snow clouds producing intermittent rain, wind South-west Force 3-4[7], visibility 10 miles. Snow lay thickly on the mountains surrounding the fiords, down to sea level.

7. At 0747 a signal was made ordering H.M.S. FURIOUS to commence air attack at the times stated in the orders for the operation (vide paragraph 3 (xi)).

8. At 0915 I made the following signal to Force "B".

"We are proceeding to attack the defences of Narvik and any German war or merchant ships met. I am sure that any resistance on the part of the enemy will be dealt with in the most resolute and determined manner. I wish you all every success."

9. At 1009 I made the following signal amplifying the operation orders issued by you.

"Operation D.W. paragraph (vi). Any sign of enemy activity on Baroy Island is to be destroyed by gunfire. Paragraph (vii). If a guide to fire distribution is necessary odd numbered destroyers take south side and even number take north side. Enemy warships take precedence over shore targets.

Paragraph (viii). On arrival east of 17° East destroyers may use high speed but should not lose the support of WARSPITE'S fire. Any enemy warship in the fiord to the north of Narvik is to be provided for before the harbour to the south is entered.

Paragraph (x). If ordered to withdraw, the signal D.B.O. by V/S and W/T will be used."

10. ICARUS, HERO and FOXHOUND in that order sweeping directly ahead of WARSPITE while the remaining five destroyers (including FORESTER, her T.S.D.S. sweep having failed) formed an A/S screen on her – one ahead and two on each bow.

11. At 1058 Force "B" was approaching ESKIMO off Tranoy Light. ESKIMO signalled "Submarine bearing 240° from me." This submarine was on the surface and flashed "U" to ESKIMO presumably thinking she was friendly. On ESKIMO turning towards the submarine dived. Although contact was not obtained depth charges were dropped by destroyers in the vicinity.

12. The area between Tranoy Light and Baroy Island had been reported dangerous due to mines. As the Force approached this area screening destroyers closed ready to form astern of the sweep.

13. At 1152 in position five miles westward of Baroy Island WARSPITE'S aircraft was flown off with instructions:-

(*a*) To carry out reconnaissance for Force "B" advancing up Ofot Fiord with particular reference to the presence of German vessels in side fiords, the movements of German forces and the position of shore batteries.

(*b*) to bomb any suitable targets.

(*c*) to return to Skjel Fiord.

I4. On reaching Baroy Island the screening destroyers moved to the van; BEDOUIN, PUNJABI, ESKIMO to starboard, COSSACK, KIMBERLEY and FORESTER to port.

I5. A "Swordfish" aircraft from FURIOUS was sighted approaching from the starboard quarter. It was believed to be that allocated to Task A in the operation orders, namely, the bombing of Baroy Island defences. Inspection of the Island however showed no sign of enemy activity and a signal was made to the aircraft "I see nothing to bomb on Baroy Island", in which the observer concurred and reported that he was returning to his ship.

I6. At I203 WARSPITE'S aircraft reported "German destroyer in position one mile north of Hamnesholm (67° 25' North I6° 36' East), steering west." At I229 BEDOUIN reported sighting the enemy bearing 073°. Fire was opened by destroyers in the van. The enemy retired at long range and fire was intermittent owing to the poor visibility and smoke.

The blackened bow of the ammunition ship RAUENFELS blown up by the 2nd Destroyer Flotilla during their retirement on I0th April, was passed in position 68° 24½' North I6° 28' East.

I7. At I240 the aircraft reported that two enemy destroyers were off Framsk (68° 24' North I6° 49' East) and at I250 that these destroyers were hiding in a bay five miles ahead of the screen, and were in a position to fire torpedoes. The number was later corrected to one destroyer.

I8. The action became more general. Enemy destroyers sighted in Ofot Fiord were engaged at long range and WARSPITE opened fire with main armament.

I9. The enemy destroyer reported by WARSPITE'S aircraft, believed to be one of the Roeder class, had manoeuvred into the small bay in a position 68° 24½' North I6° 48' East, at the head of which lies Djupvik. Her bows pointed to the eastward, and her torpedo armament bore across the fiord. She was hidden from the approaching destroyers.

20. The warning conveyed by the aircraft was therefore invaluable. The leading destroyers turned their guns and torpedo armament on the starboard tow, and before the enemy could fire more than one salvo, she was heavily engaged. Two torpedoes, one from BEDOUIN and one from ESKIMO struck the ship and in three minutes she was on fire forward and aft. A report was received, however, that a figure was seen standing by the torpedo tubes and her destruction was completed by salvos from WARSPITE'S main armament. Torpedoes fired by the enemy but passed clear of our destroyers.

2I. Meanwhile more enemy destroyers had appeared in Ofot Fiord. In the smoke and haze the targets were not clear, but at least four ships were observed. The enemy steamed to and fro across the Fiord bringing guns and torpedoes to bear and turning as the limit of the run was reached. Our destroyers, with the exception of those sweeping, adopted a loose formation from one to three miles ahead of WARSPITE altering course as necessary, to bring armament to bear and avoid shell fire. From this point Force "B" advanced up Ofot Fiord at a mean speed of I0 knots.

22. At I3I8 WARSPITE'S aircraft sighted five torpedo tracks approaching from

ahead. These passed clear to port and subsequently an explosion was observed at the water's edge on the port beam.

23. WARSPITE'S main armament engaged the enemy when a target presented itself. But owing to the smoke of the destroyer engagement fire was intermittent. Speed was adjusted to maintain support of the destroyers but to keep WARSPITE clear of the torpedo danger as far as possible.

24. At I34I FURIOUS'S aircraft were sighted on the port quarter approaching to the attack.

25. A further torpedo exploded on the foreshore bearing Red 20°.[8]

26. At I345 sweeping destroyers hauled their sweeps and subsequently proceeded in support of the Destroyers of the Striking Force.

27. At I350 COSSACK reported yet another torpedo approaching. WARSPITE was manoeuvred to present the smallest target but the track was not seen.

28. At I352 WARSPITE'S aircraft reported no destroyers in Skjomen Fiord.

29. Meanwhile the engagement with the enemy manoeuvring to the North of Narvik had become closer and another destroyer was seen leaving the harbour distant I2,000 yards from WARSPITE. She was engaged by destroyers on the starboard wing and by WARSPITE'S main armament and was soon severely damaged. The enemy's fire was becoming ragged and shots were falling round WARSPITE.

30. Gunfire was then observed in Narvik Harbour and was thought to be from a shore battery. At I402 I ordered the destroyers to engage enemy destroyers while WARSPITE engaged the shore battery.

3I. At I4I7 PUNJABI passed WARSPITE withdrawing from the action owing to hits which had put the main steam pipe and all guns temporarily out of action.

32. At the same time a heavy explosion shook WARSPITE: the cause was not ascertained.

33. At I42I WARSPITE ceased fire on the target in Narvik Bay owing to our own destroyers fouling the range. This target had proved to be a destroyer alongside the quay and not a shore battery.

34. The situation then developed as follows:-

One enemy destroyer badly on fire, ran ashore at Herjangen (68° 33' North I7° 33½ ' East) and was struck by a torpedo from ESKIMO.

The destroyer, which had just left Narvik Harbour, broke out in flames forward and aft, and was abandoned by her crew close to the shore northwest of Narvik.

An unknown number of destroyers retired up Rombaks Fiord, under cover of smoke from funnels and floats and were followed by ESKIMO, FORESTER, HERO, ICARUS and later BEDOUIN.

The destroyer alongside in Narvik Harbour continued to fire. COSSACK and FOXHOUND entered the harbour supported by KIMBERLEY, and under their combined attack the enemy caught fire. FOXHOUND approached to board but was received with Machine gun fire from the shore. Then the destroyer blew up and resistance in the harbour ceased.

While carrying out this attack COSSACK drifted on to a submerged wreck.

35. Until defensive action in Narvik ceased WARSPITE lay off the entrance and at I450 I signalled to the Commander-in-Chief:-

> "Three enemy destroyers still up Rombaks Fiord. No enemy opposition in Narvik Bay. Four enemy destroyers destroyed. Am investigating possibility of occupying the town."

36. At I500 I proceeded up Rombaks Fiord to clear up the situation there. Two enemy destroyers were reported at the head of the Fiord by the aircraft and ESKIMO was leading five destroyers to the attack.

ESKIMO passed through the narrow neck in Rombaks Fiord followed closely by FORESTER and HERO and engaged two enemy ships in sight. The enemy replied with gun and torpedo fire and at I450 ESKIMO was struck by a torpedo which removed the bow of the ship. Of the two enemy ships, one, after firing torpedoes, ran aground at Sildvika where she was destroyed by gunfire and abandoned. The other retired under cover of smoke to the top of the fiord.

37. Difficulty was then experienced owing to the congestion in the narrow neck of this fiord. ESKIMO was trying to get clear stern first assisted by FORESTER, the remaining destroyers were endeavouring to enter and continue the chase.

38. At I520 I ordered all available destroyers to concentrate in Rombaks Fiord. At I530 a report on the situation was received from BEDOUIN as follows:-

> "One aground out of action (this was at Sildvika). Two more round the corner out of sight. If they have torpedoes they are in a position of great advantage. HERO and BEDOUIN ammunition almost exhausted. BEDOUIN "A" mounting out of action. I520."

I thereupon signalled BEDOUIN:-

> "The torpedo menace must be accepted. Enemy must be destroyed without delay. Take KIMBERLEY, FORESTER, HERO and PUNJABI under your orders and organise attack sending most serviceable destroyer first. Ram or board if necessary. I540."

39. Meanwhile WARSPITE'S aircraft was recalled and hoisted inboard and preparations were made to carry out an indirect bombardment of the ships at the head of the fiord, should this be necessary. On its return WARSPITE'S aircraft reported sinking a submarine anchored off Bjerkvik, in Herjangs Fiord, by bombing. This sinking was accepted as a fact.[9]

40. While I was in communication with BEDOUIN, HERO, ICARUS and KIMBERLEY proceeded up Rombaks Fiord and, as soon as the targets could be observed in the smoke, opened fire on the destroyers at the head of the Fiord. No reply was made, however, and fire was checked. The enemy had abandoned the ships, of which there proved to be three. One was already scuttled, one sank forthwith and HERO and ICARUS sent away a boarding party to the one remaining. BEDOUIN, on arrival, ordered boarding parties to return, and the enemy was sunk by a torpedo from HERO. HERO states the boarded destroyer was the HANS LUDEMANN.

4I. As the destroyers had successfully dealt with all enemy forces at the top of the Fiord, indirect bombardment by WARSPITE was not necessary and it was decided to return to Narvik Bay to investigate the state of affairs there.

42. COSSACK was still grounded on a wreck and had been under spasmodic fire from a shore gun of small calibre. Although not definitely located, the COSSACK silenced it by retaliatory fire in its direction.

FOXHOUND, standing by, had sent her Medical Officer to COSSACK and was picking up survivors from the German destroyer abandoned on fire off Narvik.

43. At I742 I made the following report of the situation.

"WARSPITE, COSSACK and FOXHOUND in Narvik Bay. Little opposition. All German destroyers sunk, three of them after retiring up Rombaks Fiord. One submarine sunk by WARSPITE'S aircraft. Parties of men, possibly soldiers retreating over hills. One field Howitzer silenced by COSSACK. Enemy aircraft have been sighted. Damage to own ships so far reported: – ESKIMO bows blown off by torpedo. COSSACK damaged and ashore in Narvik Bay. PUNJABI one boiler out of action. I742."

44. I thereupon considered the landing of a party to occupy the town as the opposition had apparently been silenced.

With the force available only a small party could be landed and to guard against the inevitable counter-attack it would be necessary to keep the force concentrated close to the water-front and to provide strong covering gunfire. In fact I considered it would be necessary to keep WARSPITE off Narvik.

45. A signal was then received from FOXHOUND that the Officer prisoners taken had reported the presence of several German submarines in the Fiord.

46. At I800 twelve enemy aircraft were sighted approaching from the westward.

47. Apart from the above considerations I felt, that to place, at the end of a long and strenuous day, a party of less than 200 tired seamen and marines in the midst of a force of not less than 2,000 professional German soldiers, would be to court disaster, even allowing for the moral effect which the day's engagement must have had on the enemy.

48. The cumulative effect of the roar of WARSPITE'S fifteen inch guns reverberating down and around the high mountains of the Fiord, the bursts and splashes of these great shells, the sight of their ships sinking and burning around them must have been terrifying to the enemy. But such an effect cannot be of a lasting nature to the soldiers on shore, and I felt that to be taken full advantage of, it would have required a trained, organised military force, ready to land directly the Naval engagement had ceased. If such a force had been present, I believe that they would have succeeded in establishing themselves so strongly in Narvik that its eventual capture would only be a matter of time and reinforcements.

49. I thereupon decided against keeping WARSPITE stopped in the Fiord off Narvik, subject to submarine and air attack.

50. At I832 I signalled:-

"General from BC. One.[10] Am withdrawing. KIMBERLEY is to guard

COSSACK withdrawing her if possible from Narvik harbour. PUNJABI to guard ESKIMO."

51. HOSTILE (Commander J.P. Wright) and IVANHOE (Commander P.H. Hadow), based on Skjel Fiord, had been placed at my disposal by your signal. I ordered these destroyers to proceed to Narvik and reinforce those to be stationed there. IVANHOE had been ordered to patrol the entrance to the Fiord and was therefore in the vicinity.

52. I proceeded down Ofot Fiord with FOXHOUND ahead. BEDOUIN, HERO and ICARUS followed withdrawing from Rombaks Fiord. FORESTER was delayed embarking the majority of ESKIMO'S crew.

53. At 1840 when close to Hamnesholm Light (67° 25' North 16° 36' East) FOXHOUND obtained a submarine contact and counter-attacked. This submarine was apparently escaping out of Ofot Fiord. A later report received from the Hamnesholm Lighthouse keeper confirms this. I have since come to the conclusion that a submarine navigating submerged in the narrow waters of a fiord would find himself in a not very enviable position with Anti-submarine destroyers operating overhead and his desire to get out of it is therefore understandable.

54. The four destroyers then formed an Anti-submarine screen and preparations were made to repel the attack of the twelve aircraft which were still in sight to the northward. This attack did not develop although IVANHOE reported being bombed on passage up the Fiord.

55. I ordered destroyers in company to be prepared to transfer wounded to WARSPITE under cover of darkness at 2230. At 2027 I made the following report:-

"Commander-in-Chief, Home Fleet (Repeated) Admiralty from Vice Admiral Commanding Battle Cruiser Squadron.

My 1742. I am withdrawing with WARSPITE, PUNJABI, HERO, ICARUS, FOXHOUND and FORESTER when wounded are collected.

BEDOUIN and KIMBERLEY remaining to assist ESKIMO and COSSACK. Have ordered HOSTILE and IVANHOE to support them.

Seven enemy destroyers and one submarine have been destroyed. There are now no enemy warships at Narvik. No shore batteries were observed but a Howitzer on the hill behind Narvik and a field gun on the foreshore were reported to have been firing. Thirteen merchant ships in the harbour, half appeared German. Our destroyers being in occupation of the harbour these were not sunk. Formations of twelve enemy aircraft approached about 1830 but no attack has as yet been made on WARSPITE, though IVANHOE was bombed while on patrol off Tjel Sundet. Damage to ships and casualties will be reported when received. Some German prisoners have been taken, details of which will be reported later."

56. Reports which were received, however, indicated that a number of wounded remained in the destroyers at Narvik. Accordingly, at 2050 I ordered course to be reversed and signalled to COSSACK at Narvik:-

"All wounded are to be collected in PUNJABI to rendezvous with me in I7° East at midnight."

57. At 22I0 I made the following signal:-

"Commander-in-Chief, Home Fleet, (Repeated) Admiralty from B.C. One.

My impression is that enemy forces in Narvik were thoroughly frightened as a result of today's action and that the presence of WARSPITE was the chief cause of this.

I recommend that the town be occupied without delay by the main landing force.

I intend to visit Narvik again tomorrow Sunday in order to maintain the moral effect of the presence of WARSPITE and to accept the air and submarine menace involved by this course of action."

In making this signal I knew that the troop convoys making for Vaagsfiord were at sea and envisaged them being diverted direct to Narvik.

58. Meanwhile I proceeded to the Narvik area. On arrival all destroyers in company having wounded were brought alongside WARSPITE in turn to effect the transfer while the remainder carried out A/S patrol in the vicinity.

59. Transferring the wounded took a very long time, and I was acutely aware of the possibility of submarine and air attack. As regards the former I felt that Ofot Fiord had become too unhealthy an area for a submarine, witness FOXHOUND'S attack and position of submarine. As regards air attack WARSPITE was ready to go ahead at any time and slip destroyers alongside, and if air attack did develop it did not matter where it took place. In any event WARSPITE was there to support the destroyers who had done such grand work, and I was not disposed to abandon them in their distress.

60. IVANHOE had, while proceeding up the Fiord, been intercepted by a Norwegian vessel on board which were survivors of HARDY[II] and British Merchant ships. The opportunity was taken to distribute these survivors numbering about 200 men to various destroyers.

6I. Several large fires and explosions were seen in Narvik nine miles to the Eastward.

62. I received a report from COSSACK that the condition of some wounded was so serious as to make transfer by destroyer inadvisable and I therefore at 0250 closed Narvik to effect the transfer by boat.

63. During WARSPITE'S approach white Verey Lights were fired by a Merchant vessel in the harbour. This signal was presumed to be a warning to whatever shore defences were manned.

64. At 0326 COSSACK managed to draw clear of the wreck and was berthed alongside WARSPITE.

65. When all wounded were embarked I ordered withdrawal, the following disposition being made:-

KIMBERLEY and IVANHOE to remain at Narvik.

ESKIMO accompanied by BEDOUIN and COSSACK by FORESTER to proceed to Skjel Fiord.

WARSPITE and remaining destroyers to proceed to the westward.

66. At I027 in reply to Admiralty message timed 09I3/I4th April asking for an estimate of strength of enemy in Narvik area the following reply was sent:-

"Admiralty (Repeated) Commander-in-Chief, Home Fleet, AURORA,

SOUTHAMPTON from B.C. One.

Your 09I3. Information from Norwegian sources estimate I,500 to 2,000 troops in Narvik. German Naval Officer prisoner states that there are many more than this, but I think this statement was made with intent to deceive. He also states that guns on shore are being positioned with the main object of opposing a landing but COSSACK aground in Narvik Bay for I2 hours yesterday was not seriously molested.

I am convinced that Narvik can be taken by direct assault, without fear of meeting serious opposition on landing. I consider that the main landing force need only be small but that it must have the support of Force B or one of similar composition. A special requirement being ships and destroyers with the best available A.A. armaments."

General Remarks.

67. The safe return of ESKIMO and COSSACK to Skjel Fiord was a fitting conclusion to an operation which I consider was an unqualified success.

Seven or eight enemy destroyers and one submarine – the total German Naval Forces present – were sunk without the loss of a British ship.

(The enemy destroyer "already scuttled" in Rombaks Fiord vide paragraph 40 may have been abandoned after the attack by the 2nd Destroyer Flotilla on I0th April, I940.)

68. Our casualties also were comparatively small – 28 killed, 55 wounded, while the casualties amongst enemy destroyers with their complement of 280 each must have been very heavy.

69. I cannot speak too highly of the vigour and determination with which our destroyers went into the attack – they had to bear the brunt of the enemy's defence, and it was only by the skilful handling of their ships that they avoided receiving heavy damage from gunfire and torpedo.

70. Our destroyers enjoyed a tactical advantage in their ability to fire a heavy armament on forward bearings.

7I. The enemy reports made by WARSPITE'S aircraft were invaluable. I doubt if ever a ship-borne aircraft has been used to such good purpose as it was during this operation. In addition the aircraft bombed and sank an enemy submarine.

72. Apart from the effective fire developed by WARSPITE her presence undoubtedly gave great confidence to our own destroyers and put fear into the hearts of the enemy, who must have realised that they were caught like rats in a trap.

73. The precision and coolness with which WARSPITE was handled during the approach, and when both main and secondary armament were engaging the enemy was typical of the Commanding Officer – Captain V.A.C. Crutchley, V.C., D.S.C.

(Sgd.) W.J. WHITWORTH,
Vice-Admiral Commanding,
Battle Cruiser Squadron.
Commander-in-Chief,
Home Fleet.

Footnotes

[1] *Captain (D), 2nd Destroyer Flotilla.*

[2] *Sullom Voe – a harbour in the Shetland Isle.*

[3] *T.O.O. – Time of origin.*

[4] *Bow Protection Gear – Paravanes*

[5] *T.S.D.S. – Two Speed Destroyer Sweep.*

[6] *A/S – Anti-Submarine.*

[7] *Refers to the Beaufort scale of windforce.*

Force 3 – Gentle breeze (7-10 m.p.h. at sea level).

Force 4 – Moderate breeze (11-15 m.p.h. at sea level).

[8] *Red 20° = 20° on the port bow.*

[9] *It has since been confirmed that this submarine was sunk by WARSPITE's aircraft.*

[10] *A signal to all ships present from V.A.C., 1st Battle Cruiser Squadron.*

[11] *HARDY was lost in the first engagement at Narvik three days previously.*

3

ADMIRAL OF THE FLEET THE EARL OF CORK AND ORRERY'S DESPATCH ON OPERATIONS IN NORTHERN NORWAY
10 APRIL TO 8 JUNE 1940

THURSDAY, 10 JULY, 1947

NORWAY CAMPAIGN, 1940.

The following Despatch was submitted to the Lord's Commissioners of the Admiralty on the 17th July, 1940, by Admiral of the Fleet the Earl of Cork and Orrery, G.C.B.,G.C.V.O., Flag Officer, Narvik.

Be pleased to lay before Their Lordships the following Report upon the recent operations in the Narvik Area of Northern Norway.

SECTION I.
PRELIMINARY STAGES.

I. On the afternoon of Wednesday, April 10th, I received a message that the First Sea Lord would like to see me and was informed by him that a combined expedition was to be sent to Narvik and that I was to go in charge of the Naval force, etc. I then accompanied him to a meeting of the Service Ministers and Chiefs of Staff where the whole matter was discussed.

On the same evening, I attended a further meeting in the First Sea Lord's room on the subject.

I was then informed that Captain L.E.H. Maund was to go as my Chief Staff Officer, the officer I had asked for not being available.

Captain Maund who was present at the meeting left by plane the same night for Scapa, there to join the SOUTHAMPTON, which ship was conveying Major-General P.J. Mackesy, C.B., D.S.O., M.C., appointed to command the Military force, to Harstad, in Vaagsfiord, selected as the Military Base.

On the afternoon of Thursday, April IIth, I saw the First Lord for a few minutes, and left the same night for Rosyth, accompanied by Commander A.G.V. Hubback and my personal staff – (Temporary) Paymaster-Captain H.R.H. Vaughan, Secretary, and Lieutenant-Commander The Hon. D.C. Cairns, Flag Lieutenant and Signal Officer.

My impression on leaving London was quite clear that it was desired by H.M. Government to turn the enemy out of Narvik at the earliest possible moment and that I was to act with all promptitude in order to attain this result.

2. On April I2th, I embarked in H.M.S. AURORA and sailed at noon for the Narvik area. After an uneventful passage, Skjelfiord was reached at 2000, April I4th.

3. It had been the original intention to proceed to Harstad where, as already stated, the G.O.C. Troops was on passage, as was also the Military Convoy.

This destination was changed, however, on receipt of a signal from Vice-Admiral W.J. Whitworth, C.B., D.S.O., flying his flag in WARSPITE, in which ship he had carried out his successful raid on the German naval forces in Narvik Waters on April I3th.

4. In this message appeared this sentence: – "I am convinced that Narvik can be taken by direct assault now without fear of meeting serious opposition on landing. I consider that the main landing force need only be small but that it must have the support of Force B or one of similar composition . . ."

5. In order to take immediate advantage of this situation, I made the following signal:-

"AURORA and SOUTHAMPTON are to arrive at Skjelfiord by 2000 today,

Sunday . . ."

350 soldiers had been embarked in SOUTHAMPTON and it was hoped that during the night it might be possible to organise a landing force with these troops and seamen and marines of WARSPITE, SOUTHAMPTON, AURORA, PENELOPE and disabled destroyers.

6. Owing, however, to the difficult W/T conditions peculiar to this region, the message was not received by the SOUTHAMPTON until too late to take action, and her whereabouts were not ascertained until communicated by Admiralty, from whence also was received a message in which appeared:-

"We think it imperative that you and General should be together and act together and that no attack should be made except in concert . . ."

7. The AURORA proceeded for Harstad, meeting the Troop Convoy carrying the

24th Brigade, etc., off the entrance to And Fiord and leading it into harbour on the morning of the I5th.

When approaching the anchorage with the Destroyers BRAZEN (Lieutenant-Commander Sir Michael Culme-Seymour, Bt.) and FEARLESS (Commander K.L. Harkness) acting as A/S screen, the latter obtained a contact with and both smartly engaged and sank U.49, the crew being rescued practically intact.

8. The Convoy was anchored in Bygden Fiord and disembarkation carried out at once.

This operation was subjected to an air attack the same afternoon, and again on April I6th but no damage was sustained.

The transports sailed for the U.K. in the early hours of April I7th.

9. The disembarkation was effected by use of Destroyers and large numbers of local craft (small steamers and motor fishing ketches called "puffers").

Later, in order to expedite matters, the PROTECTOR (Captain W.Y. la R. Beverley) was used, and thus began a career of extreme usefulness carried out with conspicuous zeal.

I0. On April I5th, I met General Mackesy for the first time and was astonished to hear that not only was his force embarked as for a peaceful landing and consequently was unready for immediate operations but that the orders he had received, and given to him just prior to sailing, ruled out any idea of attempting an opposed landing. Thus the General and myself left the U.K. with diametrically opposite views as to what was required.

II. The arrangement of the remainder of my report is as follows:-

Section II. Proceedings from I5th April to 23rd May, together with an account of relations with the Norwegian Government.

Section III. A/A Protective Measures.

Section IV. The Development of the Base Defences.

Section V. A Summary of the Events in the Mosjoen-Mo-Bodo Area.

Section VI. The Final Operations for the Capture of Narvik.

Section VII. The Evacuation.

SECTION II
PROCEEDINGS FROM I5TH APRIL TO 23RD MAY TOGETHER WITH AN ACCOUNT OF RELATIONS WITH THE NORWEGIAN GOVERNMENT.

I. The use of Harstad – itself on an island – as Military Headquarters and main point of disembarkation for military personnel and stores meant that the Navy had a very large area to protect against submarines and aircraft, while at the same time maintaining offensive patrols to harass the enemy in the region of Narvik itself. A chart accompanies this report so that distances involved and the geographical layout of the campaign may be appreciated. The protection of Skjelfiord where the PENELOPE and other damaged ships lay, and had to be rendered seaworthy, was a commitment until I0th May.

2. The unloading of transports was a continual difficulty. There were but two wharves at Harstad and the average rate of discharge was 2 ships in 5 days. Disembarkation of personnel was done for the most part while ships were in Bygden anchorage and to facilitate this work PROTECTOR and destroyers had to be used. Large numbers of local craft were hired for this and other water transport purposes in the whole area of the operations but were not always reliable as, upon sound of an air raid warning, they scattered away into the fiords and took a considerable time to return afterwards. During the 8 weeks of the operations there were over I40 air raids in Harstad causing a considerable loss of time and work. A withdrawal of the warning system resulted in a strike among the Norwegian labourers and small craft men. The subject of A/A measures and protection is dealt with in a separate chapter of this report. In addition to the landing at Harstad, troops were put ashore at Salangen in Sagfiord on the I5th April and contact was made with Norwegian forces in that area. Advance southward was effected from both places; the Headquarters of the 24th Brigade being established at Bogen in Ofotfiord later.

3. Instead of attempting to take Narvik by assault it was decided for reasons that have been reported separately to carry out a bombardment in the hope that the nerve of the enemy already reported affected, might be so shattered thereby that he would surrender the town. The expected thaw had not come and the snow still lay everywhere several feet thick, rendering movement very difficult by any but experienced and specially equipped troops. The AURORA (Captain Louis Hamilton), was established as Senior Officer in Ofotfiord and with the ships under his orders maintained a steady and harassing pressure on the enemy. The bombardment took place on 24th April; EFFINGHAM (in which I was accompanied by General Mackesy and Brigadier Fraser), WARSPITE, AURORA, ENTERPRISE, ZULU taking part. The bitter weather conditions, heavy snowstorms and low visibility prevented any aerial activity on either side. Troops were carried in the VINDICTIVE in case the morale of the defenders should appear to be so affected as to give a promising opportunity to land. The climatic conditions were, however, entirely against any such undertaking and the low visibility entirely prevented any estimate of the effect achieved by the bombardment.

4. On the 25th April there was further heavy fall of snow and, as weather conditions compelled postponement of any direct attack on Narvik, attention was given to movements of troops designed to bring pressure on the enemy to the north and south of the Narvik peninsula. Ballangen on the south side of Vestfiord was occupied on the 26th. The first French troops were disembarked on the 28th; two Battalions to Salangen in Sagfiord and one Battalion at Bogen. I discussed the position with the British and French Generals and the latter (General Bethouart) accompanied me in CODRINGTON to reconnoitre Narvik and Herjangs Fiord.

5. On the 29th April, two weeks after our arrival in the area, there appeared the first reliable signs of the long awaited thaw and I could look forward to the conduct

of operations without the tremendous handicap of snow. On this day the A.L.C.s[1] and M.L.C.s[1] brought out in the EMPIRE ABILITY were disembarked and started a career of remarkable usefulness.

6. Affairs to the southward, in the Mosjoen, Mo and Bodo areas began to attract attention at this time. They form the subject of a separate chapter of this report.

7. On May Ist, I visited Ofotfiord in EFFINGHAM and a bombardment was carried out by AURORA, RESOLUTION and EFFINGHAM partly in support of troops skirmishing in the Ankenes area. The thaw had now set in so certainly that I ordered plans to be prepared for a direct attack upon Narvik to be staged for May 8th but, for reasons reported separately, this never materialised.

8. On May 3rd, the French Foreign Legion (2 Battalions) and the Polish Brigade arrived and on May 5th Rear Admiral A.L. St. G. Lyster arrived and assumed control of the defences and development of the bases. On May 6th, the first 3.7 in. A.A. guns (8 in number) arrived.

9. Plans were now developed for a landing by the French at Bjervik. Originally intended for the night of I0th-IIth May, this actually took place on the night of I2th-I3th. The forces employed were the two Battalions of the Foreign Legion and the Military operations were conducted by General Bethouart who was with me in the EFFINGHAM, as was also Lieutenant-General C.J.E. Auchinleck who had just arrived from England. The night was cold with low clouds but, except for 2 hours of twilight, daylight lasted throughout. The troops were embarked off Ballangen, together with tanks.[2] After retiring to the westward to mislead the enemy, the Squadron turned and steamed for a position at the entrance to Herjangs Fiord where troops were placed in the boats from which they were to land. The actual landing was prefaced by an effective bombardment (EFFINGHAM, AURORA, RESOLUTION and Destroyers taking part), after which the 3 A.L.C.s and 2 M.L.C.s landed the first flight in most spirited fashion in face of an appreciable amount of rifle and machine-gun fire. The conduct of the soldiers of the Foreign Legion, their prompt movements and good training that was evident from their action, were much admired. The first flight and supports were followed by open boats towed by ships' power boats which landed their men without any untoward incident. The whole operation went off very well and at 0600 on the I3th General Bethouart and his staff landed. He informed me that he no longer required the support of H.M. Ships beyond those normally on patrol in that area.

I0. Two Battalions of Polish troops marching from Bogen reinforced the Foreign Legion during the day. Enemy aircraft did not appear during the operation. The French were able to get into Oydejord almost at once.

II. At a conference on my return to Harstad on the I3th May, General Auchinleck informed me that he had received orders from the War Office that he was to assume command of all Military Forces forthwith.

I2. The next military objective was to obtain control of Rombaks Fiord so as to prepare the way for a direct attack on Narvik from Oydejord. FAME (Commander. P.N. Walter) conducted the Naval part of this work in most tireless and efficient manner.

13. An account of the actual final operations for the occupation of Narvik forms a separate chapter of this report.

14. Contact was maintained throughout the operation with the Norwegian High Command who were naturally very concerned about the withdrawal of troops from South Norway. The Norwegians realised that their forces were not properly armed for modern warfare and they made repeated requests for artillery, especially A/A, for the defence of Tromso and North Norway and also to equip the large number of coasting vessels upon whose movement up and down the coast depends the life of the country. These requests I passed on to the Admiralty for H.M. Government but the Norwegians, who seemed to imagine that immense reserves of guns and ammunition, etc., were readily available in England, could not understand why their requests were not immediately complied with. To ease matters I authorised the issue to them of all the war material, not required by the Army, taken in the captured German Transport ALSTER which was sent to Tromso on the 23rd April to discharge accordingly; to meet Article 39 of the Naval Discipline Act, the British Consul at Tromso was asked to watch the discharging and make an affidavit of goods handed over; a copy of this affidavit was sent to the Secretary of the Admiralty later.

15. Towards the end of the period under report it was possible, but only with the greatest difficulty and taking risks, to spare 4 heavy and 4 light A/A guns for the protection of Tromso.

16. On 16th May, I met Admiral Diesen, the Norwegian Naval Commander-in-Chief, and the same day also General Rugé, the Military Commander-in-Chief. Two days later, I was able to meet Sir Cecil Dormer, H.B.M. Minister to Norway, on his way to Tromso from England.

17. On 23rd May I went by Walrus aircraft to Storsteinnes and there met the British Minister, Sir Cecil Dormer, Colonel Pollock, British Military Liaison Officer, Admiral Boyes, Naval Attaché, and General Rugé, Norwegian Commander-in-Chief; the latter informed me he had been appointed in command of all the Norwegian Defence Forces.

18. From there, I proceeded in company with General Rugé and Colonel Pollock to visit His Majesty The King, whom I found living some miles out (1¼ hours in car) in a fishing lodge, approached by a muddy path. The Crown Prince was with him. I spent about ¾ hour with His Majesty. He told me he knew what I had come about and that I was going to see his Ministers. The object of my visit was to obtain the authority of the Norwegian Government for (1) far more drastic control in the military areas over the civilian population and the innumerable small steamers and "puffers" navigating the fiords, etc., and upon which the life and communications of the people largely depended; (2) closer collaboration between Civil Government and British Military Authorities to make this control effective. Colonel Pollock had already discussed the subject with General Rugé, who was understanding and sympathetic and undertook to insist to the Government that action in this respect was essential. General Rugé left me to go to his Headquarters when I arrived at the King's residence.

19. On leaving His Majesty I drove back with Sir Cecil Dormer to Storsteinnes from where I flew to Tromso and saw the Prime Minister, Ministers for Defence, and

for Foreign Affairs. The three Ministers also were cordial and friendly, and promised that these matters should be closely gone into – and a Government representative sent to Harstad to arrange details. This conference was somewhat rudely put an end to by an air attack aimed at DEVONSHIRE in the harbour. They had only returned to Tromso that day, and the attack that evening was unfortunate. I also saw Admiral Diesen on the subject of the control afloat who undertook to do everything necessary. Vice-Admiral Cunningham had already taken the matter up with him and accompanied me to this meeting. The Norwegian Ministers mentioned the need for A/A artillery and equipment for their troops and also the necessity of refitting their ships which they had understood the British authorities would be able to arrange. The Norwegian Ministers showed every intention of being helpful and anxious to continue the fight, but they were not unnaturally concerned about the unavoidable delay in meeting their requirements on these points.

SECTION III
ANTI-AIRCRAFT DEFENCE MEASURES

I. The enemy commenced attacks by air on the day that the first convoy arrived and continued throughout the period of the campaign. When, after the withdrawal of our forces from South Norway, the enemy was able to develop air bases in Trondheim and other places the attacks greatly increased in intensity and frequency. Our fighter craft of the Fleet Air Arm and Royal Air Force, in those periods when they were available, wrought great havoc among the enemy and afforded a very welcome relief. From the earliest days the establishment of aerodrome's was a major preoccupation, but at the beginning, the land all being covered by three or more feet of snow, the problem presented unusual difficulties. The Norwegian authorities reported Bardufoss as having been used by Gladiators. Lieutenant Francklin, R.N. (F.A.A.) organised much of the preliminary work in clearing this and also a suitable ground discovered at Skaanland, the latter having the advantage of being situated adjacent to the merchant shipping anchorage in Lavangs Fiord between Harstad and Tjeldsundet passage. The thaw was late this year and it was the 30th April before I was sure it had commenced. The flying boat "Cabot" brought Wing Commander Atcherley to the area on the 4th May and he then took charge of the finding and development of aerodromes both to the north and to the south.

2. Heavy snowstorms and bad weather in the early period interfered with good work by the FURIOUS but her aircraft operated to their full capacity at every opportunity. She was recalled on April 23rd to re-equip, having then only eight aircraft fit for service. The urgent need for A/A artillery was emphasised in a telegram to the Admiralty on April 25th.

3. After the evacuation of Namsos and Aandalsnes, the enemy air attacks in the Narvik Vest Fiord and Vaags Fiord areas were intensified and the stationing of H.M. Ships with good A/A Batteries in each area where merchant ships were anchored or troops working became more than ever necessary. The enemy steadily developed the

supplying and reinforcing of his troops in Narvik by means of troop carrying flying boats and by the method of parachutes. Minelaying was also frequently suspected but not actually proved until May 29th; when five enemy aircraft were seen to do so in Tjeldsundet. Sweepers investigated and four mines were exploded.

4. On April 30th, I was informed by the Admiralty that 48 3.7 in. H.A. Guns and 48 Bofors (making 60 in all with 12 already in the area) were to be sent, as A/A protection was of primary importance and two A/A Cruisers were also ordered to join me on completion of certain other operations. The next day, as if to emphasise the matter, the enemy obtained a direct hit on the building used for Naval accommodation in Harstad, fortunately killing only two ratings. At the same time they bombed the Hospital Ship ATLANTIS anchored wide away from all other ships and a Norwegian Hospital Ship, causing many casualties in the latter.

5. The lateness of the thaw caused a depressing delay in the preparation of aerodromes. I had hoped that Bardufoss would be ready by the 15th May, in which case Carriers with the necessary aircraft would have left England on the 11th May but on the 4th May I had to report that the snow was causing insuperable delays. Concerning the preparation and use of Bardufoss, considerable tact was necessary in dealing with the Norwegians, as they firmly wished to keep it under their control. The acceptance of Norwegian pilots and other air personnel for training in England did much to bring a convenient working arrangement into force.

6. The first 3.7 in. A/A Guns arrived in the area on the 6th May. Bofors Guns reached Bardufoss on the 7th. Four of the 3.7 in. guns were in action at Harstad on the 9th and the other four were on their way to Bardufoss. Men bombed on shore could now begin to feel that they had some chance of hitting back; a psychological factor of considerable importance.

7. The ARK ROYAL joined and was able to commence operations from a position at sea well to the northward on the 6th May and the presence of her fighter aircraft had an immediate and most noticeable effect upon the enemy's freedom of attack.

8. On the 12th May, I was informed that in view of the situation elsewhere no Fighter or A/A reinforcements beyond those already promised could be provided. It was now expected that Bardufoss aerodrome would be ready by the 19th and I accordingly requested that GLORIOUS and FURIOUS, bringing Fighter aircraft already promised, should be within 200 miles of the Lofoten Islands by that day ready to fly the machines off as soon as they could be received.

9. Every effort was now being concentrated on preparation of the Bardufoss and Skaanland aerodromes, even operations taking second place in importance. At the same time, the mounting of A/A guns was being pressed on. The speedy and efficient work of Lieutenant-Colonel H.R. Lambert, D.S.C., R.M., and his men of the M.N.B.D.O.[3] in mounting guns under difficult conditions merit the highest praise. Group Captain Moore, R.A.F., who commanded the Air Component was most assiduous in the aerodrome development.

10. On May 17th, I was again informed of the effect of the Western Front situation on the Narvik Force; the message from Chiefs of Staff, stating that my Fighter Force

would be limited to one squadron of Gladiators and one of Hurricanes and the A/A artillery to 48 Heavy and 60 Light Guns.

II. GLORIOUS and FURIOUS arrived off the coast on the I8th and 70I Squadron of Walruses flew off and arrived at Harstad, where they remained based until the final evacuation, doing most useful work – ferrying, maintaining communications and daily reconnaissances, ending with a well planned bombing attack on Solfolla most efficiently carried out. Commander R.S.D. Armour, R.N., who was in command of the Fleet Air Arm, is much to be commended.

I2. On the 2Ist of May, 263 Gladiator Squadron was flown ashore at Bardufoss from FURIOUS, I6 machines landed but unfortunately 2, and I Swordfish were lost. GLORIOUS had had to return to U.K. on account of shortage of fuel. ARK ROYAL also left for U.K. on 2Ist May.

I3. On May 22nd in reply to a question from the Admiralty concerning possible substitution of Gladiators for Hurricanes, I stated that unless the Admiralty was prepared to provide and maintain a sufficient Air Force in this area, including a Squadron of Bombers, it was my opinion that the whole policy should be reconsidered.

I4. On May 26th, the GLORIOUS was back and flew off 46 Hurricane Squadron. The first flight landed at Skaanland and the remainder at Bardufoss from which aerodrome both Squadrons worked for the remainder of the time, taking heavy toll of the enemy whenever they had opportunity. Unfortunately, however, they were upon occasion fogbound at their aerodrome, which gave the enemy working from the South opportunities he was not slow to take. Owing to the distance little could be done to give fighter protection to the troops in the Bodo area. Two Gladiators in that area did, however, destroy 4 of the enemy in one flight before the Bodo aerodrome was completely destroyed.

SECTION IV.
THE DEVELOPMENT OF THE BASE DEFENCES.

I. A preliminary telegram asking for Guns for fixed defences and for harbour defence Asdics[4] was sent on 22nd April and on the 28th April the Admiralty stated that the M.N.B.D.O. would be sent to mount guns and asked for site prospecting to be carried out. As a result, the following proposals were made to the Admiralty on the Ist May:-

2. The Main Naval Base to be in Tjeldsundet with a large ship anchorage to the west of Holsflva, other ships in Lavangsfiord and west of Skaanland: advanced anchorages at Bogen and Ballangen. A minefield extending I½ miles 3I0° from Baroen Light on Baroy Island. 6 in. Battery south of Lodingen Church. 4.7 in. Battery north of Kvitnes. I2 pdr. Battery on west side of Tjeldsundet one mile south of Staksvollholm. Further batteries are considered desirable for south and north ends of Tjeldsundet. Minefields N.E. and south of Steinvaer. Harbour defence Asdics off S.W. corner of Baroy Island and Rotvaer Island with control station off Lodingen. Port War Signal Station on Rotvaer Island. B.I Indicator Net and Gate west of

Staksvollholm. Indicator Net or Mines at northern entrance to Tjeldsundet from Taakeboen beacon to Hella.

3. On the 27th and 28th May, (fictitious) minefields were declared N.E. and S. of Steinvaer Island in Vaagsfiord and between Rotvaer Island and Baroy Island in Vestfiord.

Rear-Admiral Lyster, appointed on the 29th April, arrived by air and assumed command of the Defences and their development on 5th May.

4. M.L.Cs. arrived on the 25th April and both M.L.Cs., A.L.Cs. on the 29th. These craft, though not always reliable mechanically, were most useful in the heavy work of transporting gear and arms in the development of the Base Defences. The MASHOBRA arrived on I0th May and the work of the Royal Marine fortress unit under Lieutenant-Colonel H.R. Lambert, D.S.C., R.M., merited the highest praise. I have mentioned this also in the chapter of this Report covering the subject of A/A.

5. A scheme for minelaying by Destroyers to be sent from England was prepared but for special reasons was abandoned. Attention was also given to the matter of using a supply of some 200 Norwegian Mines at Tromso but before effective work could be done on this the operations came to an end.

6. From first to last, the maintenance of Destroyers and Trawler patrols to provide effective protection at entrances to all fiords in use as anchorages was a matter of primary importance and, whenever Walrus aircraft were available, air searches were made.

7. The final plan for the defences was as follows:-

INNER DEFENCES.

A. *HARSTAD.*

A/S Defence of Harstad Harbour is only fully possible against close range attacks. Long range attacks can only be guarded against by
H.M. Ships keeping pointed in the direction from which attack is expected.

(I) *Northern Entrance.* Closed by A/T Baffle.
(2) *Eastern Side.* Covered by line of B.I Indicator Net outside from Maagoy to Harstad Light.
(3) *Southern Entrance.* Covered by mine-loop if possible.
(4) *Patrol.* One A/S small craft, and for watching Indicator Net.
(5) *Examination Service.* Armed Trawlers.

B. *TJELDSUNDET ANCHORAGE AND BASE – NORTHERN END.*

(I) *TAAKEBOEN BEACON to HELLA.* Shallow mines. Bottom is unsuitable for nets; any S/M attempting to get in would have to be shallow owing to navigational difficulties.
(2) *TAAKEBOEN to STEGHOLM.* 4-cable wide channel, 70 to 80 fathoms deep. Deep mines or mine loop.

(3) *Patrol. One* A/S small craft.

(4) *4.7inch L.A. Battery.* ¾ mile north of Langkvitneset.

(5) *12-Pdr. Battery.* At Langkvitneset.

(6) *A/B Boom.* At Langkvitneset.

C. *TJELDSUNDET ANCHORAGE AND BASE SOUTHERN END.*

(I) *RAMSUNDET.* A/B Boom and Light Battery (further reconnaissance required).

(2) *STAKSVOLLHOLM* Net. B.I Indicator Net and Gate ½ mile south of Island.

(3) *12-Pdr. Battery on STAKSVOLLHOLM ISLAND.*

(4) *A/B Boom by STAKSVOLLHOLM Island.*

(5) *Mine Loop.* Possibly in Southern Tjeldsundet.

(6) *Patrol.* Vessel with D.Cs. watching Net.

D. *BALLANGEN.*

A/S Vessel on patrol outside when required.

E. *NARVIK* – Awaiting capture.

No defences suggested at present.

F. *TROMSO – N.E. APPROACHES.*

(I) *GROTSUNDET.* Closed with deep and shallow mines from small island with light off Sjurnes to south shore. This will leave a narrow channel close to north shore for local craft and probably warships up to and including Cruisers.

(2) *KVALSUNDET.* Shallow mines, but few will be necessary, owing to its existing navigational difficulties.

(3) *Patrols.* Armed patrol vessel to control channel by Sjurnes. Patrol at inner end of Kvalsundet would be desirable.

G. *TROMSO – S.E. APPROACHES.*

(I) *RYOY ISLAND.* Narrows controlled by a light battery on the Island and A/S Patrol craft. Deep mines might also be laid if no A/S vessel was available.

OUTER DEFENCES.

A. *TROMSO – S. APPROACH TO TROMSO AND N. APPROACH TO VAAGS FIORD VIA GI SUND.*

(I) *MALANGEN FIORDS.* H.D.A.s between Lokvik and Boenoes. Also a heavy battery (reconnaissance required). A/S Patrol. Local protection would be necessary for these defences.

(2) *Patrol.* Less effective but simpler alternative would be patrol of 2 A/S Destroyers.

(3) *GI SUND*. Norwegian patrol vessels watching narrows where S/M must pass at shallow depth.

B. *VAAGS FIORD – N.E. APPROACH.*

One destroyer off Tranoy Fiord, for general patrol duties in Vaags Fiord and backing up of other patrols.

C. *VAAGS FIORD – N. APPROACH.*

(I) *SANDSOY to LEMMINGVOER*. Fiord to be closed on this line with deep and shallow mines.

(2) *Patrol*. One destroyer inside minefield.

D. *VAAGS FIORD – W. APPROACH – TOPSUNDET.*

(I) *H.D.A.s*. Western End.
(2) *Mine Loop*. Possibly.
(3) *6-inch or 4.7 inch Battery* at Western end.
(4) *I2-Pdr. Battery and A/B Boom* at Eastern end.
(5) *Patrols*. One A/S small craft behind H.D.A.s and one standby. Detailed reconnaissance is required for all Topsundet defences.

E. *TJELDSUNDET SOUTH and OFOT FIORD.*

(I) *H.D.A.s*. Between Rotvaer and Baroy.
(2) *Deep Mines*. ¼ mile each side just inside H.D.A.s.
(3) *Shallow Mines*. Three lines I¾ miles long approximately: 3I0° from S.W. point of Baroy. (Navigation buoy S.W. of Rotvaer.)
(4) *Open Channel*. North of Rotvaer Island for small local craft. Controlled by small armed vessel at inner end.
(5) *6-inch Battery* at Lodingen.
(6) There is a possibility of effectively locating another 6-inch Battery in unfinished Norwegian emplacements at Ramnes but a further reconnaissance is required.
(7) *Patrols*. Two A/S small craft with H.D.A.s. One destroyer between Baroy and Ramsundet.

8. Of the foregoing, the patrols were established early and worked regularly. None of the guns were actually mounted but the sites had been prepared. All the preparatory planning work for the mining had been done. The B.I Indicator Net had been laid south of Staksvollholm but both ends still required completing to the shore and the gate had not been laid. A B.I Net, originally intended for Narvik, was laid in Skjelfiord early in the proceedings for the protection of the PENELOPE. The A/T Boom lay had been started in Harstad Northern Entrance but not completed. At the evacuation all nets were sunk and all traces were removed.

9. The A/S Air Patrols, when the necessary Walrus Aircraft were available, were carried out outside a circle 27 miles radius centred about the points 68 35 N I7 I0 E.

The various outer surface A/S Patrols being situated on the circumference of this circle. The sectors, centred in Harstad Harbour being:-

X. Between 060° and 300° to a depth of 40 miles.
Y. Between 300° and 245° to a depth of 50 miles.
Z. Between 245° and 225° to a depth of 100 miles.
Q. Between 225° and 190° to a depth of 80 miles.

I0. After the sinking of U.49 on I5th April, no contacts with enemy submarines were made throughout the remainder of the operations, though many reports of them being sighted in the vicinity were received. An Irish Guardsman fishing at Bogen landed a used Escape Apparatus belonging to U.64.

II. Five enemy aircraft were seen on the 29th May, apparently laying mines in Tjeldsundet South Channel, and in the subsequent sweeping operations 4 mines were exploded, 2 by non-magnetic sweep and 2, later, by magnetic.

SECTION V.
A SUMMARY OF THE EVENTS IN THE MOSJOEN – MO – BODO AREA.

I. On the 29th April, I received a message from C.I.G.S. informing me that it was essential that the Head of Saltfiord should be occupied to ensure that there should be no chance of Germans arriving by parachute. The telegram indicated that a force to occupy the area would be leaving U.K. immediately. A destroyer was sent forthwith and was followed by a detachment of the Scots Guards, I50 strong. The destroyer reported no Germans or shipping of any sort in the vicinity.

2. On the Ist May an order was received from the Admiralty to send a destroyer to Mo to prevent an enemy landing and the excellent proposal was made by the Admiralty to Commander-in-Chief, Home Fleet, that a Division of Destroyers should be established to patrol the coast from Namsos North to prevent the movement of every troopship/s by sea. This unfortunately never materialised.

3. Preparations for the embarkation in U.K. of Independent Companies of troops for Mo and Mosjoen were made known to me by signal, and I also received information that 2 Flying-Boats were coming out to reconnoitre aerodromes in the Bodo area. Their life was short. They were caught and put out of action on the water by enemy aircraft on the 4th May.

4. On May 4th, I came to the conclusion that it was time that policy and responsibility in the Bodo area was defined and I accordingly addressed the following message to the Admiralty:

"Request I may be informed of the general policy regarding Bodo, Mo and Mosjoen. It seems most important to hold in force the Mo road leading north. From Admiralty messages it appears the forces being sent are hardly adequate for this purpose and with such weak detachments in the air another naval commitment comes into being. These areas do not, I presume, come under Narvik. Are there any other allied forces to the south of me."

5. The Admiralty reply received next day was to the effect that it was not possible to maintain large forces in face of enemy air superiority well in advance of established fighter aerodromes and that Bodo was the only place south of Narvik where such could be established. That small parties only would be maintained at Mo and Mosjoen with the object of obstructing enemy advance and to prevent landings by sea and air. On the 7th May I learned that all Independent Companies operating in Northern Norway would come under Narvik Command and I was given details of their disposition under Colonel Gubbins. Anxiety was expressed by the Norwegian Commander-in-Chief as to the potential aerodromes in Bodo, Mosjoen area.

6. On the 7th and 8th the enemy advance north began to make itself felt. A French detachment at Mosjoen first reported the enemy 100 miles to the south and on the 8th I heard that Mosjoen was about to be evacuated. On the 9th the Germans were 10 miles off Mosjoen and Brigadier Gubbins reported that there was great concern amongst the Norwegians about the continued enemy advance and that he would withdraw gradually to Mo and eventually to Bodo.

7. I suggested to the Admiralty on the 7th that, if the Division of Destroyers they had originally proposed could not be provided, 2 Destroyers might be added to my force and I would manage the patrol, but on the 10th the Admiralty required me to reduce my Destroyer force by 4 vessels on account of the need for concentration in the southern part of the North Sea. On the same day, the Admiralty informed me it was essential to hold Bodo for the present.

8. On the evening of the 10th May, the enemy were successful in landing a force of 650 men at Hemnes near Mo partly from a coasting steamer which came north with aerial escort. Intelligence concerning the movements of this vessel reached me unfortunately too late for her to be intercepted by CALCUTTA and ZULU who were sent for the purpose. CALCUTTA sank the steamer at Hemnes an hour and a half after she had got alongside. Reinforcements with light A.A. guns were embarked in ENTERPRISE for passage to Mo.

9. Wing-Commander Atcherley who had visited the area reported to Air Ministry and Admiralty by W/T on the advanced state of preparedness of the aerodrome at Mo and its great value to the enemy should it fall into their hands.

10. Mosjoen was evacuated, equipment being abandoned, on the 12th May. ENTERPRISE accompanied by CAIRO landed reinforcements at Mo on the 12th and other reinforcements had reached Bodo on the 11th. The enemy was now subjecting Mo to heavy air attacks and at the same time I was informed that while no fighter or A.A. reinforcements beyond those already authorised could be expected, forces at Bodo must be supplied from the Narvik area.

11. On the 13th, it was decided to add the Irish Guards to the Bodo force and the Headquarters of the 24th Brigade. They embarked in the s.s. CHROBRY which had brought 3 Tanks from England for the Bodo Force. While on passage with STORK and WOLVERINE as escort the CHROBRY was bombed and set on fire, the four senior officers of the Battalion being killed. The troops were saved and brought back

to Harstad but their equipment was lost. It was then decided to send the South Wales Borderers in the EFFINGHAM but she grounded and became a total loss during the night 17th-18th. The troops were brought back to Harstad in EFFINGHAM's Escort, COVENTRY, CAIRO, MATABELE and ECHO, while the greater part of the Military Stores, with 4 Bren Carriers out of 10 were salved in Local Craft and landed at Bodo. EFFINGHAM was finally destroyed by torpedo.

12. During the next few days the troops after being re-equipped at Harstad were taken to Bodo by Destroyers, but news from that area was of the continual advance of the enemy.

13. On the 18th Colonel Trappes-Lomax of the Scots Guards reported withdrawing from Mo.

14. On the 21st General Auchinleck informed me that he was proposing to appoint Colonel Gubbins in command of the 24th Brigade and Independent Companies, that is, of all forces in the Bodo area. With this I fully agreed. Brigadier Fraser had had to be invalided on account of a wound received earlier when reconnoitring at Ankenes in the Narvik area.

15. Enemy air power in the Bodo area steadily increased and with corresponding harassing effect upon our forces. Only on one occasion was it possible to hit back and then (on the 27th May) 2 Gladiators brought down 4 enemy aircraft.

16. A trawler force, to work in the Bodo area, arrived at Skjelfiord from England on the 18th May under the command of Lieutenant-Commander (acting Commander) W.R. Fell, R.N. These vessels not being suitable for the work, Commander Fell organised a force of local vessels and took them south on the 24th May where they performed remarkable work and were almost continuously in action for seven days.

17. A telegram was received on the 24th May from the Chiefs of Staff ordering the evacuation of the whole of our forces from North Norway. Plans to reinforce Bodo were then abandoned and instructions were sent to Brigadier Gubbins to be prepared to evacuate.

18. On May 28 the enemy with a force of 30 aeroplanes bombed the town of Bodo, which to a greater extent than most Norwegian towns was built of stone, until it was reduced to complete ruin.

19. The evacuation of Bodo was successfully accomplished on the 29th and 31st, 1,000 men being taken direct to U.K. in VINDICTIVE and the remainder brought to Harstad in Destroyers and small craft.

SECTION VI.
THE FINAL OPERATIONS FOR THE CAPTURE OF NARVIK.

I. The landing effected by the two battalions of the Foreign Legion at Bjerkvik on the 12th/13th May, in addition to establishing contact with French troops working south, had as its object the occupation of the Oydejord Peninsula, and the northern shore of Rombaks Fiord. This was held by some to be a necessary prelude to any direct attack upon Narvik itself, allowing, as it would, of the positioning of field artillery on the peninsula to support such an attack. As soon as the necessary area had been occupied and, with the assistance of H.M.S. FAME, the northern shore of Rombaks Fiord had been cleared and occupied as far as Lillelerget, General Bethouart felt himself ready for the next stage, for which he had prepared his plan, i.e., the capture of Narvik. Commander Hubback was attached to the French Staff for this purpose; his success in this work in connection with Bjervik had been much appreciated by the French Command. My general direction to him was that he was to do everything to further the project and to promise that all possible naval support would be forthcoming. He carried out this work admirably. It was decided that the attack would take place on May 23rd/24th or on the first favourable opportunity after that date. This was the earliest date it was estimated the M.L.Cs. could be released from what, at the moment, was the all important work of preparing Bardufoss and Skaanland Aerodromes for the reception of Hurricanes and Gladiators. The conditions that were required to form a favourable opportunity were held to be either-

(*a*) Such weather conditions as were likely to largely reduce or abolish any danger of air attack; or

(*b*) The ability to provide efficient fighter protection overhead.

2. The weather, towards the date mentioned, turned fine and seemed settled and with the impending arrival of the Hurricanes on the 26th/27th it was eventually decided that the operation should take place on the 27th/28th and that date was adhered to.

3. The plan, in so far as the naval operations were concerned, is forwarded separately and, except in one or two minor details, it was adhered to.

4. The ships that took (part were CAIRO (Flag), SOUTHAMPTON (R.A.I8), COVENTRY (C.S.20) and the Destroyers WHIRLIND, FAME, HAVELOCK, WALKER and FIREDRAKE.

5. The plan is open to criticism in details – its great merit, however, was in that it was the plan of those who had to carry it out. The weak point in the plan was that owing to the paucity of transport available – a less bold man than General Bethouart might well have made this an excuse for inaction – it was necessary to leave the First Flight of 290 men unsupported for an unduly long time as the timetable in the plan indicates. Owing to the hard work to which the M.L.Cs. had been subjected in transporting guns and plant and stores of allsorts required for the completion of the aerodromes at Bardufoss and Skaanland and the sinking of one during an air raid, only two of these vessels were available – and one of these was only capable of about three knots. The A.L.Cs. similarly were reduced from four to three, one of them having been burnt out. An attempt was made to supplement the means of transport by using the two picket boats of MASHOBRA. These boats were, however, reported as unfit for action – a common complaint among all power boats during the expedition but perhaps excusable in this particular case, seeing the hard work the MASHOBRA had recently carried out.

It had been decided to land the French troops of the First Flight on a small beach east of Orneset.

The actual attack upon Narvik was to be supported by a Polish advance on the

Ankenes Peninsula in the direction of Beisford, through which ran the one road affording a line of retreat to the enemy.

6. The operation began at the appointed time of 2340 on May 27th. My Flag was flying in the CAIRO, the CURLEW in which I had intended it to be worn having been sunk the previous afternoon. General Auchinleck and General Bethouart accompanied me. The ships proceeded independently to their stations, effort being made to conceal the intention of concentrating off Narvik until as late as possible. The bombardment preceding the landing by ships' fire and that of 75 mm. battery ashore was effective and the troops landed from the A.L.C.s and M.L.C.s without, meeting the serious resistance so many had thought inevitable. The landing took place practically at one point, the training of the soldiers enabling them, as at Bjervik, to open out and obtain cover without apparent difficulty. The subsequent transportation of troops was carried out as fast as the limited means available allowed, local craft being used to a limited extent in the later stages. Two tanks were landed at Taraldvik from M.L.C.s but when ashore found the sand and mud too soft and were immobilised for some time. By soon after midnight, a battalion of the Foreign Legion and one of the Norwegian Infantry (the Narvik Battalion) with two tanks were ashore and had made good progress. The first detachment of the second Battalion of the Legion had been landed, and the remainder were being embarked and ferried across. A considerable rifle and machine-gun fire could be heard which marked the development of a counter-attack by the enemy which, however, was held by the French troops.

7. At 0420, the enemy aircraft put in their first appearance, some determined dive bombing attacks being made upon the ships. This was followed up in quick succession by high and dive bombing attacks, lasting from 0420-0626, the former by aircraft working singly and in formation. Ships for a considerable time escaped damage but only by manoeuvring at high speed in such a way as would have seriously reduced the effectiveness of bombarding and covering fire had the attack been delivered earlier. The success of these attacks, however, was largely due to the unfortunate fact that our fighters, most conspicuous and assiduous in the patrol work until 0400, were after that time fogbound on the Bardufoss Aerodrome, some 50 miles distant from the scene of battle. At 0620, CAIRO was hit by two light bombs of a pattern which fell all round her. One hit was just abaft "B" mounting, penetrating the deck and bursting among the supply party; the other hit the starboard .5 machine gun just abaft the signal deck, setting fire to the ammunition and gear in the vicinity of the gun. As a result, 8 were killed and 25 wounded. Of CAIRO's armament, only one mounting remained fully effective, two being out of action owing to the dangerous prematures being caused by the state of the guns owing to continuous firing. The ship also had considerable superficial damage to contend with and, incidentally, smartly dealt with by her fire and repair parties. I therefore determined to send her away and called a destroyer alongside to take off General Bethouart and Staff. It was also any intention to shift my Flag to STORK.

8. I had previously asked General Bethouart to let me know when he was satisfied that his troops were established and could dispense with naval aid, so that the number

of ships in a confined area could be reduced. Before leaving the ship, General Bethouart told me that he was quite satisfied and that if he were allowed to retain two destroyers that was all he asked for. On this, I ordered C.S. 20 in COVENTRY and 2 destroyers to remain in support of the French forces and the remainder of the ships to withdraw to the westward.

9. After repelling the German counter-attack, the French continued their advance throughout the day and after a few somewhat doubtful messages had been received reports became reassuring until, by a message timed 2200, General Bethouart reported that Narvik, Fagernes and Forneset were in his hands, together with some 200 prisoners, a number subsequently increased to between 350-400.

I0. The attack of the Poles on Ankenes had, after an initial setback, progressed well – a result largely due to the support received by the fire of the SOUTHAMPTON which was gratefully acknowledged.

II. That the carrying-out of this operation proved more simple than had been expected does not in my view detract in any degree from the credit due to General Bethouart for the soldierly way he had undertaken and carried out this attack, following that of Bjerkvik. He was good enough to give much credit to the naval assistance he had received. That, however, would always have been forthcoming to any force that had attempted the task.

SECTION VII.
THE EVACUATION.

I. On the night of 24/25th May, orders were received for the evacuation of Northern Norway and were contained in following message:-

"Naval Message to F.O., Narvik, from Admiralty.

Following from Chiefs of Staff.

His Majesty's Government has decided your forces are to evacuate Northern Norway at earliest moment. Reason for this is that the troops, ships, guns and certain equipment are urgently required for defence of United Kingdom. We understand from military point of view, evacuation operations will be facilitated if enemy forces are largely destroyed or captured. Moreover, destruction of railways and Narvik port facilities make its capture highly desirable.

Nevertheless, speed of evacuations once begun should be of primary consideration in order to limit duration maximum naval efforts.

2 Officers will be sent at once from United Kingdom to concert Evacuation plans with you and General Auchinleck. Evacuation of all equipment, vehicles and stores will clearly take too long. Following are required to be evacuated in order of importance from point of view of defence of United Kingdom – (*a*) Personnel; (*b*) Light A/A Guns and Ammunition; (*c*) 25-pounders; (*d*) Heavy A/A Guns and Ammunition.

Tactical conditions must rule but so far as they permit plans should be framed accordingly.

Norwegian Government have not repetition not yet been informed."

2. The following morning, I discussed the matter with General Auchinleck, and it was agreed that safety of the force made secrecy vital, and the information must only be imparted to those Senior Officers it was imperative should know it.

3. The position of the French troops, acting in conjunction with the Norwegian troops, and in actual contact with the enemy in the Gratangen district presented difficulties – as to a lesser degree did that of our own troops in a similar position in the Bodo area. That position, however, showed signs of liquidating itself. In the Ankenes peninsula also, Polish troops were pressing East in the face of enemy resistance, towards Beisfjord. It was evident that, in view of the wide area from which troops had to be evacuated, under different circumstances, the withdrawal might prove difficult more particularly in view of the increasing scale of air attack to which the whole district was being subjected. Secrecy and celerity were both called for. It was apparent that a considerable number of A/A guns would have to be abandoned, guns which had only just been installed after much labour. As, however, A/A protection must be provided to the last this loss was inevitable.

4. On May 26th, I invited General Bethouart to my house to meet General Auchinleck, and he was then told of the forthcoming evacuation. From every point of view, it seemed essential he should know. The news was received with characteristic calm, though one point upon which he was insistent was that for reasons of national honour he could not abandon the Norwegian Army he had been working with, in the lurch on the field of battle. The whole question was discussed and it was agreed that pressure on the enemy must be kept up until the last, that the attack on Narvik which had originally been fixed for the night 24th-25th but postponed 48 hours, must go on, and that this operation would of itself be the best possible way of concealing our intentions from the enemy.

5. An outline plan for the evacuation was forwarded to the Chiefs of Staff at their request.

6. It was planned that the work should be done at night – this in view of diminishing the risk of air attack as far as possible. True, it was light all night but experience had shown the night hours were a quiet time as a rule as regards air raids. The whole operation was planned to occupy five periods of ferrying. This was agreed to and was the plan followed. The dates were, however, subsequently postponed 48 hours. The measures taken to ensure secrecy worked well, so many plausible reasons were available to explain the movements of troops that for some days no suspicion was aroused.

7. Information was received that the ARK ROYAL and GLORIOUS would be in the area between the dates named for the provision of fighter protection and the retrieving of any aircraft possible.

8. The situation in the Bodo district had been causing anxiety owing to the growing pressure of enemy forces, and the reinforcement of the 24th Brigade – now intact in that area – had been in contemplation. This idea was necessarily abandoned in the

face of impending evacuation, and evacuation was ordered. This was necessary as Brigadier Gubbins had reported he must retire not later than June Ist unless reinforced.

9. The nights of May 20th, 30th and 3Ist were selected for this evacuation, which was carried out by destroyers. On the first night some I,000 troops were ferried to the VINDICTIVE in the offing, which ship conveyed them direct to Scapa. On the two subsequent nights, the troops were brought back to the Harstad area in the destroyers which had embarked them. It was decided that the Norwegian Government should be informed as soon as possible that the decision had been taken by the Allies to evacuate North Norway. The decision to do this was communicated to H.M. Government. I therefore invited Sir Cecil Dormer to Harstad for a conference on June Ist, the following day, and suggested Colonel Pollock should accompany him. This officer – in his capacity as Liaison Officer – had proved most helpful. Sir Cecil was informed of the position, and a copy of the following message given to him.

"IMMEDIATE.

To: F.O., Narvik, From: Admiralty.

Following from Foreign Office.

When Sir C. Dormer arrives Harstad you should explain the situation to him and ask him to speak to King of Norway and Minister of Defence, Colonel Ljungberg in the following sense.

H.M. Government and French Government have reviewed general position in light of recent events in Belgium and Northern France. Owing to additional strain on their resources and to necessity to defend Great Britain as well as France from invasion it is not repetition not possible for Allies to supply sufficient defence against German attack, particularly air attack, on North Norway. What has just happened at Bodo, where you have been obliged to order evacuation at short notice, is an example of what must happen elsewhere if this defence cannot be provided: and dangers of air attacks to civilian population have already been emphasised by Norwegian Government themselves. In any case restoration of Norwegian independence depends upon capacity of British Empire and France to resist present attack on them, and if this purpose is to be achieved all available Allied forces will in present circumstances be required.

Allied Governments are accordingly obliged to make arrangements for early withdrawal of their forces from Norway and will be prepared in doing so to bring away the King of Norway, Norwegian Government and as many Norwegian troops as may wish to come to the United Kingdom and continue the fight with the Allies on other battlefields.

It might be worth while to suggest to Norwegian Government, if they think there is any chance of reaching an agreement on "Mowinckel Plan," we should see no repetition no objection to their attempting this. They themselves will of course realise any hint to Germans that we had decided on evacuation would destroy any chance they may have of reaching an agreement. But evidently time for this is very short and our evacuation plan cannot be delayed."

I0. The whole matter was then discussed between Sir Cecil, General Auchinleck, Colonel Pollock and myself upon the basis of this message. It was agreed that Sir Cecil Dormer on his return to Tromso should interview privately certain Ministers, and that he should suggest the revival of the "Mowinckel Plan," as proposed in the Foreign Office Message quoted above: that the King should be told the following morning, June 2nd, and the Cabinet officially informed later in the day. Subsequently, I was told by letter that the conversations had gone off well and that, after his talk with the Foreign Minister, the latter – who already had a meeting arranged in Stockholm for the 3rd – drafted a telegram to his Swedish colleague on the subject of the "Mowinckel Plan," which draft he allowed Sir Cecil to alter as he wished. Colonel Pollock on the same day gave the information to General Rugé. Vice-Admiral Cunningham was also informed and entrusted with making arrangements for the passage of the King, Government and others who might wish to evacuate should the negotiations break down. Sir Cecil Dormer asked that there should be a delay of a day or two in order to give time for the negotiations. After ascertaining that this would entail no harmful consequences to arrangements already made, I agreed to a delay of 24 hours. The first night of evacuation was, therefore, fixed as June 3rd-4th. Naturally, at first, there was a feeling of soreness and disillusionment among the Norwegians on learning of the evacuation but on the whole the decision was received as being inevitable under the circumstances and every help was given to facilitate the withdrawal.

II. I wrote to Admiral Diesen expressing the hope that he would send all his ships to the U.K. or assure me that they should not fall into German hands. The following most satisfactory answer was received:-

6th June, I940.

"My Lord:

My very best thanks for your kind letter. It has been a great pleasure for me to meet you, my Lord, and so many officers of the grand British Navy. As a Norwegian, I can only present my thanks for all it has done.

I am preparing all the ships that may be of any use for going to the Shetlands.

You may rest assured about the submarines as well as of the rest. What cannot be evacuated will be destroyed.

To you personally, my Lord, I send my very best wishes for the future of both our countries. God bless them!

In the hope of a au revoir,

Yours very sincerely,
(Sgd.) N. DIESEN."

The Naval Attaché, Rear-Admiral Boyes, also had the matter in hand.

I2. The evacuation proceeded according to plan on the dates named. On 5 successive nights, troops to the numbers of 4,700, 4,900, 5,I00, 5,200 and on the fifth the last and most difficult 4,600, without any untoward incident. The work was almost entirely carried out by destroyers working under the orders of Captain E.B.K. Stevens,

D.S.C., Captain (D), 9th Destroyer Flotilla, in H.M.S. HAVELOCK. The presence of this energetic and capable officer ensured the programme being carried out punctually and efficiently. The destroyers were working almost continuously and, as always, rose to the occasion. Rear-Admiral Commanding 20th Cruiser Squadron was in direct charge of the transports at rendezvous and responsible for the embarkation. Up to the end, air protection was afforded by the R.A.F. and F.A.A. working in co-operation and to a programme. Owing, however, to the weather conditions that prevailed through the 5 days, low clouds and rain, the enemy air action was weak and spasmodic. Dive bombing attacks were, however, delivered upon STORK and VETERAN in Ofot Fiord during the afternoon of the 7th but the enemy did not appear to have noticed anything unusual, for no special effort was made that evening. The last men to be embarked in the Transports were the Ground Staff of the Bardufoss aerodrome. The Gladiators had been embarked in GLORIOUS but it was feared that the 8 Hurricanes that remained efficient would have to be abandoned and destroyed. The courageous action of the pilots in volunteering to fly their machines on to the flying deck of GLORIOUS and of Group-Captain Moore in allowing it to be done resulted in all 8 being safely got away – an achievement which deserved a better fate than that which befell the gallant men who had carried it out successfully.

13. The actual sailing of the various Convoys carrying the whole expedition to the U.K. was as follows:-

Group I.

MONARCH OF BERMUDA.	}
BATORY.	}
SOBIESKI.	} With VINDICTIVE.
FRANCONIA.	}
LANCASTRIA.	}
GEORGIC.	}

Group 2.

ORONSAY.	} With COVENTRY (C.S.20.).
ORMONDE.	} SOUTHAMPTON (R.A.I8).
ARANDORA STAR.	} HAVELOCK (D.9).
ROYAL ULSTERMAN.	} FAME.
ULSTER PRINCE.	} FIREDRAKE.
ULSTER MONARCH.	} BEAGLE.
DUCHESS OF YORK.	} DELIGHT.

VANDYCK should have been with this Group but failed to make the rendezvous.

Storeships (Slow Convoy left Harstad 2200/7 June).

BLACKHEATH.	}
OLIGARCH.	}
HARMATTAN.	} With
CROMARTY FIRTH.	} STORK,

THESEUS.	} ARROW,
ACRITY.	} and 10 Trawlers.
COXWOLD.	}
CONCH.	}

CAMPBELL, WALTER, ELLESMERE and THIRLMERE were sent to find and escort vessels coming from Tromso, viz., OIL PIONEER, YERMOUNT, ARBROATH (A.S.I.S.), NYAKOA (A.S.I.S.), and some Norwegian Vessels.

14. I did not consider that sailing of the 1st Group without escort as mentioned in Admiralty 1801/27 was justifiable and had originally intended to retain the ships at sea in charge of VINDICTIVE, in which ship 1,000 troops had been embarked until the whole were ready. On receipt, however, of Admiralty F.O.N.177, I resolved to sail the group under escort of VINDICTIVE if adequate protection was obtainable further south. This being guaranteed by C.-in-C., Home Fleet, the 1801/6 and 1506/5 Groups sailed for the Clyde on June 7th at 0300.

15. The RANEN (Commander Sir Geoffrey Congreve), who had been actively employed during the evacuation period delaying the enemy advance up the coast from Bodo, was sent on the night of the 7th, accompanied by NORTHERN GEM, to destroy the Oil Tanks at Svolvaer. This successful exploit ended with a most spirited engagement, on his part, with the enemy.

16. Vice-Admiral Commanding First Cruiser Squadron was in charge of the Tromso Convoy. H.M.S. DEVONSHIRE, his flagship, conveyed the Royal and Diplomatic parties, the Norwegian Government and other notables who wished to be evacuated.

17. Prior to final evacuation, the forepart of MASHOBRA, the stern of which was underwater, was blown up, the OLEANDER was sunk, disabled Trawlers destroyed and an attempt was made to tow away the A.L.Cs. but finally they and the M.L.Cs. were scuttled.

18. The whole of the Convoy (2nd Group) were clear of Andfiord by 2300/8th, the rear being brought up by the A/S Trawlers and Minesweepers. As they proceeded, they were shadowed by an enemy aircraft. After seeing these clear in SOUTHAMPTON, I ordered that ship to join the Convoy of which Rear-Admiral Vivian in COVENTRY had been placed in charge.

19. For the evacuation, I flew my Flag in the SOUTHAMPTON and was accompanied in that ship on the return voyage by Generals Auchinleck and Bethouart.

20. Being clear of Norwegian waters and operations therefore coming under Commander-in-Chief, Home Fleet, I hauled down my Flag at midnight on June 8th but directed that SOUTHAMPTON was to remain with the Convoy for passage home in view of the liveliness taking place in the North Sea. This passage was uneventful.

21. The success of the evacuation and the smoothness with which the arrangements worked was in great measure due to the unremitting work and attention of all the Staff Officers engaged upon it but primarily to those of the following Officers to whom I particularly wish to call attention. They are:-

Brigadier J.A.H. Gammell, Military Chief Staff Officer.

Captain L.E.H. Maund, Naval Chief Staff Officer.

Commander A.G.V. Hubback, Staff Officer Operations.

The latter conducted the withdrawal of the French and Polish troops that were engaged with the enemy during the concluding phase.

22. The order for evacuation, and the compliance therewith, brought this combined operation to a close – at a moment when, as a result of seven weeks' hard work, the Force seemed to be getting firmly established. To attain this result many and great difficulties had had to be overcome, due to the peculiar hydrographical and geographical conditions, but more particularly to the severe climatic vagaries, all of which were more easily realised on the spot than they could be under totally different conditions elsewhere.

23. The landing of guns, vehicles, and stores of all sorts with a minimum of facilities for doing so, imposed great efforts on all of the three Services taking part in this work.

24. Possibly, the outstanding combined effort of this sort was the preparation of the aerodromes. The initial clearing of the ground, under three to four feet of snow when work began, the water transport and landing on open beaches of all impedimenta, the positioning of the guns for defence, after much work had been expended on preparing miles of indifferent roads under "thaw" conditions to take heavy traffic called for and produced great and continued exertions from all three Services. In this as in all other activities co-operation was close and cordial – more particularly so in the later stages of the campaign. This is equally true as regards relations between the Norwegians and the various nationalities of the Allied Force. Excellent and helpful relations prevailed. I have elsewhere placed on record my appreciation of the valuable services rendered by General Bethouart. As already mentioned initially there was no means of retaliation for interference caused by enemy air attack. The Fleet Air Arm, however, did all that was possible – to the gallantry and activity displayed by that branch of the Service I desire to pay tribute.

25. The Royal Air Force when they began to arrive quickly made their efficiency and courageous skill felt – their advent was very welcome. One Officer of this Service especially attracted me by his zeal, energy, initiative and resource – Wing Commander Atcherley, upon whom fell the initial work of selection and preparation of aerodromes prior to the arrival of Group Captain Moore to the value of whose services I have already alluded.

26. Of the Army, I feel constrained to call attention to Brigadier J.A.H. Gammell – an Officer of obviously great ability whose personality contributed largely to the harmonious relations previously referred to and Colonel A.A.B. Dowler, who, in his capacity as General Staff Officer, was at Military Headquarters during the whole period of the expedition, during which his quiet efficiency and tact were of the greatest assistance – especially through one difficult period.

27. I particularly desire to mention Captain Louis Hamilton, R.N., H.M.S. AURORA, who proved himself a fine, active leader, and an Officer who could be relied upon to obtain the best results under any conditions. His sound views on all

operational matters were a great help and support to me, his desire to harass and distress the enemy never eased up.

28. Captain L.E.H. Maund acted as my Chief Staff Officer; he was assiduous and untiring in his work and in all administrative matters of the greatest help. To him can be given much of the credit for successful evacuation.

29. Finally, I must express my gratitude to Lieutenant-General C.J.E. Auchinleck in whom I could not wish for a better colleague. His sound and soldierly views on all subjects were of great assistance and support and the period of our service together will for me always be a pleasant memory.

(Signed) CORK & ORRERY,
Admiral of the Fleet.

APPENDIX "A".

REPORT ON OPERATIONS IN NORTHERN NORWAY.
I4th April to I3th May, I940.

The following Report was submitted to the Secretary of State for War on 15th May, 1940, by Major-General P.J. Mackesy, C.B., D.S.O., M.C.

Harstad, 15th May, 1940.

SIR,

I have the honour to report that I handed over command of this Force to Lieutenant-General C.J.E. Auchinleck, C.B., C.S.I., D.S.O., O.B.E., at 1830 hours on the I3th May. I submit the following brief report to the Secretary of State for War of events up to that time.

2. I arrived in the Narvik area, actually in Vaags Fjord, in H.M.S. *Southampton* at daylight on the I4th April. I was accompanied by a small staff and had on board two companies of the Ist Bn. The Scots Guards and some details.

3. Having first ascertained that Harstad was not in enemy occupation and having obtained some information from local officials at that place, I proceeded to obtain touch with the 6th Norwegian Division under Major-General Fleischer, whose headquarters proved to be in the Bardu area. The two companies Ist Bn. The Scots Guards were landed at Salangs-Verket and Sjoveien on the Sag Fjord during the afternoon and were put in touch with elements of the 6th Norwegian Division. This early contact and the subsequent co-operation of this detachment with our Allies had an important effect upon the spirit and determination of the Allied Forces.

4. During the I4th April and the following days all available information pointed to Narvik itself being strongly held and to the fact that the naval action of the I3th April had by no means demoralized the garrison as a whole. The probability was that the garrison had in fact been increased by nearly 1,000 good fighting men from the sunken German ships: this was fully confirmed by subsequent intelligence reports. My troops had been embarked for a peaceful landing at a friendly and organized port and could not be ready for active operations for some days. I decided therefore to disembark the Force at Harstad and to establish my base there also in the first instance.

5. Disembarkation at Harstad was carried out under great difficulty. Transports

had to lie at considerable distances – 10 miles and more – from the harbour and signal communication between ship and shore was impossible. Air attacks, against which my force had no defence, complicated the operation. However disembarkation of the first flight of the force was completed on the evening of 16th April.

6. Although nobody without personal experience of Arctic winter conditions can possibly picture the climatic difficulties we experienced in the early days, a word or two of description may not be out of place. The country was covered by snow up to 4 feet and more in depth. Even at sea level there were several feet of snow. Blizzards, heavy snowstorms, bitter winds and very low night temperatures were normal. Indeed until the middle of May even those magnificent mountain soldiers, the French Chasseurs Alpins, suffered severely from frost bite and snow blindness. Troops who were not equipped with and skilled in the use of skis or snow shoes were absolutely incapable of operating tactically at all. I had no such troops at my disposal when I first landed. Shelter from the weather was of vital importance.

7. It soon became certain that the enemy held Narvik in considerable strength. All the existing defences had been handed over intact by the Norwegian garrison. A personal reconnaissance convinced me that topography favoured the defence and that an opposed landing was quite out of the question so long as the deep snow and existing weather conditions persisted and so long as my force lacked landing craft, tanks, adequate artillery support, adequate anti-aircraft defence and air co-operation. The problem was, of course, not merely one of landing, but one of carrying out a subsequent advance of several miles; yet, owing to the configuration of the ground, not even during the first mile could support be given by ships' guns.

I decided therefore that my first objective must be to secure the Oijord and Ankenes peninsulas, North and South of Narvik, from which in due course observed artillery fire could be brought to bear on the enemy defences. Both these peninsulas were held by the enemy.

With this in view I moved the Ist Bn. The Irish Guards to the Bogen area and (at a later date) the 2nd Bn. The South Wales Borderers to Ballangen. The detachment of the Ist Bn. The Scots Guards, under Major L. Graham, M.C., which I had landed in the Sag Fjord on 14th April, moved forward to co-operate with the 6th Norwegian Division in the Forsbakken area. The state of the roads, lying under 2 to 4 feet of snow and ice, and the impossibility of moving across country without skis, prevented further progress by these forces for the time being.

8. On the 20th April Admiral of the Fleet the Earl of Cork and Orrery was placed in sole command of the operations. It may however be convenient to have on record a brief summary of the subsequent operations from an army point of view. On 24th April a naval bombardment of the Narvik defences was carried out with the object of making the enemy surrender. The Ist Bn. The Irish Guards, embarked in one of H.M. Ships, were held ready to land and occupy the town in the event of such surrender. Other troops were at short notice to follow the Irish Guards. The bombardment, however, did not achieve the result hoped for by the naval commander. Subsequent reports indicated that the defences were not seriously impaired, though some casualties were inflicted upon the enemy.

9. My hopes of prosecuting the land operations more vigorously were raised by the arrival on the 28th April of General Bethouart with a Demi-Brigade of Chasseurs Alpins. Two battalions of these were directed to advance, in co-operation with Norwegian forces, from the Gratangen area to Bjerkvik at the head of Herjangen Fjord. One battalion co-operated with the South Wales Borderers on the Ankenes peninsula where the latter had been landed without opposition although counter-attacked later.

Even those first class troops, the Chasseurs Alpins, trained as they are, to snow conditions, found themselves very seriously hampered, indeed almost immobilized, by the soft deep snow. Their small proportion of ski troops in each battalion and a lack of snow shoes for the remainder proved serious handicaps. They suffered severely from frost bite and snow blindness. The troops in the front line were subjected to continual low-flying air attacks against which, owing to the state of the ground, they could not adequately protect themselves either by digging or by dispersion. (Later when I was enabled to allocate a small number of light anti-aircraft guns to the French troops, the effect was excellent.) Nevertheless they made some progress and took no little toll of the enemy.

10. On 29th April I was ordered to send troops to Bodo. I accordingly despatched one company of the Ist Bn. the Scots Guards. A few days later developments at and South of Mosjoen were brought prominently to my notice by the serious effects they were having upon our Norwegian Allies, and I soon found myself concerned with two fronts – the Narvik area in the East and Mosjoen and Mo in the South. For the reasons indicated in paragraph I2 below, the Southern front caused me increasingly greater concern.

II. The arrival of a Demi-Brigade of the Foreign Legion and of a Polish Brigade, coupled with gradually improving weather conditions and an accession of much needed equipment (notably anti-aircraft artillery, a very limited number of landing craft and a French company of light tanks) facilitated the undertaking of more active operations on the Narvik front. On 8th May I instructed General Bethouart to clear up the Gratangen – Bjerkvik area and to establish artillery on the Oijord peninsula. He was then to explore the possibility of moving through the mountains against the strong German concentration in the Hundalen area East of Narvik. At the same time I instructed the 24th (Guards) Brigade (with one battalion of Chasseurs Alpins under command) to hold the Northern end of the Ankenes peninsula firmly and to advance on Beisfjord as soon as weather conditions should permit. At 0I00 hours I3th May, accordingly, General Bethouart landed the Demi-Brigade of the Foreign Legion at Bjerkvik. The landing was preceded by a naval bombardment. An enemy machine-gun on the left flank was knocked out by a destroyer's guns. At this point three light tanks from motor landing craft and about I20 infantry from assault landing craft (followed by infantry from ships' boats) were able to land with little loss and so to work their way round the head of the Fjord to deal with the remaining machine-guns, on the beaches, which had not been affected by the naval bombardment. Distant machine guns were still in action when the second battalion landed on the East shore about 2 hours later. The operation was entirely successful. Without the use of tanks and armoured landing craft it might very easily have ended in a costly failure. It was fortunate indeed that low clouds prevented hostile air attack during the landing.

Touch was made with the force operating from Gratangen. The Oijord peninsula was seized. The stage was now set for the capture of Narvik.

12. Meanwhile the situation in the South was causing me some concern. Continued German advances in that area were having most serious results upon our Norwegian Allies and, indeed seemed likely to result in the withdrawal of all Norwegian support from the Allied forces. I considered that the time had come to stop these enemy advances and I welcomed Lord Cork's suggestion on 9th May that troops should be despatched with that object. I had been in constant touch with Colonel Gubbins and two companies of Scissors Force at Mosjoen and with one company of that Force, under Major May, at Mo. After the abandonment of Mosjoen I decided that energetic measures must be taken and accordingly sent the Ist Bn. the Scots Guards (less one company already at Bodo), with field and anti-aircraft guns, to Mo. Mo was doubly important as being the terminus of the most northerly road into Sweden and as covering the Norwegian aerodrome a few miles to the North. Should this aerodrome fall into the hands of the enemy it would afford him just that extra stepping stone he needed to bring further air forces into action in the Narvik area.

This detachment arrived at Mo at 0400 hours 12th May without loss. Colonel Gubbins with his two companies from Mosjoen had meanwhile withdrawn to Bodo.

At the same time I instituted arrangements for reinforcing the detachment at Mo with Headquarters 24th (Guards) Brigade and Ist Bn. The Irish Guards. Before these arrangements were completed and put into effect (they were subsequently modified) I handed over command to my successor.

13. It will be apparent from the preceding paragraphs that the period of my command was perforce chiefly one of reconnaissance and planning and of carrying out such initial offensive operations as the climatic conditions and the gradual building up of my force to a reasonable fighting organisation permitted. At the same time the task of setting the administrative organisation on a sound basis fitted to deal with projected operations and with future expansion made tremendous calls upon the initiative and powers of improvisation of my staff, all under Arctic conditions of great, though decreasing, severity. Subsidiary bases were established at Skaanland on Sundet Fjord and in Ballangen south of the Ofot Fjord.

14. I wish to place on record my deep appreciation of the co-operation and assistance afforded by the Royal Navy at all times to the troops under my command. Without that help it would have been impossible to make any progress. The Royal Navy carried and escorted the Allied troops and, pending the arrival of anti-aircraft guns, took over the duties of anti-aircraft protection under the most difficult circumstances. The naval staff, particularly Captain Maund, R.N., and Commander Hubback, R.N., worked in intimate and unflagging co-operation with my own staff: I owe these officers a deep debt of gratitude for their ever close and cordial assistance.

15. Relations with the French were most happy throughout. The loyalty and efficiency displayed by General Bethouart were of the highest order. It was a very great pleasure to be so closely associated with so fine an officer.

I6. Major-General Fleischer and the troops of the 6th Norwegian Division under his command co-operated at all times willingly and effectively with the Allied forces. Without that co-operation the British and French troops engaged on the mainland would have been faced with a number of additional difficulties.

I7. The period of planning and of consultations with the Royal Navy and with the Allied Forces threw a great strain and weight of responsibility upon any General Staff. The establishment of a base and the supply and movement of troops with limited and difficult means of transportation made equally heavy demands upon my Administrative Staff and Services. All these demands were met in a most praiseworthy manner. All concerned displayed powers of improvisation of the highest order.

I8. I would draw special attention to the fine work of my General Staff Officer (First Grade), Colonel A.B. Dowler and of my A.A. and Q.M.G., Colonel J.F.W. Allen, M.C. These officers were faced with unusual problems and responsibilities They dealt with them all in a truly admirable manner.

I9. That I once commanded an Allied Force containing such fine troops, British, French and Polish alike, will for ever remain a source of great pride to me.

I have the honour to be,
Sir,
Your obedient servant,
P.J. Mackesy,
Major-General.

German infantry advance past burning buildings in a Norwegian village during the fighting in April 1940. (Historic Military Press)

German parachute troops, or *Fallschirmjäger*, pictured landing during operations in the area of Narvik in 1940. (Historic Military Press)

The aftermath of the Battle of Narvik. The wrecks still present in the harbour include both merchant vessels and warships (British, German, Swedish and Norwegian). (Deutsches Bundesarchiv)

German mountain troops, or *Gebirgsjägers*, deployed in the countryside surrounding Narvik. (Bundesarchiv, Bild 183-2005-1202-500/CC-BY-SA)

A Bristol Blenheim of 254 Squadron in the spring of 1940. Operating from Hatston in the Orkney's, this squadron was one of many from Coastal Command deployed on operations during the Norwegian campaign. (Historic Military Press)

Blohm und Voss seaplanes moored at Stavanger, as photographed by a Lockheed Hudson of 18 Group, Coastal Command, during an early morning reconnaissance on 10 April 1940, the second day of the German invasion. (Historic Military Press)

The original wartime Ministry of Information art work, which was drawn to illustrate a part of the actions for which Lieutenant Richard Been Stannard was awarded the Victoria Cross. Here Stannard can be seen on the bows of HMT *Arab* fighting the fires on the quayside at Namsos, Norway, in April 1940. (Historic Military Press)

Lieutenant Richard Been Stannard, RNR – the only member of the Royal Naval Patrol Service to be awarded the Victoria Cross. Stannard died in Australia in 1977. (Historic Military Press)

The crew of HMS *Curacoa* at action stations in Romsdalsfjord, Norway, during 23 or 24 April 1940. Note the quadruple 0.5 inch machine-guns in the right foreground. (IWM; HU71299)

Lockheed Hudsons of 224 Squadron flying up Romsdalsfjord on 23 April 1940. The lead aircraft is N7264, flown by Pilot Officer O'Neill; the second is N7249, which was flown by Pilot Officer Hector Webb. This photograph was taken from Sergeant A. James' Hudson with literally just seconds to go until disaster struck – a disaster in which the aircraft nearest the camera was shot down by the guns of HMS *Curacoa*. (Historic Military Press)

The crew of 224 Squadron's Hudson Mk.I N7264 pictured together at RAF Wick following their safe return from operations over Norway on 23 April 1940. The damage was caused by the guns of HMS *Curacoa*. (Historic Military Press)

British prisoners of war being processed by their captors in the Norwegian port of Drontheim, April 1940. (Bundesarchiv, Bild 183-L03926/CC-BY-SA)

A contemporary artist's depiction of the action during the First Battle of Narvik for which Captain Bernard Armitage Warburton Warburton-Lee was awarded the Victoria Cross. On 10 April 1940, in Ofotfjord, Warburton-Lee, of HMS *Hardy*, commanded the British 2nd Destroyer Flotilla in a surprise attack on German warships and merchant ships in a blinding snowstorm. This was successful, but was almost immediately followed by an engagement with more German destroyers during which Captain Warburton-Lee was mortally wounded by a shell. (Historic Military Press)

British commandos in action during the attack on the island of Vaagso, Operation *Archery*, on 27 December 1941. (Historic Military Press)

A Messerschmitt Bf 109 attempts to take off from the Norwegian airfield of Herdla during a raid by Bristol Blenheim Mk.IVs of 114 Squadron, which were operating in support of the Combined Operations attack on Vaagso, 27 December 1941. Note how bombs can be seen exploding. (Historic Military Press)

A survivor of the Norwegian campaign – the remains of a 263 Squadron Gloster Gladiator, Mk.II N5628, which can be seen in the RAF Museum at Hendon. This aircraft was one of those flown off from HMS *Glorious* on 24 April 1940, landing at the airstrip on the frozen Lake Lesjaskogsvatnet. Damaged during the German air raids the following day, N5628 eventually sank through the melting ice. (Courtesy of Michael Matthews)

APPENDIX "B".

REPORT ON OPERATIONS IN NORTHERN NORWAY.
13th May to 8th June, 1940.

The following report was submitted to the Secretary of State for War on 19th June, 1940, by Lieutenant-General C.J.E. Auchinleck, C.B., C.S.I., D.S.O., O.B.E.

Receipt of Instructions.

I. On the evening of 28th April I was summoned by the Chief of the Imperial General Staff (General Sir E. Ironside) to the War Office and informed by him that I, with part of the 4th Corps Staff, would be required to go to Narvik in the immediate future. I returned to my headquarters at Alresford and arranged for an advanced headquarters to be established in the War Office.

2. For the next week, my staff were fully employed collecting and collating information concerning Northern Norway and the existing situation in that theatre.

In this task they received every possible assistance from the staff of the different departments and branches of the War Office.

3. On the 6th May, I received my instructions from the Secretary of State for War. These instructions were to the effect:-

(*a*) That the object of His Majesty's Government was to secure and maintain a base in Northern Norway from which it would be possible:-

    i. To deny iron ore supplies to Germany via Narvik.
    ii. To interfere with ore supplies to Germany from Lulea in Sweden,
    iii. To preserve a part of Norway as a seat of Government for the Norwegian King and Government.

(*b*) That the forces, assembled for this purpose were under the command of Admiral of the Fleet Lord Cork and Orrery; the Military Commander Major-General Mackesy being subordinate to him, and that this system of unified command was to remain in being until such time as His Majesty's Government decided to terminate it and revert to the usual system of having independent commanders of the sea and land forces.

(*c*) That I was appointed G.O.C.-in-C. designate of the Anglo-French land forces and of the British Air Component in the theatre of Operations.

(*d*) That I was to proceed to the area with an officer detailed by the Chief of the

Air Staff and in conjunction with the Earl of Cork and Orrery, report for the information of the Chiefs of Staff, the forces required to attain the objects outlined in sub-paragraph (*a*), and the area which should be occupied.

(*e*) That I was to consider the possibility of shipping any iron ore now at Narvik to the United Kingdom, and of resuming a supply of iron ore from Swedish mines at Gallivare, and to report on the feasibility and desirability of repairing the railway from Narvik to the Swedish frontier.

4. I received also an instruction from General Sir John Dill, Vice-Chief of the Imperial General Staff, to the effect that it was the intention of the C.I.G.S. that I should take over command of the Anglo-French forces when His Majesty's Government decided to end the system of unified command, but that, if on arrival in the Narvik area, local conditions appeared to me to necessitate the step, I was to assume command of the Anglo-French troops, placing myself under Admiral of the Fleet Lord Cork and Orrery.

5. Before leaving London I appreciated the situation in Northern Norway in the light of such information as was available on the spot, and informed the C.I.G.S. that in my view, the implications of the objects given to me were:-

(*a*) The establishment of aerodromes necessary for the effective operation of an air component. These would include one at Bardu Foss, another in the neighbourhood of Harstad and probably a third further south possibly at Bodo, with the necessary complement of anti-aircraft artillery.

(*b*) The protection of the naval anchorage which could be defended economically against surface, under water and land attack, and around which ground anti-aircraft defences could be installed.

(*c*) The selection and occupation of an area which could be adequately defended against sea, land and air attack and within which suitable base installations could be developed to supply a force of approximately three divisions through the port of Narvik and the railway to Lulea.

I estimated that this area would have to include not only an area South of Narvik at least as far as the Tysfjord (40 miles South of Narvik) but also an area East of Narvik along the frontier. Further, that the Northern portion of the area would have to include Hatten which lies 80 miles North of Narvik at the head of the Lyngen Fjord and covers the approaches to Tromso.

6. I submitted also to the C.I.G.S. a provisional estimate of the forces which I considered would be required. These in general, apart from air forces and troops required for administrative purposes, amounted to twelve infantry battalions, one or two machine gun battalions, a divisional cavalry regiment (mechanised) with a due proportion of artillery and engineer units.

In conjunction with the technical experts available in the War Office, I estimated the requirements in anti-aircraft artillery at I44 3.7 guns and II2 Bofors Light Guns.

Departure for and arrived in Norway.

7. I embarked with an advanced headquarters staff at Leith in the Polish liner *Chrobry* on the 7th May and landed, after an uneventful voyage at Harstad on the IIth May.

8. Lord Cork was away in his flagship at Skaanland when I landed, but I met Major-General Mackesy and his General Staff Officer, Colonel Dowler, at once, and learned the situation from them. Hearing that a landing operation by the French contingent was about to take place near Bjerkvik at the head of Herjangs Fjord, and that Lord Cork was to direct the operation in person, I at once went to Skaanland with my Brigadier General Staff, Brigadier Gammell, and met Lord Cork.

I explained my position to Lord Cork, and with his approval, remained in H.M.S. *Effingham* with him. Neither General Mackesy nor any member of his staff was present on the Flagship, though General Bethouart, Commanding the French Contingent and his staff embarked just after myself and remained aboard throughout the operation.

9. The landing took place under a heavy bombardment from the guns of the Fleet in cold and cloudy weather in the early hours of the I3th May, and, in spite of the fact that there was now continuous daylight throughout the twenty-four hours and appreciable opposition from enemy machine guns on shore, was completely successful. The enemy was ejected from the area North and East of Herjangs Fjord and the French landing parties not only effected a junction with their own troops advancing from the North from the direction of Gratangen but also cleared the country down to Oijord immediately across the Rombaks Fjord from Narvik.

Although I was present in the capacity of a spectator only, I am constrained to express my admiration for the way in which the whole operation was conceived and effected by all concerned. I was particularly struck by the business like efficiency of the French Foreign Legion which carried out the landing. That the landing was not interfered with by enemy aircraft was almost certainly due to the fortunate weather conditions prevailing at the time. At this period, there were no land based aircraft available in Norway with which to counter enemy air attacks and a bombing raid might well have turned the operation from a success into a failure.

I0. I returned with Lord Cork to Harstad in H.M.S. *Effingham,* arriving on the afternoon of the I3th May.

Assumption of Command.

II. Immediately H.M.S. *Effingham* reached Harstad, Brigadier Fraser, Commander of the 24th Guards Brigade, came on board with Colonel Dowler of the General Staff, to discuss plans for operations in the Mo and Bodo areas with Lord Cork. Owing to ill health, Major-General Mackesy was not present.

I2. With the concurrence of Lord Cork I listened to the ensuing discussion which centred round the question whether reinforcements already embarked at Skaanland should be sent to Bodo or to Mo, where an advanced detachment consisting of Ist Battalion Scots Guards and some "Independent Companies" had already been landed under heavy enemy air attack. At this conference I told Lord Cork that, in accordance with my instructions from the War Office, I proposed to assume command of all military forces forthwith.

13. I then gave verbal orders to Brigadier Fraser that he was to proceed at once with Ist Battalion Irish Guards and other troops to Bodo and not to Mo, and that he was to hold Bodo permanently, and Mo, for as long as he could. These orders were subsequently confirmed in writing.

14. On landing from H.M.S. *Effingham* I at once informed Major-General Mackesy that I had assumed command. Throughout my dealings with Major-General Mackesy I found him uniformly helpful and informative. In fact, many of my subsequent actions were based on information and advice received from him.

Situation on 13th May, 1940.

15. Briefly the dispositions, on the 13th-14th May, were:-

(*a*) In the Narvik area:-

    i. One battalion Chasseurs Alpins and the 2nd Battalion South Wales Borderers on the Ankenes Peninsula in touch with enemy detachments but not yet in possession of Ankenes itself.

    ii. The enemy still in possession of Narvik and the whole peninsula on which it stands.

    iii. Two battalions of the Foreign Legion and one battalion of the Polish Contingent holding the area Bjerkvik-Qijord, and in contact with the enemy to the Eastward.

    iv. One battalion Chasseurs Alpins to the North of the Foreign Legion, having advanced from the direction of Gratangen, and in contact with enemy elements about Hartvigvand.

    v. The Norwegian 6th Division (5 bns. of infantry and a few mountain guns) under General Fleischer to the North and East of the Chasseurs Alpins and in touch with the enemy in the Graesdalen valley and to the East of it.

    vi. A battalion Chasseurs Alpins near Gratangen.

    vii. A Polish battalion near Harstad and another at Ballangen on the south shore of Ofot Fjord and a third at Salangen.

(*b*) In the Mo-Bodo area dispositions were:-

    i. Ist Battalion Scots Guards less one company and one Independent Company at Mo and in contact with enemy forces which had landed on the Hemnes Peninsula 20 miles south of Mo. This force was under the command of Lieutenant-Colonel Trappes-Lomax, Scots Guards, and included also one troop 203rd Field Battery (four 24-pdr. guns) and one troop 55th Light Anti-Aircraft Regiment (four Bofors guns).

    ii. In the Bodo area, one company Scots Guards and three "independent" companies.

iii. En route to Bodo in *M.V. Chrobry* the Ist Battalion Irish Guards, H.Q. 24th Guards Brigade and detachments of the 230th Field Company, R.E., and 137th Field Ambulance.

iv. Brigadier Fraser proceeded ahead of *Chrobry* in H.M.S. *Somali* to Mo, visiting Bodo on the way. At Mo, news of the bombing of *M.V. Chrobry* was received, and H.M.S. *Somali* at once left to render assistance. On the way, however, H.M.S. *Somali* was bombed and had to return to Scapa. Later Brigadier Fraser succeeded in transferring to H.M.S. *Curlew* and arrived back at Harstad. It was evident that he had not recovered from a wound received at Ankenes, and it was therefore necessary to convene a medical board. The Board found that he was unfit and he had unfortunately to return to U.K.

16. The force was maintained through the Base Area which had been established from the outset at Harstad, the forward delivery to Units and Formations in contact being made by locally procured water transport to Fjord Head, where approximately 10 days' reserve supplies, etc., were held.

Inland Water Transport was thus the main agency for forward maintenance. Yet, although a study of the map would have shown that this was so, no provision had been made to send with the Force at the outset the necessary personnel to organize and operate Inland Water Transport in the way that railway units are sent to operate railways in a theatre where the railway is the main transport agency.

17. The policy of the War Office and the French Co-ordinating Staff in London by which the French maintenance system was to be welded into the British system and controlled by Force H.Q. had not been fully realised.

This was necessary as the items of supply common to both and all reserves of ammunition and fighting equipment were to be held in a common Base Area, whilst Force Headquarters were to be responsible also for forward maintenance.

In actual fact the French had been permitted to commence the establishment of a separate Base Area at Ballangen, and provided with water transport under their own control. As the French Administrative Staff was very small, and had at its disposal only a few issuers and checkers, and no personnel for handling stores, there was a great delay in dealing with their store ships; in fact 5 had remained near their Base Area only partially unloaded for 16 days or more.

18. The reserve of supplies, ammunition and general stores was low for the whole force, this situation being aggravated by the fact that the French had not arrived with 60 days' supplies as had been arranged. Motor Transport repair facilities and spares were almost non-existent.

19. At Harstad itself, the number of quays available for unloading ships was sufficient for the amount of stores going through the Base Port at that time, but the facilities for clearing and holding the stores up to the scale of reserves to be held, was quite inadequate. The port had not sufficient accommodation for the number of personnel required to be accommodated in the Base Area, nor were there storage facilities available in sufficient quantity or in dispersed areas.

The Medical plan for the evacuation of Allied casualties through British Medical

Units back to the Base was working efficiently, but the number of beds available in the General Hospital at Harstad was inadequate, as only approximately 500 beds were available in three buildings.

General survey of events during the period.

20. The principal military activities during the period under review were the attempt to stabilise the position on our Southern front in the region of Mo and Bodo, the establishment in the theatre of war of land-based aircraft, the organisation of a base and its protection against attack from the Air. These activities are dealt with separately in subsequent paragraphs. Other events of interest are described briefly in the following paragraphs.

2I. Throughout the period the enemy was active in the air and carried out numerous attacks of varying intensity and duration against H.M. Ships and other vessels in the area. Attacks on ships and other craft in the Ofot Fjord and off Narvik were of daily occurence, and several attacks were made on Harstad itself and on shipping in the harbour. On May 20th enemy bombers succeeded in setting light to an oil tank at Harstad and two oil tankers moored in the vicinity were also set on fire and burned out. On the whole, however, except for the damage to shipping which was considerable, little harm was caused to Harstad by these attacks and casualties were few. The effect on the morale of the troops and civil population, however, was considerable.

22. In spite of arrangements made for co-operation with local military and civil authorities by Major-General Mackesy and his staff prior to my arrival, the relations between the Allied Forces in Norway and the Norwegian authorities, civil and military, had never been regularised through the proper diplomatic channels, and co-operation with such Norwegian forces as remained in being was not made easier by this omission to place matters on a proper political footing. On the I6th May, however, I had a cordial and satisfactory interview at my Headquarters with General Rugé, Commander-in-Chief of the Norwegian army, and General Fleischer, Commander 6th Norwegian Division, acting in close co-operation with the French forces to the North of the Rombaks Fjord.

The Norwegian Generals were insistent on the need for preventing Mo and Bodo falling into the hands of the enemy and stressed their desire to pass from the defensive to the offensive and recapture Mosjoen. I explained the Allied situation to them fully.

On I5th May Colonel R.C.G. Pollock, M.C., Head of a Military Mission sent out to assist my Headquarters to maintain close relations with the Norwegian Government, reported to me and was informed of the situation before he left for Tromso.

Sir Cecil Dormer, British Minister in Norway, also arrived from the United Kingdom and discussed the situation with Lord Cork and myself before proceeding to take up his post with the King and Government of Norway. The opportunity was taken of impressing on him the urgent need of a closer control of the civil population in militarily occupied areas.

On 23rd May Lord Cork flew to Tromso and discussed the general situation with the King and members of the Government. As a result of these activities relations with the Norwegian authorities began to assume a more businesslike and realistic aspect, particularly in respect of the necessary provision of facilities for the establishment of a base at Tromso. These the Norwegians were reluctant to concede on the grounds that our presence there would expose the town to enemy air attack; in fact, they went so far as to stipulate that unless we provided adequate anti-aircraft artillery protection in the area, base facilities could not be provided.

With the help of Colonel Pollock these objections were eventually overcome, but part of my already inadequate allotment of anti-aircraft artillery had to be diverted to Tromso as the War Office could not spare any for this purpose.

23. On the 16th May I completed and despatched the Report to the Chiefs of Staff called for in my original Instructions from the Secretary of State for War. The Report was to the effect that provided the situation generally remained unchanged it should be possible to maintain the integrity of Northern Norway with the forces outlined below, and, as well, develop a limited offensive so as to deny the landing ground at Mosjoen to the enemy.

FORCES REQUIRED.

(*a*) *Sea.*

> Four cruisers.
> Six destroyers.
> Four escort vessels.
> Twelve anti-submarine trawlers.
> Two submarines.
> Auxiliary vessels as at present.

(*b*) *Land.*

> One Divisional Cavalry Regt.
> One Squadron Armoured Cars.
> One Mounted Infantry Unit (Lovat's Scouts).
> Five Batteries Field Artillery.
> Two Batteries Medium Howitzers.
> Thirteen Batteries (104 guns) Heavy Anti-Aircraft Artillery.
> Eight Batteries (96 guns) Light Anti-Aircraft Artillery.
> Five Companies Engineers.
> Seventeen Infantry Battalions.
> One Machine Gun Battalion.

(*c*) *Air.*

> Two Squadrons Hurricane Fighters.
> One Bomber Squadron.
> One Army-Co-operation Squadron.

I also pointed out, that the first object, namely, the denial of iron ore to Germany through Narvik, seemed already to have been achieved by the destruction of the facilities at the port, partly by the Germans themselves and partly by naval bombardment; secondly, that the interference with the supply of ore to Germany through Lulea did not seem to be a practical proposition unless the active and full co-operation of the Swedish armed forces could be assured; and that therefore the third object, namely, the maintenance of the integrity of Northern Norway seemed to be the only one of the three that required immediate consideration.

The need for Tromso as a base port in addition to Harstad was also indicated, as was the urgency of arriving at some adequate arrangement with the Norwegian Government so as to ensure the efficient control of the civil population in the theatre of operations and the desirability of placing all the armed forces in Norway under a single Commander-in-Chief.

The interdependence from a strategical point of view of Bodo, Narvik and Tromso, and the impossibility of treating the defence of any one of them as an isolated problem was also pointed out, as was the potential threat involved in the present defenceless state of the landing grounds in Northern Norway at Laxelvn and elsewhere.

24. Throughout the period I was in constant touch with Lord Cork from whom as Commander-in-Chief I received my general instructions. On 16th May Lord Cork established his Headquarters ashore, and a joint Navy and Army Operational Office was set up at Force Headquarters in Harstad. Co-operation was greatly facilitated by these measures.

25. During this period General Bethouart perfected his plans for the achievement of the objects assigned to him by me, and his troops, assisted by the Norwegians under the Command of General Fleischer on the eastern flank, continued steadily to press back the Germans North of the Rombaks Fjord and South of the Beis Fjord in circumstances of considerable difficulty of terrain and maintenance.

26. On 17th May a telegram was received from the Chiefs of Staff to the effect that, owing to events in France and Belgium, my Force would be limited to 12 French and 3 British Battalions, with ten independent companies with proportionate artillery, engineers and services, 48 heavy and 60 light anti-aircraft guns, one Hurricane Squadron, one Gladiator Squadron and, possibly, one Army Co-operation Flight. The telegram also stated that only the first object, namely, the denial of iron ore supplies to Germany through Narvik, and the third, the preservation of the integrity of Northern Norway, could be accomplished at present, but that the possession of a base in Narvik might make the second object, namely, the interference of ore supplies to Germany through Lulea, possible in time. The telegram concluded by requesting my views as to the retention of Narvik in these circumstances.

27. On 21st May, after consultation with Lord Cork and Group Captain Moore, R.A.F., I sent a reply to the effect that my considered opinion was that the land forces suggested by His Majesty's Government might be sufficient with certain small additions, that the provision of anti-aircraft artillery was unlikely to be adequate should the enemy make heavy air attacks and that I adhered to my original estimate of the minimum air forces required, namely; two Hurricane Fighter Squadrons, one bomber Squadron and one Army Co-operation Squadron.

28. Throughout this period the installation of such anti-aircraft artillery as had been made available for the force, namely, 48 heavy and 58 light anti-aircraft guns, was pushed forward with skill and energy by Brigadier Rossiter, commanding the Anti-Aircraft Defences. Except at Harstad itself the disembarkation of these guns had to be carried out by transferring them into motor landing craft and then ferrying them ashore. The extremely mountainous nature of the country increased the difficulty of finding suitable positions for the guns, and the indented character of the coast complicated the maintenance of isolated detachments. In spite of these obstacles the establishment of the anti-aircraft artillery was effected with commendable speed and efficiency and materially added to the security of the Force and its bases.

The allotment of the limited guns available was made on the principle that it was only possible to give a minimum degree of protection to really vital areas and that smaller and less important areas must go without.

On 20th May I decided that the best disposition of these guns would be:-

Situation	Heavy Guns	Light Guns
Bardu Foss	8 (16)	12 (24)
Harstad and Skaanland	24 (48)	18 (36)
Bodo	8 (16)	12 (12)
Tromso	8 (24)	16 (24)
	48 (104)	58 (96)

The figures in brackets show the number of guns considered necessary to give really adequate protection to each area.

In addition, there were demands for anti-aircraft artillery to protect French troops in the forward areas round Narvik, at Lodingen at the mouth of Tjelsundet Fjord to protect the coast and naval anti-submarine defences there, to cover the R.D.F. stations to be installed in the Lofoten Islands and elsewhere, and also for the protection of a third landing ground under preparation at Elvenes, near Salangen.

In actual fact these proposed dispositions did not materialize and the distribution of anti-aircraft artillery at the end of May was:-

Situation	Heavy Guns	Light Guns
Bardu Foss	12	12
Sorreisa	—	2
Elvenes	—	4
Tromso	4	4
Harstad	12	5
Skaanland	15	10
Ballangen	—	4 } (Protecting
Ankenes	—	4 } French
Bjerkvik	—	4 } forward troops)
Bodo	—	2 (Two lost at Mo)
Loaded for Bodo	4	4
With the Navy	—	1 (in a "Q" Ship)

The despatch of the guns to Tromso was in response to a Norwegian demand for protection as already recounted.

29. On 24th May telegraphic instructions were received from the Chiefs of Staff that Northern Norway was to be evacuated as soon as possible.

The Reinforcement of Bodo.

30. The security of the vital base area round Harstad was essential to ensure the success of the operations and was now threatened by the rapid Northward advance of the enemy from Mosjoen. It was necessary, therefore, to check this advance, and it appeared to me that it was essential to hold the port of Bodo so as to ensure adequate depth in the defence and because it was the only port available for use as an advanced base which still remained to us, Mo being already threatened by enemy forces in its immediate proximity. I therefore decided that an adequate force must be established in the area.

I determined to transfer the British Contingent to that area and to use the French Contingent, helped by the Norwegian Army, to continue the pressure on the enemy in the Narvik area. I issued instructions to this effect to General Bethouart on I4th May and gave him as his task the destruction of the enemy forces in that area and the capture of Narvik.

3I. It has already been mentioned that the Ist Battalion, Irish Guards, and other troops sailed from Harstad on I4th May in the *Chrobry.* The ship was attacked and set on fire by German aircraft when nearing Bodo. Six officers of the Irish Guards were killed, but nearly all the troops were saved by H.M. Ships *Stork* and *Wolverine,* whose complements showed the greatest courage and resource in the work of rescue, and were brought back to Harstad having lost practically the whole of their equipment.

Realizing the urgency of the situation at Mo, I then arranged to send the 2nd Battalion, South Wales Borderers, to Bodo as soon as they could be relieved at Ankenes by a French Battalion. This unit left for Bodo in H.M.S. *Effingham* on I7th May. When H.M.S. *Effingham* was within an hour's steaming of Bodo she struck an uncharted rock and eventually became a total loss. The South Wales Borderers and other troops on board were rescued by the Navy without loss of life, but with the loss of much of their equipment, though the Navy by the most strenuous exertions managed to save much of it, including even some Bren gun carriers, which was taken to Bodo in a small craft. A duplicate consignment of stores and ammunition was at once despatched to Bodo in small Norwegian fishing boats ("puffers").

I also appointed Colonel Gubbins to the command of the troops in the Bodo – Mo area in place of Brigadier Fraser, who, as already mentioned, had proceeded to Scapa Flow in H.M.S. *Somali.*

32. On I5th May as the enemy had outflanked the Scots Guards in their positions, South of Mo, Brigadier Gubbins ordered them to withdraw.

On the next day this detachment, which was commanded by Lieut.-Colonel Trappes-Lomax of the Scots Guards, evacuated Mo under pressure. Brigadier Gubbins went to Mo to acquaint himself personally with the situation, and asked for the support of fighter aircraft, of which there were none to be had, excepting those in the carriers of the Fleet Air Arm which could not be made available at that time.

On the same day I despatched the Headquarters of the 24th Guards Brigade (for the third time) and half the South Wales Borderers in destroyers to Bodo which they reached safely on 20th May. They were followed on 21st May by two Companies of the Irish Guards in "puffers", the journey by "puffer" taking about 24 hours against nine by destroyers.

Two more Companies of the Irish Guards arrived the same day at Bodo in destroyers, accompanied by Colonel Dowler of the General Staff, sent by me to make personal contact with Brigadier Gubbins.

The troops at Bodo were bombed that day by enemy aircraft.

Brigadier Gubbins had now at his disposal the three Battalions of the 24th Guards Brigade, three independent companies, one troop of Field artillery and one troop of Bofors guns; and seemed satisfied with the situation for the moment. There is no doubt, however, that the retardation of the reinforcement of the force by the sinkings of the *Chrobry* and H.M.S. *Effingham* had adversely affected the chances of stopping the enemy in the narrow defile North of Mo.

Enemy air attacks on the long and attenuated line of communications of the Scots Guards at Messingletten were causing anxiety to Brigadier Gubbins, who was also in urgent need of small armed vessels to prevent enemy landings at will in his rear. He informed me that he considered the enemy's comparative freedom to move troops by sea the most serious feature of the situation.

33. On 23rd May I formed the troops in the area into "BODOFORCE" under Brigadier Gubbins and amalgamated his Staff with that of the 24th Guards Brigade.

Brigadier Gubbins asked for reinforcements of infantry, field and anti-aircraft artillery and mechanical transport. Arrangements were made to embark these at Harstad, except as regards the infantry, it being my intention to send him three more independent companies which were due to arrive from England on 30th May. A Company of 25 millimetre French anti-tank guns, borrowed from General Bethouart were also embarked for Bodo.

34. On 23rd May reasonably reliable information was received of the concentration in the Mo – Mosjoen area of about 4,000 Germans with tanks and artillery. This day the Scots Guards withdrew from their position and Brigadier Gubbins decided to relieve them by the Irish Guards. On 24th May the Scots Guards withdrew under orders from Brigadier Gubbins towards Rognan.

On 24th May intimation of His Majesty's Government's intention to evacuate Northern Norway was received, and I at once sent Colonel Dowler of the General Staff to acquaint Brigadier Gubbins of the new situation and to concert with him plans for the early withdrawal of all his troops from Bodo.

35. The operations for the stabilization of the position in the Bodo area were marked throughout by an unrelenting pressure on the enemy's part, both on the ground and in the air, and by a steady resistance by our troops, handicapped as they were by an almost complete absence of any support in the air or any means of hitting back at their enemy.

The evacuation of our troops from Bodo is described in paragraphs 72 to 79.

36. The reinforcement of Bodo and the maintenance of troops in that area, caused certain administrative difficulties. The *Chrobry* conveying the Irish Guards to Bodo having been sunk, the Irish Guards returned to Harstad by destroyer and had to be completely re-equipped, even down to personal clothing of Officers and men. There were sufficient reserves in the Base to carry out 75 per cent. of this re-equipping, with the exception of certain items of personal clothing which were not available.

After H.M.S. *Effingham* conveying the South Wales Borderers to Bodo had been sunk the South Wales Borderers returned to Harstad minus their equipment – although much was salved from the H.M.S. *Effingham* subsequently. This Battalion had to be re-equipped almost completely as they were required at once. Reserve stocks were not sufficient to allow of this and equipment had to be withdrawn from Base Units. Even then the Battalion could not be completed with all items. The chief deficiencies were Mortars, Signalling equipment, Web equipment, Revolvers, Field Glasses, Compasses and Bren guns (these were, however, made up from other sources).

There were considerable difficulties in supplying "BODOFORCE". Destroyers could take personnel but very small quantities of stores. Puffers could take stores but no guns or vehicles, and had to have guards on board. Even then the reliability of the civilian crews was doubtful. There was only one coastal steamer which was capable of carrying guns and vehicles and this was in constant demand in the Harstad area. Any boat larger than a puffer had to proceed with Naval escort, which was not always available at the time required. This problem of supplying "BODOFORCE" was never solved satisfactorily before the evacuation.

The Establishment of the Air Component.

37. On 13th May the Germans had a powerful air force in Southern Norway and several excellent air bases from which to operate it. We, on the other hand, had not a single aerodrome or landing ground fit for use. The enemy thus had complete mastery in the air, except on the somewhat rare occasions when the Fleet Air Arm were able to intervene with carrier-borne aircraft. The vigour and daring of the pilots of the Fleet Air Arm when they were able to engage the enemy earned the admiration of the whole Force, but even their strenuous efforts could not compensate for the absence of land based aircraft owing to the unavoidable relative weakness of performance of carrier-borne aircraft.

38. Shortly before Group Capt. Moore, R.A.F., who had been selected to command the Air Component, and I arrived in the theatre of operations, an energetic and inspiring start in the selection and preparation of possible landing grounds had been made by Wing Comd. Atcherley, R.A.F., who carried out this difficult task with great energy and perseverance.

Group Capt. Moore pushed on the work with the utmost determination and was ably assisted by Brigadier Pyne, my Chief Engineer. The work of preparation was hampered by much of the country being still under deep snow, making it impossible to determine whether expanses of a reasonable size and flatness would prove suitable for landing grounds in respect of their surfaces. The mountainous nature of the country forced upon us the selection and development of the most unlikely sites, of which that at Skaanland was an example. Few laymen would have thought it possible that this site could possibly be made into a landing ground for Hurricane fighter aircraft.

39. The need for some support in the air for both the sea and land forces was urgent, particularly for H.M. Ships which were suffering heavily from the daily and almost continuous attacks made on them in the narrow waters round Narvik by the thoroughly efficient enemy bomber aircraft. Nevertheless, Group Capt. Moore rightly, in my opinion, resisted all pressure to induce him to call for the aircraft to be sent before he was quite satisfied that the landing grounds could be said to be reasonably ready to receive them.

The existing landing ground at Bardu Foss, 50 miles north of Narvik, was selected to be the main air base and work to make it fit for fighters was pressed on with the utmost energy and in face of considerable difficulties, not the least of which was the conditioning of the road to it from Sorreisa at which place all stores, vehicles and equipment had to be disembarked from the ships in landing craft.

The preparation of the new landing ground at Skaanland also presented great difficulties and even the laying of a specially prepared mat brought out from the United Kingdom failed to overcome the softness of the surface caused by the peaty nature of the soil.

Another possible site was found at Elvenes near Salangen, north-east of Harstad, and was put in hand as an alternative landing ground, while work was also commenced at Elvegaard, near Bjerkvik, as soon as the enemy had been ejected from this area by the successful French landing on 13th May.

The possibility of operating aircraft from Lakelvn on Forsanger Fjord, east of Hammerfest was also considered as there is an excellent landing ground there capable of taking two squadrons and relatively free of snow, but it was too far from the scene of active operations.

40. Eventually the first Squadron of Gladiator Fighters flew off one of the aircraft carriers on the 21st May and was safely established at Bardu Foss, with the loss of two aircraft from crashes into the mountain side in bad weather. Just, before their arrival anti-aircraft artillery, heavy and light, had been installed at Bardu Foss after much labour and energy had been expended in their disembarkation and subsequent transport by road from the sea. The importance of giving this one and only aerodrome the maximum degree of protection against air attack was so great that its defence was given priority over all other needs. Twelve heavy and sixteen light anti-aircraft guns were installed there.

It was not until 26th May, that is two days after the orders to evacuate Norway had been received, that it was possible to receive the second squadron, consisting of Hurricane fighters, at Skaanland. Even then, this landing ground proved unequal to the weight of these aircraft and they too had to be operated from Bardu Foss which remained the sole landing ground in regular use until the final evacuation.

41. At the cost of a great amount of skill and energy on the part of Wing Commander Maxton, R.A.F., an advanced landing ground was got ready at Bodo and

used with great effect by our aircraft in support of the troops in that area until it was so heavily bombed by enemy aircraft as to be unusable without extensive repairs.

42. Once established, the R.A.F. soon proved their superiority over the enemy bombers and fighters, and I have no doubt that the comparative immunity from air attack enjoyed by the forces during the later phases of the campaign was due to the severe losses inflicted by our aircraft on those of the enemy. The effect on the morale of the force as a whole of their vigorous and successful operations was most marked.

In general terms, my instructions to Group Capt. Moore for the employment of his fighter aircraft were:-

(a) To protect from hostile air attack the following:-

    (i) The Naval anchorage at Skauland and its approaches.
    (ii) The base at Harstad.
    (iii) Allied sea and land forces in contact with the enemy.
    (iv) Airfields occupied by the R.A.F.

(b) The primary aim of fighter aircraft should be to destroy enemy aircraft approaching the areas to be protected.

(c) To co-operate closely with the land forces operating against the enemy when required.

Organization of the Base.

43. A Maintenance Project had been prepared by my Administrative Staff whilst waiting in London before we sailed. This envisaged the creation of a main Base Area at Skaanland with a Hospital Area at Harstad, and personnel on the coast road running South. Skaanland would have come under the same A.A. protection as the Naval Anchorage.

44. Previous to my arrival, owing to the poor result of a reconnaissance of the Skaanland Area, a representative party of the Services had proceeded to Tromso with a view to investigating what facilities existed there. They had reported that provided assistance was forthcoming from the Norwegian authorities, Tromso was suitable for the handling and storage of large quantities of stores, and could probably provide sufficient accommodation for the General Hospital, but that labour was scarce. Immediately on arrival the D.A. & Q.M.G. visited the Skaanland Area after having seen the facilities available at Harstad, and reported to me that Skaanland could not be developed as a Base Area before the arrival of the winter snows owing to the large amount of constructional work on unsuitable ground that would be necessary. It was therefore decided to send a further reconnaissance to Tromso with a view to establishing a Base Sub-Area there to include the General Hospital, Supply Depot, Ordnance Depot, and certain reserves, the remainder of the base facilities being located at Harstad with an Ammunition Depot at Fjeldal near Skaanland.

45. This layout was about to be implemented when it was decided that the operations were not to be proceeded with.

46. During the period Harstad was being bombed from the air, i.e. up to the end

of the third week in May, certain dispersion of stores at Harstad was made by increasing the reserves held forward and moving certain Base stocks into the surrounding countryside.

General Remarks on Administration 13-24 May.

47. As will be seen from paragraph 16, the weak link in the administrative system was the locally procured Inland Water Transport which the Navy and Army had improvised. It was weak because the crafts were owner-driven Diesel engined fishing craft of 10 to 50 tons and also because of the lack of adequate control or organization. In consequence, though willing workers, the personnel could not be relied upon, whilst the distances to be covered were great. All immediately procurable craft ("puffers") and seven small coastal steamers, two of which were used as Hospital Carriers, were located at Harstad and in the vicinity of the forward Field Supply Depots.

48. Owing to the lack of control, the crews and Dock Labourers at one time stood down during the period of the bombing attacks on Harstad. It was decided that the Army should take over the running of Inland Water Transport, and procure British personnel from home for this purpose. In the meanwhile, the Navy would continue to run it under Force Headquarters through the A.D.Tn. with certain Army personnel placed on board to ensure a measure of availability of the crafts themselves, together with their personnel.

49. Great difficulties were experienced in the handling of heavy equipment and stores at places other than Harstad, as there was no means of putting them ashore except by Motor Landing Craft. These were few in number and were also required for tactical operations. Inconsequence the establishment of A.A. Guns in position and the creation and stocking of aerodromes at Bardu Foss and Skaanland were seriously delayed. Labour for the creation of the aerodromes and for working in the Base installations was procurable and generally worked well, though it would not have been sufficient to maintain the roads and assist on a large scale scheme of hutting.

50. It was soon realised that a comprehensive scheme for the control of the civil population and that certain evacuations in the Base and forward areas would be required for security reasons. An added reason was to ensure that maximum use could be made of existing accommodation for the housing of personnel and stores during the coming winter in order to reduce the hutting programme to a minimum. Negotiations were going on with this in view when operations ceased.

General Survey of Events during the Period from 25th May to 2nd June 1940.

51. The principal military operations during this period were the capture of Narvik and the evacuation of Bodo. These are described in subsequent paragraphs.

52. During the period our fighter aircraft were exceedingly active and caused heavy casualties to the enemy. As already mentioned, the Hurricane fighter squadron arrived on 26 May, and, after an abortive attempt to base it on Skaanland, was finally located at Bardu Foss with the Gladiator squadron.

Enemy activity in the air was increasingly evident at the commencement of the period under review and there were several heavy raids on Harstad, Bardu Foss, Skaanland and Bodo, the newly-prepared landing ground at the last named place being so badly cratered as to be unusable.

As a result of these attacks H.M.S. *Southampton* and *Cairo* were damaged and sustained a number of casualties in personnel, while on 26 May H.M.S. *Curlew* was hit by a bomb at Skaanland and became a total loss. On 29 May the *Mashobra,* mobile base ship, had to be beached as the result of bombing attacks and also became a total loss.

Towards the end of the period enemy air activity was less noticeable, presumably owing to the activity of our fighters and the prevalence of low clouds and mist.

53. Throughout this period close touch was kept with Colonel Pollock, Head of the Mission at Tromso, and much valuable information regarding the trend of Norwegian politics and opinion was obtained from him.

54. On 29th May, after consultation with General Bethouart and myself, Lord Cork telegraphed to the Chiefs of Staff requesting that the decision, as to how and when the intention to evacuate Norway was to be communicated to the Norwegian Government and military commanders, should be left to him, otherwise the tactical situation might be gravely compromised to the detriment, not only of our troops, but also the Norwegian troops.

On the same day information received from Colonel Pollock at Tromso indicated that owing to the evacuation of Bodo, the Norwegian Government were greatly disturbed and might possibly ask for a separate armistice regardless of the military situation.

I received an urgent request from General Fleischer on 30th May to reconsider the decision to evacuate Bodo and for protection of his troops in that area. In actual fact, all Norwegian troops withdrew from the neighbourhood of Bodo without loss and escorted by a destroyer.

On Ist June Sir Cecil Dormer, H.M. Minister in Norway, and Colonel Pollock flew from Tromso and discussed His Majesty's Government's instructions regarding the procedure to be adopted towards the Norwegian Government with Lord Cork and myself and then returned by air to Tromso.

On 2nd June a telegram from Sir Cecil Dormer urging postponement of the commencement of the evacuation for twenty-four hours to enable the Norwegian Government to get into touch with the Swedish Government was received. Lord Cork discussed the suggestion with me, with General Bethouart present, and, as a result, the postponement was agreed to.

55. In order to make it easier for the Norwegian troops to extricate themselves when the French finally withdrew from the neighbourhood of Narvik, I wrote to General Fleischer on 2nd June asking him to withdraw his battalion in Narvik to North of Rombaks Fjord.

The Capture of Narvik.

56. After the successful landing near Bjerkvik and the subsequent operations which

resulted in the clearing of the Oijord Peninsula and the North shore of the Rombaks Fjord as far East as Lilleberget, General Bethouart continued, in accordance with my instructions, to perfect his plans for the capture of Narvik. Until the ground North of the Eastern entrance of the Rombaks Fjord had been cleared an assault on Narvik would have had to be launched on difficult beaches which were believed to be strongly defended by machine guns. Furthermore, such an operation could not have come as a surprise, since the ships and landing craft would have had to be marshalled in Ofot Fjord in daylight in full view of the enemy.

57. Our hold on the Northern shore of Rombaks Fjord widened the front on which the attack could be launched and permitted it to be supported by French field artillery, established North of Oijord. The first echelon of attackers, with the necessary landing craft could now be assembled secretly under cover of Oijordneset point and emerge thence less than a mile from their objective behind the bombarding ships of the Royal Navy.

58. After careful reconnaissance, General Bethouart decided to land the first flight at a beach East of Orneset, and subsequently to transfer a total of three battalions, including a Norwegian battalion, across the Rombaks Fjord from Oijord by motor landing craft. When established ashore, this force, having first blocked the approach of enemy reinforcements from Sildvik by securing a strong position astride the railway, was to advance across the Peninsula and take the town from the rear.

59. The assault on Narvik was to be accompanied by an attack towards Beisfjord by the Polish troops established on the Ankenes Peninsula, with the objects of containing enemy troops in that area, and of threatening the enemy's line of retreat from Narvik by the road running along the North shore of the Beisfjord.

60. The landing operation was rendered particularly hazardous by the scarcity of landing craft which, owing to enemy action and mechanical breakdown, had been reduced to three assault landing craft and two motor landing craft. This meant that the number of men in the first landing party had to be reduced to 290, the numerical weakness of which caused considerable anxiety both to General Bethouart and myself.

6I. The operation was originally intended to take place on the night 24/25th May, but at a conference with General Bethouart on 23rd May I came to the conclusion that unless the weather was very propitious it would be an unjustifiable risk to undertake it with the support of only one fighter squadron of aircraft, in view of the strength and efficiency of the enemy bombers. I decided therefore that it should be postponed until after the arrival of the Hurricane fighter squadron which was due on 27th May. Lord Cork agreed with this decision.

62. After taking this decision the news of the intention of His Majesty's Government to evacuate Northern Norway was received, and it became necessary to consider whether the operation was to be proceeded with or not. After consulting General Bethouart, I recommended to Lord Cork that it should be carried out as intended on the night of 27/28th May. In doing so I considered that, apart from the desirability of making sure whether the facilities for shipping ore from Narvik had in fact been destroyed as thoroughly as had been reported, the chances that a

successful attack would do much to conceal our intention to evacuate the country in the immediate future would outweigh the possible disadvantages involved in extending our commitments by establishing troops in close contact with the enemy on the Narvik Peninsula, where his main force was thought to be located.

63. The operations were timed to begin at 2340 hours on 27th May when three cruisers and five destroyers steamed into position in the mouth of the Rombaks Fjord and commenced their bombardment. Admiral Lord Cork flew his flag in H.M.S. *Cairo* in which ship I accompanied him, together with General Bethouart and his Staff. H.M.S. *Southampton* was detached to work at the mouth of Narvik Harbour to afford support to the Polish troops on the Ankenes Peninsula. The Naval bombardment on the Narvik Peninsula was on a wide front, the targets selected being the mouths of the tunnels of the railway and other suspected machine gun and artillery positions. The fire of the guns of the ships and the French field artillery was heavy and accurate, but close support of the attacking troops was hampered throughout by the broken nature of the terrain and the difficulty of accurate observation in the birch scrub which covered the lower slopes of the hills.

64. The initial landing was hardly opposed and was accomplished with little loss, the first contingent of troops quickly being successfully established on shore. The subsequent movement of troops across the Rombaks Fjord was hampered for short periods by a small gun firing from further to the East on the South shore. This gun caused some casualties, but was soon silenced by Naval gun fire, and by 0330 hours one battalion of the Foreign Legion and the Narvik battalion of the Norwegian Army were ashore on the Peninsula.

65. While this operation was in progress, the enemy launched a strong counter attack from the East, and the forward troops had to fight hard for a time to maintain their positions; this forward movement by the enemy enabled him to bring the landing beach under fire for an appreciable period during which Commandant Paris, Chief of Staff to General Bethouart, was killed in a landing craft. The counter attack was beaten off, and the advance inland resumed. Two French tanks were also ferried across in motor landing craft and landed successfully, but unfortunately they were bogged on the beach and played no part in the operation for the capture of the town.

66. Arrangements had been made for a continuous patrol to be flown by our two squadrons of fighter aircraft over the area throughout the operation. This was carried out from 1915 hours on 27th May until 1615 hours on 29th May with the one brief enforced interval mentioned below. No enemy aircraft appeared in the area until about 0500 hours, a circumstance which seems to show that the operation came as a surprise to the enemy. Unfortunately just about this time our own aircraft became fogbound on Bardu Foss aerodrome, 50 miles to the North and could no longer protect the ships and troops. From 0500 hours to 0700 hours numerous enemy aircraft, often flying in formation, made repeated bombing attacks upon H.M. Ships round Narvik and on the troops on shore. By this time, however, the task of the ships had been substantially completed, and, by constant manoeuvring, they succeeded in avoiding serious damage, though the flagship, H.M.S. *Cairo,* was hit by two bombs and lost 30 men

killed and wounded. The casualties to the landing forces from bombing amounted to only one small craft loaded with ammunition.

67. Once the initial landing had succeeded the progress of General Bethouart's troops was steady and continuous. From reports subsequently received it appears that the enemy withdrew in considerable haste eastwards along the Beisfjord, and by 2200 hours the whole Peninsula west of a line from Fagernes to Forsneset was in French hands, together with some 200 prisoners.

68. After an initial set-back the Polish troops also pressed forward along the Ankenes Peninsula and established themselves on high ground overlooking Beisford.

69. Thus ended an operation which, in my opinion, reflects great credit on the judgment and pertinacity of General Bethouart and on the fighting qualities of his troops. Reconnaissance after the capture of the town revealed the full difficulties of landing on the beaches close to the town and the wisdom of the plan finally adopted. Though he knew of the decision to evacuate Norway before the operation started, General Bethouart persevered with his plan and the vigour with which the advance eastwards was pressed after the capture of the town drove the enemy back on to his main position covering Sildvik and Hundalen, thus making it difficult for him to attempt a counter-attack against Narvik at short notice; this enabled the subsequent evacuation to be carried out under more favourable tactical conditions than at one time seemed likely.

70. Nevertheless, it is my considered opinion that the operation was carried out with the barest margin of safety, and for this reason might well have resulted in failure. Not only had the strength of the first echelon to be put ashore to be limited to 290 men, but this small force had to maintain itself unsupported for forty-five minutes. Had the enemy been able to launch an immediate counter attack the result might have been disastrous. It must always, in my opinion, be unwise to embark on operations of this character unless landing craft are available to land a first flight of adequate strength, and, in addition, provide an adequate floating reserve to meet unforeseen contingencies. Moreover, the absence of bomber aircraft deprived the attack of one of the most effective means of repulsing an enemy counter attack, as has already been mentioned the broken and intricate nature of the ground prevented accurate observation by the supporting ships and artillery. The risk, however, was, in my opinion, worth taking, and, as things turned out, was justified.

7I. I wish particularly to commend the work of Commander Hubback, R.N., of the Naval Staff, upon whom rested practically the whole responsibility for the co-ordination of the Naval share in the operation with that of the French troops. It is no exaggeration to say that the success of the operation was largely due to his unremitting application to the work in hand, and his excellent judgment and sound common sense. The work of the Naval officers and ratings who manned the landing craft and supervised the difficult task of embarkation and disembarkation on open beaches, often under fire, was, in my opinion, magnificent and deserving of the highest praise.

The evacuation of Bodo.

72. Prior to the receipt of instructions from His Majesty's Government to evacuate

Northern Norway, it had been my intention to use every means to reinforce the troops in the Bodo area. I had already in mind a plan to send down a battalion of Chasseurs Alpin, in order to have troops specially trained in mountain warfare to oppose the advance of the German infantry which was being carried out with great skill and vigour. Once the decision to evacuate Norway had been made however, it was obvious that the evacuation of the troops from Bodo must be carried out as promptly as possible, as I had already received reports from Brigadier Gubbins that, without further reinforcements, he was doubtful whether he could hold on for more than a few days.

73. On receipt of the instructions for evacuation from the Chiefs of Staff I therefore immediately despatched Colonel Dowler, my G.S.O.I, to Bodo in a destroyer, which was conveying the last company of the South Wales Borderers to join the rest of its battalion, to concert plans with Brigadier Gubbins for the withdrawal of his force.

74. In view of the heavy and repeated air attacks which were being made upon the town, docks and aerodrome at Bodo, it was decided in consultation with Lord Cork, that evacuation by destroyers provided the best chance of evacuating personnel without serious loss. This decision meant abandoning the few wheeled vehicles and guns with the force, but in view of my instructions that the first consideration was to save personnel, and also in view of the fact that no suitable ship for embarking wheeled vehicles and stores was immediately available, no other course was practicable.

75. Arrangements were therefore made to send two destroyers to embark 500 men each at 2300 hrs. 29th May and three destroyers on each of the two succeeding nights 30th and 31st May, to embark two further parties of 1,500 men each. Early on 26th May when the orders to prepare for the evacuation reached Brigadier Gubbins, the main position held by his Force was some 40 miles from Bodo, in the neighbourhood of Fauske.

Orders were issued by Brigadier Gubbins for two Independent Companies and administrative details to concentrate at Bodo at once and for the withdrawal from the position north of Fauske to start next day.

76. The general plan was that the Ist Bn. Irish Guards and three Independent Companies, which were all under the command of Lt.-Col. Stockwell, should withdraw from the position held north of Fauske and pass through the Scots Guards who were to be placed in position on a neck of land between the sea and a lake near Hopen.

Having passed through the Scots Guards the Irish Guards and the Independent Companies were to move straight to Bodo and embark.

The third battalion of the 24th Guards Brigade, namely the 2nd Bn. The South Wales Borderers, was to be placed in position across the Bodo peninsula further to the west astride Lake Soloi.

The withdrawal of the Irish Guards and the Independent Companies was carried out without interference from the enemy's land forces, though the rear party passed through the Hopen position less than an hour before the enemy's advanced troops, consisting of cyclists and machine guns, made contact with the Scots Guards.

The enemy were at once engaged and the bridge at Hopen was destroyed. This checked the pursuit and the Germans made no movement during the next day.

During the withdrawal on the last night the enemy again followed up with cyclists and machine guns, but no serious pressure developed and no delay occurred.

One company from the Scots Guards and one company from the South Wales Borderers with four 25-pr. guns were placed in position some 4 kilometres east of the town and formed the final rearguards. These companies withdrew to the quay without difficulty by previously reconnoitred routes.

77. During the three days covering the period of the re-embarkation several bombing attacks were carried out by the enemy on Bodo and its vicinity, but during none of the three periods when the actual embarkation of troops was in progress was there any interference from enemy aircraft in spite of the fact that there was continual daylight. This was probably due to unfavourable flying conditions during the first two days. On the last day however, the weather cleared.

The times chosen were round about midnight when enemy air activity was normally at its lowest.

Fortunately the quay at Bodo had not suffered from enemy air attacks and this enabled destroyers to go alongside without difficulty. The embarkations were carried through with great rapidity, 500 men of one battalion embarking with their kits in less than ten minutes.

78. The swiftness and efficiency with which the evacuation was carried out reflects great credit on Brigadier Gubbins and his staff. The destroyers of the Royal Navy were very well handled and carried out the programme laid down to the minute. Four 25-pr. guns, four Bofors guns, and three Bren carriers which had been salved from H.M.S. *Effingham* had to be abandoned together with such material as could not be moved by the men, but some wireless sets and all the arms and equipment, including Bren guns and anti-tank rifles, which could be carried by the men, were brought away.

79. The first echelon to be embarked were transferred at sea from the destroyers to H.M.S. *Vindictive* and conveyed direct to the United Kingdom. Owing to the fact that transports for the second and third echelons had not arrived in time to admit of their direct transhipment, the troops comprised in these were landed at Borkenes to the east of Harstad and re-embarked later as part of the general evacuation programme.

General considerations in the evacuation of Norway.

80. As mentioned already His Majesty's Government's orders to evacuate Northern Norway were received by Lord Cork and communicated at once by him to me. The information was passed on by me to a few selected senior staff officers. General Bethouart was informed by me in Lord Cork's presence.

The news was not imparted to my heads of services or to junior staff officers until May 29th. In the meanwhile, though many steps were taken in preparation for evacuation, such as the loading of arms and stores in ships and the embarkation of certain personnel, the deception was maintained and fostered by all possible means that these activities were concerned with the reinforcement of Bodo, the establishment of the Tromso base or the occupation of Hammerfest and the landing ground in the far North. Thanks to the loyalty and discretion of those concerned, the secret was well kept, and even those who might have suspected were kept constantly confused by conflicting rumours and bogus instructions sedulously circulated by those staff officers in the know.

81. The successful French operations round Narvik resulted in there being three Polish battalions in the area Ankenes – Beisford in touch with the enemy north east of the latter place. East of Narvik the Foreign Legion had made steady progress toward Sildvik and had met with increasing enemy resistance. A Norwegian battalion was in Narvik. On the north shore of the Rombaks Fjord a battalion of Chasseurs was in close touch with German outposts opposite Stromsnes, while General Fleischer's 6th Norwegian Division (5 battalions) were holding from the left of the Chasseurs to the Swedish frontier north of Bjornefjell, also in touch with the enemy.

General Bethouart was particularly anxious that the withdrawal of his troops should not compromise or endanger the Norwegian troops in his sector. The original programme of evacuation was timed to begin on the night 2nd/3rd June, but was postponed 24 hours at the urgent request of Sir Cecil Dormer in order to enable the Norwegian Government to try to implement the so called "Mowinckel Plan" through the Swedish Government and so ensure that Narvik should become a neutral area under Swedish protection. In view of the probability of heavy enemy air attacks on Harstad I agreed to this postponement with great reluctance.

82. The Norwegian high command was informed by its Government of the impending evacuation and after a very natural display of great disappointment, continued to co-operate loyally to the end, although they might with some justification, have decided to lay down their arms at once and so gravely prejudice our withdrawal. It was a trying period for all concerned, throughout which Colonel Pollock, head of the Military Mission at Tromso, was of the greatest assistance to Lord Cork and myself; in spite of everything he managed to maintain cordial relations with the Norwegian authorities to the last.

83. Bodo having been evacuated there was a distinct though not perhaps grave, danger that the enemy working up the coast might appear on the south shores of the Ofot and Vest Fjords and embarrass our withdrawal from there; all craft carrying French troops from the Narvik – Ankenes area had to pass through the Tjelsundet Fjord past Harstad and beyond before re-embarkation into transports could take place. There was also a risk that enemy detachments, sea or air borne, might effect a landing on the long indented coast line of Hinnoy Island on which Harstad stands and directly interfere with our main embarkation centre.

To counter these possible dangers, patrols by warships and aircraft of the Fleet Air Arm and by motorised troops on the island of Hanoy, were organised and maintained throughout the evacuation period.

The telephonic communications with Bodo and the south were also forcibly severed, much to the annoyance of the local Norwegian authorities who had no understanding of the needs of war.

In actual fact the Germans did work up the coast as fast as they could in the face of interference by the Navy, but only succeeded in reaching the neighbourhood of Ballangen with a few parachutists on the final evening of the evacuation.

The weather throughout the evacuation period (June 3rd to 8th) remained generally overcast and dull. I can only assume that it was to this factor and to the genuine fear which our fighter aircraft had succeeded in inspiring in the German bombers that the embarkation of some 27,000 men was carried out with practically no interference from the air.

It was lucky that this was so, as a well directed attack on the quays at Harstad or the beaches round Narvik might have had a very serious effect on the completion of the programme. As it was, the embarkation proper was carried out without a casualty, though there were losses from enemy air attacks during the period.

84. My instructions from the C.I.G.S. were to the effect that the primary object was to save and bring away personnel, and that the salvage of arms, equipment and stores was a secondary object. With this in view I gave orders that if necessary all anti-aircraft artillery was to be kept in action till the last moment and that all fighter aircraft were to be kept in operation till the last man was evacuated and then destroyed.

In actual fact, owing to the inactivity of the enemy it was found possible to save anti-aircraft guns and to fly all the aircraft on to the aircraft carrier *Glorious,* which was, however, unfortunately sunk later by enemy warships on her way to Scapa Flow.

85. My chief preoccupation from the tactical point of view was the disengagement, withdrawal and embarkation from open beaches into fishing boats, re-embarkation into destroyers and final embarkation into transports at sea, of the French troops in contact with the enemy round Narvik. This was most carefully and successfully effected by General Bethouart ably assisted by Commander Hubback, R.N., to both of whom great credit is due.

86. The personnel who had already been sent to Tromso in connection with the organization of a base and the installation of anti-aircraft artillery at that place, together with the members of the military mission, the King and the Government were evacuated in H.M.S. *Devonshire* under arrangements made by Lord Cork and the authorities on the spot.

The anti-aircraft guns (4 heavy and 4 light) were handed over to General Rugé, Commander-in-Chief of the Norwegian Army.

87. The entire process of embarkation, whether from beaches or quays, in fishing boats, destroyers or directly into transport went with the greatest smoothness and celerity and reflects the greatest possible credit on all concerned. The morale and cheerfulness of the troops remained high throughout, although their destination was not known to them until they were actually on the high seas so well was the secret kept.

88. The French Chasseurs furnished the final rear-guard round Harstad but the actual rear party round the quays was found by the Royal Engineers and Military Police. There was no disorder or unpleasantness of any kind.

Evacuation of Personnel.

89. The problem was examined in conjunction with the Navy after an estimate had been made of the numbers to be evacuated, and the probable dispositions at the time of breaking contact. As a result of this the F.O. Narvik sent an agreed wire to the Admiralty outlining the suggested proposals for evacuation. This was agreed to and a sufficient number of large liners was despatched from the United Kingdom together with three store ships and one horse ship. The time taken for us to evacuate the personnel was five days.

90. In the case of Harstad parties embarked direct on to destroyers, whilst at Skaanland and in the Narvik and Sorreisa areas embarkation was by means of "puffer" from land to destroyers lying off. The destroyers then proceeded approximately 70 miles to rendezvous where they loaded direct to liners, three of which were filled at a time. These in turn moved to anchorages in the Fjords awaiting orders for the forming of the main convoy, which was done during the night 7th /8th June. At each embarkation place, alternative points for embarkation were selected in case of bombing, whilst a reserve of "puffer" craft was held at each locality to meet all probable eventualities. These craft were formed into small fleets with an Army officer in charge, and two British O.Rs. on board each ship.

9I. Troops in contact in the Narvik area were embarked on the last day into six destroyers under the control of Commander Hubback, R.N., who supervised with the assistance of certain British officers, the embarkation of the 2,500 French troops.

Losses and Casualties.

92. The total losses apart from Naval and Air Force casualties, incurred during the period I3th May-8th June were approximately 235 all ranks killed, 535 wounded and 200 missing. Of the above French casualties amounted to I70 killed and 360 wounded and missing.

Conclusion – Lessons of the Operations.

93. The predominant factor in the recent operations has been the effect of air power. In the operations which culminated in the evacuation of Bodo the enemy had complete initiative in the air, and used it, first, to support his troops:-

(*a*) By low-flying attacks.
(*b*) By bombing.
(*c*) By surprise landings of troops by parachute and from seaplanes.
(*d*) By supplying his advanced detachments by air.

And secondly, to deny us the use of sea communications in the narrow coastal waters in the theatre of operations.

94. The actual casualties caused to troops on the ground by low-flying attacks were few, but the moral effect of continuous machine-gunning from the air was considerable. Further, the enemy made repeated use of low-flying attacks with machine guns in replacement of artillery to cover the movement of his troops. Troops

in forward positions subjected to this form of attack are forced to ground, and, until they have learned by experience its comparative innoccuousness, are apt not to keep constant watch on the enemy. Thus the enemy were enabled on many occasions to carry out forward and outflanking movements with impunity.

The second effect of low-flying attacks was the partial paralysis of headquarters and the consequent interruption in the exercise of command.

Thirdly, low-flying attacks against transport moving along narrow roads seriously interfered with supply, though this was never completely interrupted.

95. Bombing was not effective against personnel deployed in the open, but this again interfered with the functioning of headquarters and the movement of supplies.

The enemy's use of aircraft in these two methods of offence was obviously most closely co-ordinated with the action of his forward troops, and showed a very high degree of co-operation between his Air Force and his Army, particularly in view of the fact that his aerodromes were distant from the actual fighting.

96. Surprise landings from aircraft had far reaching effects owing to the ability they conferred on the enemy to outflank positions or take them in the rear.

The action on the Hemnes Peninsula, South of Mo, provides an outstanding example of these tactics. The sequence of this action was first bombing and low-flying attacks on our troops holding the position. These attacks were followed almost immediately by landings from seaplanes in two places on each flank of the peninsula. Once these landings had been secured they were promptly reinforced by small coastal steamers and further reinforcements were brought up to the outflanking detachments by seaplanes on succeeding days. In addition, seaplanes were used to ferry troops for further outflanking movements. Bicycles, mortars and motor cycles were carried in the seaplanes for this purpose.

The possibility of the enemy carrying out such outflanking movements caused continuous dispersion of the troops trying to hold defensive positions during the withdrawal and prevented sufficient concentration to enable any of the positions selected to be held successfully.

97. The enemy's ability to supply detachments by air enabled him to neglect or overcome many of the obstacles put in his way by demolitions.

The outstanding example of the supply by air is the maintenance of the German detachments in the Narvik area. In this area his troops to the number of three or four thousand have been successfully supplied by air for many weeks, partly by seaplanes landed on the Beisfjord, partly by aircraft landed on frozen lakes or small landing grounds, and partly by the dropping of containers attached to parachutes.

From the reports received, the enemy operating in the mountainous country 12 to 15 miles North of Narvik were plentifully supplied with all their requirements. A large number of cardboard containers were found in Narvik, and it is reported that large quantities of perishable foodstuffs, such as vegetables, eggs and butter from Denmark, were successfully dropped in Narvik from the air.

98. As regards the control of sea communications, the enemy's supremacy in the air made the use inshore of naval vessels of the type co-operating with this force highly dangerous and uneconomical. Though it might have been possible to use high

speed coastal motor boats armed with small guns to prevent movement of enemy craft in these waters, the use of trawlers, owing to their extreme vulnerability to air attack, was not considered practicable. On the other hand, the inshore waterways were used at will by the Germans, who constantly employed local boats and steamers to ferry their troops about thus entailing more dispersion of the defending forces on land.

In an attempt to send considerable reinforcements and wheeled vehicles to Bodo, the Polish steamer *Chrobry* was sunk before she reached port. The unloading of large supply ships which, owing to the limited faculties available, would have taken many hours, had to be ruled out as impracticable and reinforcements to Bodo could therefore be sent only by destroyer or by small local craft. Thus the provision of adequate reinforcements in guns and vehicles was made extremely difficult.

99. The second main factor which has affected the operations in this theatre has been training. It has been brought out that for operations of this nature thoroughly trained soldiers only are of any real value, and that every officer and man must be physically hard and fit.

The first need is for troops trained to move freely over hilly country and physically fit to carry the "soldier's load" for long periods under active service conditions. The enemy appeared to be superior to our troops in this respect, and his mobility and powers of endurance were remarkable. In this connection I wish to record my opinion that the "soldier's load" is still far too great.

The second need is a proper appreciation of the value of ground and the willingness to quit valleys and get up on to high ground with confidence and determination.

The third need is the vital necessity for initiative and self-reliance on the part of subordinate commanders, and the necessity for teaching them that a weak threat to a flank can be ignored and need not be a menace entailing general retirement.

100. As regards equipment, the following lessons emerged:-

(*a*) The need for an automatic weapon capable of producing sustained and accurate fire at long ranges that is the medium machine-gun. The lack of such a weapon was severely felt, and the Bren gun was not adequate to perform many of the fire tasks which it was called upon to undertake. The Germans continually employed overhead fire from long range automatic weapons.

(*b*) The Bren gun tripod was found too heavy to move about over the hills for the "independent companies" which had no special transport for it. In such theatres as this, pack transport for this purpose would seem essential. "Tommy" guns were invaluable, and were successfully used by the enemy.

(*c*) The two inch mortar was found to be effective, but should have been supplied with a greater proportion of H.E. bombs. The German mortar, which appeared to have a range of about 1,500 yards, was reported as being not particularly successful as the shell seemed to have very little killing power, possibly due to over-fragmentation.

(*d*) Bicycles. The Germans made extensive use of these for their advanced guards, and the mobility thus achieved was remarkable.

(*e*) Three Bren gun carriers of one of the battalions proved of great value, particularly in assisting the withdrawal of rear parties.

(*f*) 25 pounder field guns proved efficient and were found to be more manoeuvrable than was expected. No difficulties of crest clearance were reported.

(*g*) Signal equipment. The Marconi sets supplied to the Independent Companies were useless. They were too heavy to be carried, and had insufficient range. No. 18 set as used on the frontier of India, would have been more suitable. No. 11 set proved most useful, and also the Lucas signalling lamp. Personnel were insufficiently trained to get the best value out of heliographs.

101. The Arctic boots were reported in all cases too big. Boots two sizes only above the normal are needed to ensure a correct fit.

Skis are essential for operations in snow, but the men must be really well trained and specially selected. Only a portion of a unit, however, need be fitted with skis if the remainder are equipped with snow shoes. The battle dress and leather jerkin proved most serviceable, but a proportion only of fur-lined coats, sufficient for guards and sentries, need have been issued.

It is considered that gas masks and steel helmets need not usually be worn in operations of this nature.

In country such as this, some form of pack transport is essential to ensure full mobility. The Germans made considerable use of impressed ponies, and also of Norwegians impressed as porters.

102. Such demolitions as were carried out had surprisingly little result in stopping the enemy even though effected with complete thoroughness. It is believed that the Germans made extensive use of improvised rafts and rubber boats to cross rivers and narrow fjords. In fact the enemy's thoroughness and foresight in providing everything required for fighting were extraordinary.

103. Co-operation with the Navy in the landing operations carried out by the French Army has been close and effective, but the operations have been handicapped to a marked degree by lack of suitable equipment.

For the landing in the Herjangs Fjord on the 13th of May only four Assault Landing Craft and two Motor Landing Craft were available, and many of the troops had to be taken ashore in open boats.

Thanks to the weakness of the enemy's resistance at the points selected for landing and the skill and determination with which the operation was carried out it was successful, but had the resistance proved to be more serious the results might well have been very different.

Again, the plans for the landing on the peninsula North of Narvik had continually to be changed and postponed owing to the lack of proper landing craft, particularly of Motor Landing Craft which were required to land tanks. These Motor Landing

Craft were also in constant demand for the vital task of landing heavy anti-aircraft guns for the protection of the base area.

The landing at Narvik was also successful thanks to the most effective co-operation of the Royal Navy, the excellent support given by the guns of H.M. Ships and the skill and determination of General Bethouart's troops, but with the facilities available the transfer of three battalions across a narrow fjord some 1,500 yards wide took over seven hours, and the strength of the first flight had to be limited to 300 men.

The landing of such a small advanced party on a hostile shore entailed considerable risk, and in view of the likelihood of such operations having to be repeated in other theatres of war it is urgently necessary that an ample supply of modern landing craft should be provided without further delay. It is unfair to expect any troops to undertake such hazardous operations with such inadequate means.

104. The control of the civil population in a war zone is always a matter of great difficulty and particularly so in an Allied country, and it was found almost impossible to impose any restrictions upon the movement of civilians by land or water or upon telephone and telegraphic communication.

There have been therefore ample opportunities for the enemy to obtain military information from agents or to organize sabotage. Had the campaign been continued it would have been essential to obtain full powers from the Norwegian authorities to put security measures into force, but it is doubtful whether these measures would have been effective had they been carried out through the Civil Authorities, which is the ideal method. It is probable that a complete Military Government would have had to be set up unless the civil population had been completely evacuated from all areas in close military occupation. Again, had sustained air attack been directed against towns such as Harstad, civil resources could not have met the demands for hospital accommodation, food, light and sanitation which would have resulted.

It is recommended, therefore, that full weight should be given to these considerations when planning a campaign of this nature, and that a definite policy of evacuation or military control of all civilian activities in the theatre of war should be insisted upon from the outset.

105. The Force relied mainly upon local hired craft, such as Diesel-engined fishing boats, and small steamers, for the distribution by water of food, ammunition and stores of all kinds. This system proved very unsatisfactory, and at one time, after comparatively light bombing of the base area, threatened to break down completely owing to the defection of the civilian crews, even though military guards were placed on board. It is unreasonable to expect civilian hired personnel to incur the risks inseparable from such work under heavy air attack, and the replacement of these civilians by skilled and enlisted personnel subject to military law and discipline would have become inevitable.

In any future expedition of this nature, this important subject must receive full consideration before the expedition is launched and adequate provision of suitable craft, including fast motor-boats for inter-communication and control, together with trained crews must be made.

106. In conclusion, the first general lesson to be drawn is that to commit troops to

a campaign in which they cannot be provided with adequate air support is to court disaster.

The second lesson is that no useful purpose can be served by sending troops to operate in an undeveloped and wild country such as Norway unless they have been thoroughly trained for their task and their fighting equipment well thought out and methodically prepared in advance. Improvisation in either of these respects can lead only to failure. Our preparation and provision for ensuring the comfort of the troops were magnificent, too good perhaps; it was in respect of fighting equipment that we compared unfavourably with the enemy.

I07. As will be seen from what has previously been stated in this report, the two outstanding difficulties from the administrative point of view, were, first, shortage of administrative transportation and movement control staffs, and, secondly, the entire lack of any organization to operate what was, perforce, the main transportation agency, namely, inland water transport. In the main, although the role of the force since its inception had been changed several times, its composition remained substantially as originally designed.

The first difficulty, except in respect of movement control staff, was to some extent overcome on my arrival by the additional administrative and transportation staff that I brought with me. Pending the arrival of personnel and staff of the Inland Water Transport organization, the steps taken to set up some form of organization were as follows:-

On his arrival the Assistant Director of Transportation took over the control of the improvised organization which had previously operated the Inland Water Transport fleet. A part of the railway operating company was used on its arrival to form the nucleus of an inland water transport organization. All craft were numbered, organized into fleets, and their movements recorded. The captain of each craft was given written orders each time he was detailed for duty, and a system of leave for "puffer" crews was started, otherwise they would not work for more than a limited period. One soldier was placed on board each "puffer" and most of the steamers were manned by naval crews.

During the evacuation the armed guard in each "puffer" was increased to two, and each fleet was placed under the command of an army officer.

Even with this amount of control it was difficult to prevent the "puffer" crews absenting themselves with their craft, especially after a bombing attack, and the Inland Water Transport situation remained precarious up to the end.

Summary.

I08. I trust it will be clear from this report that although my command in Norway lasted for about four weeks only, the problems which my staff officers and the troops under my command had to face were complex and unusual. That they were solved and, so far as lay in their power, solved successfully, is, I submit, the best tribute I can offer to those who served under me.

I09. In the strategical and tactical sphere, the outlook changed rapidly from a situation in which I had every hope of receiving the forces and resources for which I had asked to enable me to maintain the integrity of Northern Norway, recapture Narvik and assume the offensive against the enemy to the southward, to one in which it appeared as if the Force would have to fight hard to retain a fringe of the coast round Narvik and Harstad with inadequate support in the shape of ships, artillery and aircraft. This phase again quickly gave place to the final problem of complete withdrawal from Norway in the face of increasing enemy pressure on the sea, in the air and on the ground.

I fully realise that these changes were inevitable and essential, and I mention them only to stress the efficiency and loyalty with which every one in the Force responded to what must have been to those not in the possession of inside knowledge, a bewildering and possibly disheartening succession of changes of plan on the part of the higher command.

II0. Co-operation between the three services and within the Force itself was excellent throughout, which is perhaps remarkable considering the very mixed composition of the Force.

III. I have already had occasion to mention certain individuals by name, but I desire specially to bring to notice the services of the following officers:-

Captain L.E.H. Maund, R.N. and Commander G. Hubback, R.N. were closely associated with the operations and planning side of my headquarters throughout the operations, and rendered invaluable assistance to me and my staff and to the troops, British and French.

Group Captain M. Moore, O.B.E., R.A.F., commanded the air component and it is due very largely to his energy, determination and tactical ability, first that it so quickly and decisively gained superiority over the enemy air forces.

I cannot speak too highly of this officer's services.

Brigadier C. McV. Gubbins, D.S.O. commanded the forces round Bodo in most difficult circumstances with the greatest skill and determination, and it was largely due to his devoted efforts that a premature withdrawal, which might have seriously compromised the whole campaign, did not occur in this area.

Brigadier J.A.H. Gammell, D.S.O., M.C. acted throughout as my Brigadier General Staff and Chief Staff Officer with marked success. His energy, determination and devotion to duty were remarkable, and the success of the operations was due in no small measure to his untiring efforts.

Brigadier R.M. Wootten, M.C. as my chief administrative staff officer, bore practically the entire burden of responsibility for coping with the many and varied problems to which the rapid changes of policy gave rise. The results of his work speak for themselves and, in my opinion, stamp him as an officer of outstanding ability and firmness of character.

II2. I need not again mention the services of General Bethouart, commanding the Franco-Polish Expeditionary Force, as their outstanding nature should be evident from the accounts of the operations conducted by him. I would, however, like to bring to notice, the work of Major D.A.W. Watney, O.B.E., liaison officer with General Bethouart, whose fluent knowledge of French and sound tactical sense, added to his quick understanding and engaging personality, were largely responsible for the cordial and constant co-operation which obtained between my headquarters, French headquarters, and the Royal Navy.

II3. I have to acknowledge the close and unfailing support I received, often in very difficult circumstances, from the following Norwegian officers:-

General Rugé. Commander-in-Chief, Norwegian Army.
General Fleischer. Commander, 6th Norwegian Division.
Colonel H. Finne. Liaison Officer at my Headquarters.

II4. Finally, I wish to record my deep sense of gratitude to the Commander-in-Chief, Admiral of the Fleet the Earl of Cork and Orrery, G.C.B., G.C.V.O., under whom I served throughout the campaign, for his quick understanding of the problems before me, his unfailing consideration, and the generous and ready help which he gave me on all occasions, thereby making it possible for me to carry out my task.

C.J.E. AUCHINLECK.
Lieutenant-General,
General Officer Commanding-in-Chief,
Norwegian Expeditionary Force.
London,
I9th June, I940.

Footnotes

[1] *A.L.C. s and M.L.C. s – Minor Landing craft for landing troops and mechanized vehicles respectively.*
[2] *This was the first occasion on which tanks were landed in a combined operation*
[3] *M.N.B.D.O. – Mobile Naval Base Defence Organisation.*
[4] *Asdics – Anti-Submarine detecting device.*

4

ADMIRAL SIR JOHN C. TOVEY'S DESPATCH ON CARRIER-BORNE AIRCRAFT ATTACK ON KIRKENES (NORWAY) AND PETSAMO (FINLAND)

22 JULY AND 7 AUGUST 1941

THE CARRIER BORNE AIRCRAFT ATTACK ON KIRKENES AND PETSAMO.

The following Despatch was submitted to the Lords Commissioners of the Admiralty on the *12*th September, *1941,* by Admiral Sir John C. Tovey, K.C.B., D.S.O., Commander-in-Chief, Home Fleet.

Home Fleet.
12th September, 1941.

Forwarded. The material results of this operation were small and the losses heavy. This had been expected. The heaviest losses occurred in the squadrons from the VICTORIOUS and there is no doubt that some of the survivors felt that an attack on such poor targets against heavy opposition was not justified and their morale was rather shaken until they appreciated the political necessity for the operation.

2. Attacks by low performance aircraft in broad daylight where fighter opposition is present can only hope to achieve results commensurate with their losses if complete surprise is obtained. On this occasion the force was extremely fortunate in the weather conditions which allowed it to make the long approach to the flying-off position without being seen; but the good fortune did not last quite long enough, and they were reported by an enemy aircraft just before the Striking Force left.

3. It would perhaps have been better to time the attack to take place during the night, even in this region of perpetual summer daylight, in the hope that the enemy reconnaissance and defences would then be less alert. This would also have avoided an approach directly into the sun.

4. The lack of enterprise on the part of the enemy which enabled the force to withdraw without being attacked by aircraft is encouraging.

5. I concur in the remarks of the Rear Admiral Commanding, First Cruiser Squadron, in paragraph 53 of his report. The lack of time for training and preparation was mainly responsible for such small errors in execution as took place. I concur also in paragraph 54. It was not possible for the force to provide its own reconnaissance without sacrificing the vital factor of surprise. I consider it essential that steps should be taken to remedy the present complete lack of air reconnaissance in Northern and Northwestern Norway.

6. With reference to paragraph 52 of the report of the Rear Admiral Commanding, First Cruiser Squadron, the importance of the Command being in the carrier in purely air operations is appreciated; but, although the question did not arise on this occasion, it is considered preferable in the case of surface attack that the Senior Officer, should be in a ship of the supporting force.

7. The gallantry of the aircraft crews, who knew before leaving that their chance of surprise had gone and that they were certain to face heavy odds, is beyond praise. The conduct of the operation by the Rear Admiral Commanding, First Cruiser Squadron, the handling of ships by their Commanding Officers in most difficult conditions, the keenness and efficiency of all officers and men, especially of the deck handling parties in the carriers, are much to be commended. I trust that the encouragement to the morale of our Allies was proportionately great.

(Signed) JACK C. TOVEY,
Admiral,
Commander-in-Chief.

H.M.S. *DEVONSHIRE.*
15th August, 1941.

Operation "E.F." was carried out with the object of making attacks by carrier-borne aircraft on German shipping in the waters adjacent to Kirkenes (Norway) and Petsamo (Finland).

Forces Taking Part.

DEVONSHIRE	INGLEFIELD
(Flag of Rear Admiral	(Captain (D), 3rd
Commanding, First	Destroyer Flotilla).
Cruiser Squadron)	INTREPID
SUFFOLK	ICARUS
	ESCAPADE
FURIOUS	ECLIPSE
VICTORIOUS	ECHO
R.F.A. BLACK	ACTIVE
RANGER[1]	ANTHONY
	ANTELOPE
	ACHATES

2. ADVENTURE was placed under the orders of the Rear Admiral Commanding, First Cruiser Squadron, so that she might make her passage to North Russia under cover of the forces taking part in Operation "E.F."

Narrative.   *22nd July.*

3. Force "Q", consisting of ECLIPSE, ECHO, and BLACK RANGER, left Scapa at 0001 on 22nd July and proceeded to Seidisfiord,[2] where the destroyers fuelled from R.F.A. WAR SUDRA, and the Force then proceeded to the rendezvous at Position "X" (70 degs. 28 mins. N., 08 degs. 00 mins. E.).

23rd July.

4. ADVENTURE left Scapa at 0030 on 23rd July and arrived at Seidisfiord before Force "P".

5. Force "P", consisting of DEVONSHIRE, SUFFOLK, FURIOUS, VICTORIOUS, INTREPID, ESCAPADE, ANTHONY, ACHATES, ACTIVE and ANTELOPE, sailed from Scapa at 2300 on Wednesday, 23rd July, and proceeded at 20 knots to Seidisfiord. A/S[3] air escort was provided by the Commander-in-Chief, Rosyth.

24th July.

6. At 0856 on the 24th DEVONSHIRE detected an aircraft approaching. A fighter patrol was flown off from FURIOUS but it quickly became obvious that

DEVONSHIRE had detected the A/S patrol. The incident was of value in that it brought out various small points of co-operation between R.D.F. ships[4] and the two aircraft carriers. One Fulmar landed on when FURIOUS was stern to wind and crashed.

7. The whole of this day was very overcast. In the afternoon visibility decreased and varied from one mile to five and it was not possible to operate an A/S patrol. I regarded this as rather a blessing as it reduced the possibility of our being sighted by enemy aircraft.

25th July.

8. At 0258 ACHATES, which was starboard ship of the screen, struck a mine. ANTHONY immediately went to her assistance, and ACHATES reported that she was badly damaged forward but that her engines would still work. The Squadron at the same time was turned away, and soon after, as it became thicker, it was obvious that with an uncertain position Seidisfiord could not be made in safety. I accordingly turned to the southward looking for clear weather, and after crossing the hundred fathom line turned to the westward at 0730.

9. The coast was sighted at 0833 but the exact position could not be ascertained as it was shrouded in shifting fog and only the mountain tops were occasionally visible. The Force was turned to the northward and later to the north-eastward on soundings. A destroyer was sent inshore at 0951 to try to identify the land, and about 1100 an aircraft was flown off. At about 1130 ANTHONY and ACHATES were sighted. The tow had just parted, and they were then about 40 miles from Seidisfiord.

10. It had been my original intention to send VICTORIOUS and SUFFOLK into Reydarfiord,[5] but I decided that it was unwise to leave them to make this difficult entrance under the prevailing conditions. At 1400 the Force was off Seidisfiord. The coast was still completely shrouded in fog, and INTREPID was sent in and told to proceed with great caution and endeavour to find the entrance, of which she was given the approximate bearing. At 1415 Glettinganes Light was sighted and it was possible to fix our position. The Force then proceeded into Seidisfiord, DEVONSHIRE and FURIOUS anchoring above the minefield, and VICTORIOUS and SUFFOLK joining ADVENTURE near the entrance to the fiord.

11. An A/S patrol was carried out by destroyers in the mouth of the fiord. On anchoring I was told by the Examination Officer, Lieut. R.P.B. Veal, R.N.R., that a U-boat had been operating in the neighbourhood during the preceding two or three days. I was surprised that I had no information of this from the Admiral Commanding, Iceland, but I supposed he thought it was a false report. My investigations, however, did not at all convince me that it was false and I ordered VICTORIOUS, SUFFOLK and ADVENTURE to move further up the fiord where they had to anchor in forty fathoms. In the fiord were two A/S trawlers, WASTWATER and SEALYHAM. I ordered these to carry put an A/S patrol off the entrance.

12. I had arrived at Seidisfiord eleven hours late on my programme and I decided that it would be better to hold over the whole operation for twenty-four hours and thus retain its original timing. This had been arranged so as to pass the track of the

Zenit Flight[6] at a time when it was least likely to be operating. ADVENTURE's departure was accordingly delayed to conform with the new programme. This also gave me time to oil SUFFOLK in addition to DEVONSHIRE, FURIOUS and the four destroyers, INTREPID, ESCAPADE, ANTELOPE and ACTIVE.

I3. At midnight ACHATES, in tow of ANTHONY, arrived in harbour and berthed alongside DEVONSHIRE. Before sailing next day all possible assistance was given to her, arrangements were made for the accommodation of her ship's company, and such measures were taken as were necessary until the Salvage Officer arrived. In this the local military authorities gave great assistance.

26th July.

I4. In addition to the destroyer patrol an A/S air patrol was arranged, using SUFFOLK's and DEVONSHIRE's Walruses.

I5. ADVENTURE sailed at I745 on the 26th July with ANTHONY in company. In view of the possible presence of an enemy submarine in the neighbourhood I considered it unsafe to send her unescorted, at I5 knots. ADVENTURE had orders to send ANTHONY back after 24 hours. An air A/S patrol from SUFFOLK was also told off to accompany her to the limit of its endurance.

I6. Force "P" sailed from Seidisfiord at 2300 on the 26th July at 20 knots. An A/S air patrol had been asked for from the Admiral Commanding, Iceland, and on leaving Seidisfiord this was provided by a Northrop. The patrol was later to have been taken over by a Catalina, but as the weather closed down the Catalina was not seen.

27th July.

I7. At 0345 the Force ran into fog. This continued, except for short intervals, until the afternoon, after which the visibility varied from two to ten miles with low cloud overhead.

28th July.

I8. Position "B", where ADVENTURE should have been overtaken, was reached at 0200 on 28th July. Some time previously the Force had been spread five miles apart with the R.D.F. cruisers[7] on the flanks, thus covering a front of about 30 miles. Nothing was seen of ADVENTURE until 0550, and the Squadron proceeded at I5 knots towards Position "X". During the period of thick fog I had come to the conclusion that my orders for Force "Q" might produce an uncomfortable situation if there was fog at "X".

I had accordingly at 20I2 on 27th signalled amended instructions to ECLIPSE regarding the use of D/F[8] procedure in such weather conditions.

Force "P" was a little ahead of its programme and I expected to meet Force "Q" about I200. Up till this time no sights had been obtained, and not only was the position of Force "P" doubtful but I knew that Force "Q's" would also be very doubtful.

I9. On arrival in the vicinity of Position "X" a search was commenced. While so doing the sun appeared and sights were obtained, and the search was re-arranged.

The Squadron was spread to cover a front of about 40 miles, with aircraft patrolling on the wings and ahead. At I5I5 Force "Q" was sighted some twenty miles ahead. With Force "Q" was Captain (D), 3rd Destroyer Flotilla, in INGLEFIELD and ICARUS, who had been sent to replace ACHATES and ANTHONY.

20. Oiling then took place as follows. DEVONSHIRE gave 60 tons each to ECHO and ECLIPSE who had been the escort for Force "Q" and had filled up recently from BLACK RANGER. SUFFOLK oiled ESCAPADE and INTREPID with I50 tons each, and BLACK RANGER was ordered to oil ADVENTURE. Oiling commenced at about I820 but unfortunately the wind was from the south-west and the oiling course was therefore directly opposite to the future course. During oiling FURIOUS and VICTORIOUS acted independently and maintained an A/S patrol in the air.

29th July.

2I. I estimated from the time taken to oil the first destroyer that SUFFOLK would complete oiling at 0I30, ADVENTURE had only 3I0 tons to take, but at 0022 she reported she had received only I50 tons and that it would take another I6 hours at her present rate of oiling to complete. She put down the slow rate to the cooling of the oil. The temperature of the sea was 50 degs. I did not consider that I could afford this time and I therefore told her to discontinue oiling at 0I30. At 0058 FURIOUS reported fog ahead and I immediately gave orders for ADVENTURE to cast off. She was then I30 tons short.

22. At that time the Force was spread about, DEVONSHIRE was close to BLACK RANGER and ADVENTURE, SUFFOLK seven or eight miles away to the south-westward, FURIOUS and VICTORIOUS with two aircraft up were five miles to the southward. Thick fog was met almost immediately. Previous to this the carriers and ADVENTURE had been told that the Force would be turned to 050 degs. at I5 knots at 0I30. On entering the fog I made by syren "course 050 degs.", and turned to that course myself. I also made course and speed by low power W/T. As I was uncertain of the reception of this signal, which was broadcast, I also made a wireless signal to shore addressed Force "P" giving a rendezvous at 0300 on 30th July in Position "C", allowing a speed of I5 knots to that position.

23. Nothing more was seen of the Squadron until 0900 on the 29th when the aircraft carriers formed up, followed by SUFFOLK and 6 destroyers at I047. At that time visibility was only about I mile but it shortly increased to about four or five miles. I was glad to learn that VICTORIOUS had succeeded in landing on her aircraft. The Force had been largely kept together by R.D.F.[9] and this showed of what immense value R.D.F. can be in such a situation. ADVENTURE was not sighted until 2I50 that night by which time visibility had increased to ten miles. She was some distance astern.

30th July.

The Force passed through Position "C" about 0300 on the 30th July and

ADVENTURE was detached. As she was only one hour behind her programme I did not consider it necessary to make an amended time for her rendezvous.

24. The weather continued overcast and from the point of view of evasion it could hardly have been better; the conditions were such that it was extremely unlikely that the Force would be sighted by aircraft. My experience of the weather had made me realise the possibility that fog might come down in the middle of flying off. I therefore made a plan by which one carrier operated on one side of a line parallel to the wind through the flying-off position and the other carrier on the other side, and I arranged that, so far as possible, DEVONSHIRE and VICTORIOUS should operate on the inshore side of this line, thus giving FURIOUS a clear run to seaward. After discussion with VICTORIOUS the original Position "M" was decided on for the flying off position and a position 30 miles, 040 degs. from Position "M" was fixed for flying-on. I also made 1400 the zero hour, half an hour later than my original intention.

25. During the approach German destroyer wireless signals had been heard, and by the use of the HF/DF set[10] in INGLEFIELD it had been possible to place them as operating off Tana Fiord.[11] At one time I had an idea that they were escorting a convoy towards Kirkenes, but eventually came to the conclusion that they were probably hunting a Russian submarine off Tana Fiord. Considerable interference was also experienced on the R.D.F. This seemed to come from a station of sorts at Vardo. As we approached the coast R.D.F. transmission was stopped as I felt it was possible that it might lead to our detection.

26. The weather was at first favourable, overcast, low clouds and visibility not too good, but about 1200 the clouds thinned and finally cleared away with good visibility. Still, the Force had not been sighted and there appeared every reason to hope that the attack would be launched without it being detected. The wind was off shore and this facilitated the approach. These hopes, however, were doomed. At 1346, just as FURIOUS was flying off two Hurricanes, which had to be got off the deck before her T.S.Rs.[12] could fly off, an He.III was sighted. An enemy report was made by this aircraft and from that moment the German destroyers operating off Tana Fiord ceased to transmit. I considered it was too late to call off the attack and it was accordingly launched as originally arranged.

27. Detailed reports of the attacks are given in FURIOUS's and VICTORIOUS's reports attached (Appendices I and II). VICTORIOUS flew off twenty T.S.Rs. in one range, followed by twelve Fulmars eighteen minutes later. FURIOUS commenced ten minutes before VICTORIOUS by flying off four Hurricanes and nine T.S.Rs. These were followed by a second range of nine T.S.Rs. and finally by six Fulmars.

28. The Striking Force went into the attack as planned at 1429 (Z + 29) followed seven minutes later by the fighters. Three of the Fulmars from VICTORIOUS and the four Hurricanes were kept for the protection of the Force. During the attack the Hurricanes were refuelling in VICTORIOUS.

29. The Striking Force knew before leaving that the Force had been sighted and that they must meet fierce opposition. Nevertheless the attack was pressed home

courageously and gallantly in face of great odds and VICTORIOUS's aircraft suffered heavy casualties.

30. The material results were disappointing. The attack by VICTORIOUS's aircraft was thought to have achieved results as follows:-

BREMSE.	Two torpedo hits.
2 Merchant Ships.	At least one torpedo hit each.
2 Merchant Ships.	Probably one torpedo hit each.

Aircraft.	Probable.	Damaged.	Certain.
ME.I09	1	1	-
ME.II0	2	I	-
JU.87	I	-	I

It has since been learnt that BREMSE was not hit.

3I. FURIOUS had the misfortune to find Petsamo empty of shipping and her torpedoes had to be expended on easily repairable wooden quays, but it is probable that her bombs did considerable damage to the oil tanks and ship yard.

32. Captain (D), 3rd Destroyer Flotilla in INGLEFIELD was sent shorewards to visibility distance to act as a guide to returning aircraft and remained there until completion of flying-on.

33. At I6I2 aircraft were seen to be returning from the attack and it soon became apparent that many were missing from VICTORIOUS. At I735 VICTORIOUS reported that she was still short of eleven Albacores and two Fulmars, who had petrol till about I900. FURIOUS had completed landing on at I657 and reported the loss of two Fulmars and one Albacore. I informed the Force that I should remain in the vicinity until I900.

34. During the flying-off and flying-on operations, the two divisions of the Force had operated independently, the cruisers conforming to the carriers' movements. VICTORIOUS had orders to remain as near as possible to FURIOUS. These operations were very satisfactorily carried out and at no time were the garners more than six or seven miles apart.

35. At I900 the Force withdrew to the northward. No attempt was made by the enemy to locate the Force or to attack it. I had previously arranged for a Walrus aircraft from SUFFOLK to be available for picking up any survivors, but the only reports of aircraft down were from FURIOUS. Two of her crews were known to be in the water in position 260 degs. Heinasaari 6 miles, but as this was only five miles off the shore and a long way from my position it would have entailed fighter protection and remaining for several hours longer near the flying-off position. I did not therefore consider it justifiable to send the Walrus in.

3Ist July.

36. The activity of the destroyers off Tana Fiord had made me suspicious that they might be using Smalfiord as an anchorage for supply ships or other such vessels. As this might form a possible target for a second attack I arranged for a Fulmar with its

distinguishing marks erased as far as possible to reconnoitre this fiord during the night. Accordingly at 0316 on the 31st July one Fulmar was flown off from VICTORIOUS. This Fulmar returned at 0455 and reported that she had found four twin-engined aircraft patrolling off the entrance and had not therefore been able to reconnoitre the fiord. Five minutes after this Fulmar returned the Squadron ran into thick fog.

37. FURIOUS's fuel situation at this time made it necessary for her to return immediately, as she would have little more than 500 tons on arrival at Seidisfiord and had no margin for possible loss of fuel due to damage. I accordingly arranged to complete VICTORIOUS as far as possible with aircraft from FURIOUS. Owing to the fog this could not be commenced until 1215 when it cleared sufficiently to enable the operation to proceed.

38. Whilst transfer was in progress the Force was sighted by a Dornier 18. At about 1300 FURIOUS flew off two Hurricanes which shot it down, but not before it had had time to make a report of our presence. As the whole Force was then steering west in company I was not unduly disturbed as I wanted the enemy to think that the Force was returning together.

39. Transfer of aircraft was completed at 1530 and course was then altered to 305 degs., i.e., to the northward, in order to get further away from the coast and avoid observation by the enemy. At 1633 a report of another aircraft was received, and fighters were again flown off, but saw nothing and returned. This report of aircraft, I am sure, was false, and due to an inoffensive skua gull.

1st August.

40. The course of 305 degs. was held until 0001 on the 1st August, when FURIOUS[13] was detached in a position 40 miles north-east of Bear Island. This was to be followed by another signal in naval cypher to Commander-in-Chief, Home Fleet, on H/F from such a position as to give the impression that she was proceeding towards the Faeroes. This second signal would be made using a naval general call sign requesting that my delivery group be included in certain signals on H.D. broadcast. The object of these signals was to deceive the enemy into thinking that the whole Force was on its way back and thus to disguise my continued presence in the area. The making of these signals was governed by the proviso that they were only to be made in conditions of low visibility, since they were liable to lead to FURIOUS being found by aircraft in which case the whole ruse would have been exposed. This in fact occurred and she was sighted four hours after making the first signal. It is probable therefore that the enemy had a shrewd suspicion that I was still about.

41. On parting with FURIOUS I remained to the north-north-east of Bear Island and oiled destroyers during the course of the 1st August. I did not consider in any case that an attack was possible on this day as the chance of surprise did not arise until sufficient time had elapsed for us to have left the area.

42. I had asked VICTORIOUS to prepare plans for possible operations against Tromso, Hammerfest, Tana Fiord, Honningsvaag or shipping along the coast and I wished very much that I was in VICTORIOUS at this time so as to be able to discuss

the project at first hand. The Captain of the VICTORIOUS informed me that he had an urgent letter to send over and I decided to visit him instead. I accordingly transferred to INGLEFIELD by DEVONSHIRE's crane, and intended to board VICTORIOUS in a similar manner. Unfortunately INGLEFIELD appeared to be sucked in towards VICTORIOUS and fouled one of her gantries, which smashed INGLEFIELD's .5 machine gun. I therefore abandoned the project and exchanged letters with the Captain of the VICTORIOUS.

2nd August.

43. DEVONSHIRE oiled the three destroyers, giving them 200 tons each, and the whole operation took 13 hours. The Force then proceeded to a suitable position from which, the attack on Tromso might be made, passing 40 miles north of Bear Island at 0342 on the 2nd August. Visibility was good and Bear Island was clearly visible.

44. At 1033 on 2nd August a signal was received from Force "A" addressed to TARTAR reporting that they were being shadowed by aircraft. At that time Force "A" was 138 degs., 148 miles distant from Force "P" and on a similar course. VICTORIOUS stated that fighter support could be given from a distance of 50 miles, and I accordingly informed Force "A" of this fact and of my position, course and speed, by W/T using low power.

45. Force "A", which had previously been steering to the south, altered course to the north at 1245, on receipt of my signal and reported that they were still being shadowed. I followed suit with Force "P" and turned in towards Force "A" so that at 1352 I was 50 miles away. Force "A" were also informed of the fighter wave so that they could direct them. Two Fulmars were flown off at 1335 Just as Force "A" reported that they were not wanted, and almost at the same time VICTORIOUS reported aircraft two miles away by R.D.F. and a doubtful sighting. Two more aircraft were flown off for the protection of Force "P". The first pair of fighters located Force "A" and then returned. Nothing further was seen of any shadower. In the interchange of signals, Force "A" used C.S.I's call-sign on one occasion and it seems probable that owing to the use of power necessary for reception at over 100 miles, both forces were detected by D/F at this time. I am not certain that Force "P" was actually sighted but it seems likely that the aircraft shadowing Force "A" took a further look to seaward before returning to its base, and visibility at this time was such that it may well have sighted Force "P". During this period homing signals from shore stations were heard and detected by D/F, and I think the aircraft must have been at the limit of its endurance.

3rd August.

46. Force "A" having reported that it was proceeding to the northward and then towards Bear Island, I turned Force "P" to the southwest again to get towards a position approximately 300 miles off Tromso in readiness for an attack on that place. Several signals had passed between me and VICTORIOUS on the subject of the attack and I came to the conclusion that the only satisfactory thing was to shift my

flag. On the morning of the 3rd I informed VICTORIOUS that I intended to do so and made arrangements to board her with certain of my staff in DEVONSHIRE'S cutter. Unfortunately it blew up very hard and I did not consider the weather suitable for a cutter in view of the inexperienced crews that are nowadays available. I accordingly flew over in the Walrus with my Flag-Lieutenant at 1415.

4th August.

47. In the course of the day the Force closed in towards the flying-off position, which had been fixed as 100 miles from Tromso. During the last two hours a speed of 25 knots was maintained. Three Fulmars were flown off at 0106 on the 4th August with orders to attack Tromso, the sea-plane station and any shipping being given as their objective. After flying-off, the Force moved to the westward at 20 knots for two hours to the flying-on position.

48. At 0303 the first Fulmar returned, followed by the second at 0325. Both these machines reported that they had seen someone bale out of the remaining machine and there seemed little doubt that it had been brought down. The Flight had found two armed trawlers just short of Tromso and had attacked them. It was the Flight Leader who had been lost, and he appears to have continued the attack too long. As the attack was made out of sight of Tromso no information of shipping in the harbour was obtained.

49. The Force withdrew at 25 knots for two hours, and reducing to 20 knots at 0600 set course for Seidisfiord. I was unable to pass the report of the attack until 1700 on the 4th August. At the same time I informed the Commander-in-Chief, Home Fleet, that I did not require Force "Q" and requested that they should be ordered to return unless required for ADVENTURE.

5th August.

50. During 5th August various exercises were carried out by DEVONSHIRE and VICTORIOUS and her aircraft. The Force arrived at Seidisfiord at 1800 on the 5th August, and I transferred my flag to DEVONSHIRE. The Force completed with oil from the oilers ALDERSDALE and WAR SUDRA.

6th-7th August.

51. At 1500 on the 6th August the Force sailed for Scapa. An A/S patrol was maintained by VICTORIOUS during passage and air exercises were carried out on the forenoon of the 7th August. The Force arrived at Scapa late on the 7th August.

Command.

52. The experience of this operation brought out very clearly the importance of the Command being in the carrier when air operations are under consideration. For the conduct of an operation already planned and discussed it is not so necessary, though even then there is much to be said for it as otherwise a large degree of discretion may

have to be given to the carrier Captains at the last moment. Captain Bovell[14] was in this case put in a difficult position and in my opinion acted very properly on the knowledge at his disposal in putting forward the view he did.

Planning and Preparations.

53. By force of circumstances this operation was carried out in a hurry. Neither VICTORIOUS nor FURIOUS was really ready for such an operation, and some of the pilots had never deck-landed, before. During the six days in which the operation had to be planned VICTORIOUS was frequently at sea exercising, as also was DEVONSHIRE for some days. FURIOUS was only in company for two days and was at sea exercising most of that time. This made it very difficult for any consultations to be held as to details of the plan. The capabilities of the two carriers were so different that the scheme of fly-off presented considerable difficulties and was only decided at the last minute.

Intelligence.

54. For operations in this area to be effective in doing material damage, far better intelligence than was available in this case is necessary. The presence of such a force must always be an embarrassment to the enemy, but without intelligence it is like looking for a needle in a haystack to try to locate the small amount of shipping that may be strung out along the inner leads and open sea between say, Narvik and Kirkenes. That much can be done in this way I am certain, if the appropriate force is employed and routine reconnaissance can be made.

Conclusion.

55. The brunt of the operation fell upon the personnel of the naval aircraft and the carriers. The way in which the attack was pressed deserves high praise and I do not doubt that amongst those lost are many who deserve recognition.

   56. The ships engaged in the operation were ably handled by their Captains and their ready co-operation called for a minimum of signalling. Sudden fog several times produced conditions when timely orders were impossible, but I was always able to feel complete confidence in their actions. During flying on and off the divisions were operated independently by the carriers with great efficiency. The destroyers under Captain Todd[15] as usual carried out their duties with great efficiency and particularly the oiling from cruisers and BLACK RANGER.

(Signed) W.F. WAKE-WALKER,
Rear Admiral Commanding,
First Cruiser Squadron.

APPENDIX I.

H.M.S. *FURIOUS.*
5th August, 1941.

OPERATION "E.F."
*Attack by FURIOUS' Aircraft on Petsamo on Wednesday,
30th July,* 1941.

I have the honour to forward herewith a report of Operation "E.F."

NARRATIVE.

Flying Off.

2. Zero hour for the Operation was 1400B/30.

The T.S.R. striking forces from both carriers were due to leave Force "P" for their objectives at 1429B.

3. At 1349 one enemy aircraft was sighted right ahead. The Hurricanes of the first range, which was at that time being flown off, endeavoured to locate it but without success.

4. The aircraft were flown off in three ranges, the last aircraft leaving the deck at 1436. The total time taken to fly off all aircraft was one minute inside a programme based on the best times for ranging, etc., which had been noted in rehearsals.

Passage to the Objective.

5. 812 Squadron left at 1425B, 817 Squadron at 1432B, and 800 Squadron at 1442B, the ship then being in approximate position 70 degs. 42 mins. N., 33 degs. 00 mins. E.

6. On passage, FURIOUS Squadrons passed, as planned, twelve miles West of Majakkaniemi, flying low on the water in an effort to avoid visual and R.D.F. detection. They climbed whilst proceeding to the entrance to the Gulf of Petsamo. The Squadrons had concentrated, 812 Squadron leading and followed by 817 Squadron, both at about 2,000 feet, with 800 Squadron above and astern of them.

7. At approximately 1450B, single engined monoplane aircraft were observed by

FURIOUS Squadrons flying over Majakkaniemi at a height of 1,500-2,000 feet. It is thought, but not yet confirmed, that these were Fulmars of 809 Squadron from VICTORIOUS; if this was the case, presumably they had lost their way. By flying above the agreed height and over the land, they frustrated all efforts to evade detection.

8. One Fulmar of 800 Squadron forced landed in position 260 degrees, six miles from Heinasaari Island Light with smoke pouring from its engine. The crew were seen to get into their dinghy.

The Approach.

9. At the entrance to the Gulf of Petsamo, the bomber sub-flights were detached and proceeded independently.

10. The Torpedo Striking Force proceeded to Huutoniemi Point in sub-flights in line astern and then headed South, using the hills on the East side of the Gulf as cover until they were approximately due East of their targets. They then crossed the sky-line and came down on to the water as quickly as possible, using the background of the hills as cover during the attack.

11. It was the intention for 812 Squadron to proceed to the Trifona anchorage, had there been targets there, and for 817 Squadron to attack targets at Liinahamari. It was thus hoped that the torpedo attacks of these two Squadrons, developing from the East would be synchronised with that of the bomber force from the West.

In the event of there being no targets at Trifona, it was planned that both Squadrons should attack Liinahamari from the East, there being insufficient manoeuvring space for attacks on the harbour to be carried out from more than the one general direction.

12. The leader of 812 Squadron saw that Trifona anchorage was empty of shipping and led his Squadron to attack the jetties at Liinahamari, as no shipping was seen to be present. Thus all torpedo aircraft attacked from approximately the same direction, with the exception of three aircraft of 817 Squadron which approached from the South of Ristmiemi, one attacking the Swedish Quay and the other two a small ship which was a doubtful target of about five hundred tons lying off Paksuniemi.

13. The bomber sub-flights after being detached, proceeded to the West of Nurmensatti and approached over the lakes and behind the hills to the West of Liinahamari whence they made their final approach along the line of targets from the ship repair yard to the oil tanks.

14. The fighter escort proceeded South keeping to the West of the torpedo aircraft and climbing above them.

They patrolled to the Southward of the target area, keeping between it and the nearest aerodrome some fifteen miles to the South. They then acted in accordance with the general plan, in which, if no enemy aircraft were encountered, they were to assist the striking force by attacking ground targets with bombs and machine-gun fire, with the restriction that not more than half their ammunition was to be expended on ground targets.

The Attack.

15. There were no suitable ship targets for torpedoes at either Trifona or Liinahamari. One small ship off Paksuniemi was unsuccessfully attacked and a photograph reveals that another small ship, unseen by aircraft, was actually berthed alongside Number I pier. One torpedo was fired at this pier and seen to run. A second observer saw an explosion at this pier, but he also failed to see this ship.

Other than the above, there were only small harbour craft present at Liinahamari, and three motor-boats, possibly E-Boats.

The quays which formed the only alternative torpedo targets were mainly pile jetties, and it was problematical whether torpedoes fired at them would explode, but in all the cases observed, it appears that they did so.

16. The attack was carried out by all aircraft according to plan.

In only one case, where the pilot of an aircraft was grazed by a shell splinter at the time of releasing his torpedo, was the accuracy of the attack affected.

17. One Albacore was shot down by enemy fighters after making his attack, and one Fulmar which is missing is thought to have met the same fate.

One other Fulmar engaged an M.E.I09 without definite result, and was in turn attacked by another M.E.I09 which was driven off by means of a "Tommy" gun from the back seat.

Return to Ship.

18. On making their getaway out of the Fjord, several aircraft machine-gunned a small vessel near the entrance, gun positions, huts, etc.

19. Returning aircraft were landed on from 1615 to 1658. The time taken in landing on twenty-one aircraft, some of them in damaged condition, in forty-three minutes without any mishap was the result of good backing up by pilots and of good drill by the handling parties on deck and in the hangars.

SUMMARY OF RESULTS.

20. (*a*) *Attacking Force:-*

> Twelve torpedo bombers.
> Six bombers.
> Six fighters.

(*b*) *Results obtained:-*

> (i) *Torpedo* – Two certain hits on New Quay (Number 2 Jetty). Two probable hits on other quays. Further possible hits on quays. Two small craft probably destroyed.
> (ii) *Bomb* – Damage to oil installation. At least one tank destroyed. Minor damage to ship repair yard. Fires started.

(*c*) *Casualties:-*

    (i) *Aircraft* – Three missing. Four damaged.

    (ii) *Personnel* – Three pilots missing. Two observers missing. Two air gunners missing.

General.

2I. For the last nine months, FURIOUS has been employed as a Transport Carrier, and it was a tonic to all concerned to learn that once more she was to be used operationally.

22. A full scale rehearsal, as carried out by VICTORIOUS had to be abandoned as far as FURIOUS was concerned. No flying, except for action purposes, could be carried out on passage, owing to the necessity of conserving fuel.

23. On the day, the work of the Flight Deck Party and Squadron personnel, coupled with the close backing up by pilots when landing on, was excellent, and this alone enabled a most exacting programme, which allowed no latitude, to be adhered to in every detail.

24. The Squadrons carried out their plan without a hitch; their navigation was accurate and their timing was exact. Their air discipline was of a very high standard.

(Signed) A.G. TALBOT,
Captain, R.N.
Commanding Officer.

APPENDIX II.

H.M.S. *VICTORIOUS.*
30th July, 1941.

The following brief report of the part taken by aircraft from H.M.S. VICTORIOUS in Operation "E.F." is submitted.

2. A striking force consisting of 12 Albacores of No. 827 Squadron and 8 Albacores of No. 828 Squadron was flown off in one range at 1400 on 30th July. All aircraft were armed with torpedoes fitted with duplex pistols set to noncontact at 14 feet. At 1430 a fighter escort of 9 Fulmars of No. 809 Squadron, and a fighter patrol of 3 Fulmars of 809 Squadron was flown off, the former having been ordered to over-take the striking force en route for the objective and the latter to patrol over the Fleet.

3. The fighter escort on making a landfall proceeded at a height of 4,000 feet to a position between Renoy and Prestoy Islands where heavy anti-aircraft fire was encountered. It was therefore decided to circle this area in the hope of drawing the fire from the striking force.

4. Approximately ten minutes later at least three M.E.109s and six M.E.110s were seen approaching from the direction of Vadso and Kirkenes aerodromes.

5. During the ensuing combats two M.E.110s and one M.E.109 were shot down for certain and confirmed, and a further M.E.110 was possibly shot down. Two of this Squadron are missing, but the pilot of one was seen to escape by parachute.

6. 827 Squadron, on making a landfall at Rabachi peninsula, formed sub-flights astern, proceeded at low altitude down Jarfjord, climbed the intervening hills, and then attacked shipping in Bokfjord.

7. Five aircraft fired at the BREMSE and two hits were reported. The remaining aircraft fired at shipping anchored N.E. and N.W. of Prestoy. Torpedoes were observed running correctly towards two targets but owing to heavy fighter opposition encountered at this time it was impossible to observe the results. During the retirement heavy fighter opposition continued and one JU.87 was shot down for certain by a front gun, and a probable M.E.109 with a rear-gun. Six Albacores were lost. The air gunner for whom the probable M.E.109 is claimed, died in the aircraft and was buried at sea after the aircraft had returned to the ship.

8. 828 Squadron which approached Rabachi peninsula about half a mile astern of the leading squadron, formed sub-flights in line astern and led away through the hills to attack shipping at the northern end of Bokfjord.

9. Two ships (of about 2,000 tons each) under way, were attacked by, it is thought five air- craft. Both ships were on fire when last seen, nothing was seen of the attacks

made by the last three aircraft. Five out of the eight air-craft of this squadron were lost.

10. It is hoped that further damage was done by the aircraft which did not return, but observation was most difficult for all aircraft on account of the fighter interference.

General remarks.

11. The enemy reconnaisance aircraft sighted Force "P" at the most unfortunate moment, as it was too late to call off the attack and yet gave the enemy plenty of time to prepare for the arrival of the striking force. With all chance of surprise gone, and with a cloudless sky, heavy casualties were inevitable, yet the attack was pressed home with great determination and gallantry and I consider that the conduct of all who took part is deserving of the highest praise.

12. From a military point of view the attack was a failure as we lost eleven Albacores and two Fulmars and had eight Albacores damaged, while we shot down two M.E.110s, one M.E.109, one JU.87, probably one M.E.110 and one M.E.109 and damaged one JU.87. We also obtained hits with two torpedoes on BREMSE and at least one each on two Merchant Ships and probably one each on two more Merchant Ships. It is a pity that there were not more torpedo targets.

13. The fact that the Fighter Squadron climbed to 1,000 feet before reaching the Ribachi peninsula might have led to their being detected by the enemy's R.D.F. and so giving away surprise. In the event, due to Force "P" having already been sighted, I do not think it mattered. It was none the less a mistake.

14. It is interesting to note that the Germans used all types of aircraft to engage our attacking force. It is reported by our aircraft crews that the JU.87s were armed with extra machine guns and possibly with cannon as well. It is much to the credit of the crews of our Fulmars that they shot down three enemy aircraft of superior types for the loss of only two Fulmars.

15. Should it be found necessary on a future occasion to carry out a similar attack, i.e. one where complete surprise is unlikely and where lack of reconnaisance leaves both the strength of the defence and the number of targets in doubt, it is suggested that there would be better chances of success by using a smaller force of T.S.R.s and a large force of fighters.

16. It was arranged to refuel the Hurricanes in VICTORIOUS while the striking force was away. Two of them would not start after refuelling and had to be kept on deck. The resulting congestion caused a delay in the landing-on programme just at the time when (but for lack of initiative) the German bombing attack should have developed. Thus this delay might have had serious consequences.

(Signed) H.C. BOVELL,
Captain, R.N.
Commanding Officer.

Footnotes

[1] *An Admiralty oil tanker.*

[2] *Seidisfiord – on the east coast of Iceland.*

[3] *A/S – Anti Submarine.*

[4] *R.D.F. ships – those ships fitted with radar equipment.*

[5] *Reydarfiord – about 25 miles south of Seidisfiord.*

[6] *The Zenit Flight – a routine German meteorological aircraft reconnaissance.*

[7] *R.D.F. cruisers – those fitted with radar equipment.*

[8] *D/F – direction finding by W/T.*

[9] *R.D.F. – radar.*

[10] *HF/DF set – High Frequency Direction Finding equipment.*

[11] *Tana Fiord – northwest of Kirkenes and Petsamo and about 90 miles from the area in which the aircraft carriers were to operate.*

[12] *T.S.R. – Torpedo/Spotter/Reconnaissance aircraft.*

[13] *FURIOUS with SUFFOLK and Destroyers returned to base in advance of the remainder, reaching Seidisfiord at 0830 on 3rd August.*

[14] *Commanding H.M.S. VICTORIOUS.*

[15] *Captain (D), 3rd Destroyer Flotilla.*

5

ADMIRAL SIR JOHN C. TOVEY'S DESPATCH ON THE RAID ON THE LOFOTEN ISLANDS,
4 MARCH 1941

RAID ON MILITARY AND ECONOMIC OBJECTIVES IN THE LOFOTEN ISLANDS.

The following Despatch was submitted to the Lords Commissioners of the Admiralty on the 4th April, 1941, by Admiral Sir JOHN C.TOVEY, K.C.B., D.S.O., Commander-in-Chief, Home Fleet.

H.M.S. *KING GEORGE V.*
4th April, 1941.

OPERATION "CLAYMORE"

Be pleased to lay before Their Lordships the enclosed report of Operation "Claymore"[1] prepared by the Captain (D), 6th Destroyer Flotilla, H.M.S. SOMALI, in command of the operation. I concur fully in the report and in the remarks of the Rear Admiral (D), Home Fleet, in his Minute II, particularly in paragraph 2.

2. Among the factors which contributed to the success of this small combined operation I would draw attention to the following:-

(*a*) The excellent co-operation between all ranks and ratings of the Navy and Army taking part. Each single phase required a joint decision to be taken, and in each phase Naval units and Army units were working side by side in complete agreement and harmony. It is appropriate to record the appreciation of the Naval officers and ratings who took part for the qualities of their soldier opposite numbers.

(*b*) The weather. It had not been practicable to carry out more than elementary drills in the short time at Scapa, and it was a great relief to me that the landing craft did not have to contend with swell, strong wind or tide. I would stress moreover that any less time than was allowed for rehearsal and planning, and it was two days less than originally planned, would have been quite unacceptable.

3. I would mention the valuable part played by the submarine SUNFISH in her role as a D/F beacon.[2] This scheme worked well, and although in the event the force was able to fix by sights, had this not been possible they would have been in an uncomfortable position without the SUNFISH'S aid.

4. With reference to paragraph 29 of Captain D.6's report, I had laid particular emphasis in my verbal instructions on the importance of punctuality in withdrawing all forces at the end of the agreed time, and I endorse the opinion that it was necessary to sink the HAMBURG rather than to attempt to steam her down the Vestfjord and then some 750 miles to the Faroes with the resources available, but she should first have been boarded and searched for papers or other material likely to be useful.

(Signed) JACK C. TOVEY,
Admiral,
Commander-in-Chief,
Home Fleet.

MINUTE II
H.M.S. TYNE.
15th March, 1941.

Forwarded.

1. Great credit is due to Captain C. Caslon, Royal Navy, for his part in the efficient planning and execution of this operation.

2. It was fortunate that the conditions were ideal. The weather throughout the passage could not have been better, and the opposition was negligible.

3. It is thought that future operations of this nature will not only need equally efficient and careful preparation and execution, but also adequate air support, if the geographical position is not so favourable to us.

(Signed) L.H.K. HAMILTON,
Rear Admiral (D),
Home Fleet.

H.M.S. *SOMALI.*
8th March, 1941.

OPERATION "CLAYMORE" – REPORT OF PROCEEDINGS

I have the honour to forward the following report of the proceedings of Force "Rebel" in Operation "Claymore".

2. Force "Rebel" consisted of the following ships:-

Destroyers
SOMALI – Captain C. Caslon (Captain (D), 6th D.F.).
BEDOUIN – Comdr. J.A. McCoy, D.S.O.
TARTAR – Comdr. L.P Skipwith.
LEGION – Comdr. R.F. Jessel.
ESKIMO – Comdr. E.G. Le Geyt.

Troop Carriers
QUEEN EMMA – Comdr. C.A. Kershaw.
PRINCESS BEATRIX – Comdr. T.B. Brunton.

3. During the afternoon of Friday, 28th February, Brigadier J.C. Haydon, D.S.O., O.B.E., embarked in SOMALI with his headquarters staff which consisted of Major A.R. Aslett (Brigade Major), 2nd Lieutenant L.M. Harper-Gow (interpreter in Norwegian), and four other ranks

4. Force "Rebel" sailed from Scapa at 0001 on 1st March, 1941, and proceeded to Skaalefjord, Faroes, arriving there at 1900 on the same day. Destroyers refuelled from WAR PINDARI and the force sailed at 0001 on 2nd March. Course was set for position L (64° 00' N. 3° 00' W.) and thence for position P (67° 12' N. 02° 00' W.).

5. After clearing the Faroes a speed of 20 knots was maintained until 1100 on 2nd March in order to be as far to the northward as possible by that time. It was hoped that, by so doing, the force would evade detection by the Zenit flight.[3] No aircraft was in fact sighted.

6. After passing through position P at 0130 on 3rd March course was shaped for position Q (67° 09' N. 11° 55' E) which was reached as planned at 0001 on 4th March, speed having been adjusted as necessary.

7. Up to this time the passage had been uneventful and the weather conditions very favourable. These were particularly so while making the approach to position Q from the westward. The sky was, for the most part, overcast with low cloud and frequent snow showers were experienced which tended to reduce the chances of detection. The weather cleared sufficiently at intervals, however, for navigational observations to be taken to fix the position of the force.

8. During the passage from P to Q the wind was from E.N E., force 3, and the state of the sea 24.[4] It was unnecessary, therefore, even to consider postponing the operation as conditions promised to be excellent. Special weather reports made by

Admiralty were received, also reports of air reconnaissance patrols from the Commander-in-Chief, Rosyth.

9. During the approach to position Q, D/F bearings were obtained of SUNFISH at the expected times and these bearings confirmed the position obtained by astronomical observations. It is estimated that the force passed 2 miles south of SUNFISH at 2335. This method of checking the position was most valuable in making the landfall. Had no sights been obtained, it would have been the only means of fixing the position of the force at this critical stage of the approach.

I0. From position Q the force moved up Vestfjord towards position C (68° 05' N. I4° 29' E.), continuing in night cruising order until 0300 when ships formed into single line ahead. Position C was reached without incident at 0430 when the force split, SOMALI, BEDOUIN, TARTAR and QUEEN EMMA proceeding to position D (68° I4' N. I4° 42' E.) and LEGION, ESKIMO and PRINCESS BEATRIX to position E (68° 08' N. I4° 0I' E.). It is believed that the force was observed by coast-watchers during this passage, but that no reporting message got through to the mainland. This point may be mentioned by the military who gave me the information after our return to Scapa.

II. Passage up the Vestfjord was much simplified by the fact that all lights were burning at full brilliancy and with normal characteristics, with the following exceptions:- Skomvaer, Tennholm, Grytoy. By 0445 the outline of the coast could be distinguished.

I2. After the splitting of the force, SOMALI, with BEDOUIN, TARTAR and QUEEN EMMA in company, moved towards position D where the landing craft for X landing were lowered by 0508. These were taken in charge by TARTAR while SOMALI, BEDOUIN and QUEEN EMMA proceeded to position F (68° I2' N. I4° 52' E.).

I3. The weather conditions now were – wind E N.E , force 3, sea I0 to 20.[5] It was intensely cold, the temperature being between 20° and 25° F. The weather continued to be fine and very clear throughout the day, with brilliant sunshine.

I4. By this time it had become apparent that, in view of the lightness of the dawn and the perfect visibility, the landing of troops could, with advantage, have been made earlier than at 0645, the projected time. No alteration, except in the case of X landing, was however possible owing to the distances to be covered by landing craft after having been lowered.

I5. Craft for X landing, covered by TARTAR, were comparatively close to their objective on being lowered and must have been clearly visible to those ashore. To avoid the loss of the element of surprise, therefore, they moved off to Port X[6] at 0530 and arrived there approximately half an hour before the planned time.

I6. In the meantime LEGION, ESKIMO and PRINCESS BEATRIX had reached position E at 0540. Landing craft were lowered and led inshore to Ports A and B by LEGION and ESKIMO respectively. Disembarkation proceeded in accordance with the timetable and landings were made at 0645.

I7. At 06I0, shortly before the arrival of BEDOUIN and QUEEN EMMA at position F, SOMALI parted company to proceed to Ports A and B to see if the landings were being effected satisfactorily there. On passage, an armed trawler, later found to be the KREBS, was sighted steering away from Port X. Fire was opened at a range of 3,000 yards at 0620 and the enemy very quickly hit. Our fire was returned by three rounds fired from a small gun in the bows of the trawler, but no hits were obtained on SOMALI. Immediately afterwards three shells were observed to be effective, one apparently exploding the ready-use ammunition, another bursting in the wheelhouse and the third in the boiler room. A considerable volume of smoke was seen to be coming from the trawler which was clearly out of control. Fire was accordingly checked. Five survivors were then seen to be swimming in the water; they were picked up by 0655.

18. At this time gunfire could be heard at Port X. As W/T communication with the landing places had not yet been established and the Brigadier was anxious to find out if any landings had been opposed, SOMALI left the now helpless trawler, which had run aground on a small island, and proceeded to ascertain the state of affairs at Ports X, B and A.

19. At 0710 SOMALI, made the negative W/T silence sign and from then on, throughout the operation, satisfactory W/T communications were maintained with all landing places. V/S[7] communication was also established at each landing place.

20. At each port, operations were proceeding according to plan and by 0735 reports had been received that at all four ports landings had been effected successfully without opposition and that relations with the Norwegian population were most cordial. From this time onwards, reports came in from all military landing parties that allotted tasks were being earned out successfully and the Brigadier, from his position on SOMALI'S bridge, was kept in continual touch with the progress of operations.

21. By now the local Norwegian fishing fleet had put to sea; there were literally hundreds of little fishing smacks and small puffers beginning to fish in the adjacent waters. It quickly became clear to them that our operations were directed against the Germans and that they were not to be molested. They showed their friendliness and enthusiasm by cheering and waving and hoisting Norwegian flags.

22. From Port A SOMALI then proceeded back to Port X. During the passage the trawler KREBS, still burning, was seen to have refloated and to be drifting towards the centre of the fjord. As SOMALI closed, a white flag was seen being waved and at 0910 a boarding party was sent over in a Norwegian fishing boat who volunteered their services. The survivors consisted of five ratings, all of whom were wounded by gunfire, two seriously. The balance of the crew, consisting of the captain and thirteen ratings, had been killed in the action.

23 The boarding officers, Major A.R. Aslett, Lieutenant Sir Marshall G.C. Warmington, Bart, R.N , the Signal Officer on my staff, and 2nd Lieutenant L.M. Harper-Gow, searched the ship so far as was possible.

24. The wheelhouse was found to have received a direct hit and nothing could be recovered from there, other than a number of charts. The captain and one rating were found dead by the wheel; one or two bodies which could not be identified were also in the wheelhouse.

25. The ship was still on fire below and no entry could be made into the fore-peak or the engine room.

26. The search of the KREBS occupied three quarters of an hour and while SOMALI was stopped, numbers of fishing craft took the opportunity to come alongside and throw their fish on board as gifts to the ship's company. The fishing boat which took the boarding party was rewarded with gifts of food and cigarettes.

27. At I0I5 the KREBS was sunk by gunfire after an unsuccessful attempt had been made to destroy her by depth charge fired from the port thrower. She finally disappeared at I030. Her armament consisted of a 3 or 6-pdr. gun forward, a 2-cm Madsen machine-gun aft and eight depth charges in two chutes.

28. A summary of the happenings at the various ports is given in the ensuing paragraphs.

29. At Port X an important success was the destruction of the HAMBURG by gunfire from TARTAR. This was a ship of 9780 tons which had been specially converted into a fish-refrigerating and factory ship. From the report of the officer in charge of the naval demolition party at Port X it appears that a plan was made to take possession of this ship and to steam her as a prize to England and that this plan was frustrated by TARTAR opening fire and destroying her. I consider that the Commanding Officer, H.M.S. TARTAR, was justified in the action he took, having regard to the general instructions for the conduct of the operation and to the fact that no information of the plan to seize the ship had been communicated to him. Nor was I, myself, aware of it.

30. In addition, TARTAR sunk the PASAJES, I996 tons, and completed the destruction of the FELIX HEUMANN, 2468 tons, which was still floating after partial destruction by the naval demolition party. The latter, from H.M.S. NELSON, under the command of Lieutenant D.D. Bone, R.N., sank the EILENAU, I404 tons, the trawler RISSEN and, as stated above, commenced the destruction of the FELIX HEUMANN. The work performed by this party was most creditable. It is believed that the large majority of the crews of all these ships were made prisoners by the military landing parties and brought back in QUEEN EMMA.

3I. At I035 the Norwegian trawler MYRLAND, whose crew wished to proceed to England and asked for instructions, was directed by TARTAR to proceed independently to Skaalefjord in the Faroes. This was reported in my signal timed I444 of 6th March, I94I. She arrived safely today, 8th March.

3686 SUPPLEMENT TO THE LONDON GAZETTE, 23 JUNE, 1948

32. At Port Y, BEDOUIN at 0626, while leading the landing craft in towards the shore, intercepted the Norwegian ferry steamer MIRA flying the Norwegian flag and endeavoured to stop her by firing a shot across her bows. As this had no effect a second shot was fired into the fore part of the ship, but as the ship still did not stop effective fire was opened. One shot entered the ship below the funnel, steam poured from her and she lost way. BEDOUIN then left her to see the landing parties safely ashore. This done, BEDOUIN, acting in accordance with my instructions, returned to sink the MIRA. It was seen that she was being abandoned and, when this was

completed and the rafts were clear, fire was opened. MIRA was very soon severely damaged and started to sink slowly.

33. I was subsequently informed by a military officer of one of the landing parties that the captain of the MIRA was forced at the pistol-point by a German officer on board to continue on his course, despite BEDOUIN'S warning shots. It is believed that this officer and 12 German soldiers who were also on board were later taken prisoner and brought back in QUEEN EMMA. It is feared that there were some casualties to Norwegian civilians as a result of BEDOUIN'S gunfire.

34. By 0840 it had become evident that the work of the landing parties at Port Y would shortly be completed. QUEEN EMMA, who had been lying off Port X, was accordingly directed to proceed to Port Y to commence re-embarkation of A.L.C.s.[8] This was completed at 1024 when QUEEN EMMA, with BEDOUIN, returned to Port X who had reported all tasks completed at 1011 and parties ready to re-embark.

35. By 1030 SOMALI was proceeding to cover the landing parties at Port A as LEGION had moved southward to investigate two trawlers which subsequently proved to be Norwegian puffers. During this passage, dense columns of heavy black smoke could be seen at Ports X and A rising to the tops of the surrounding mountains, a height of several thousand feet, sure evidence of the thoroughness with which the landing parties were carrying out their tasks of destruction.

36. At Port A the military completed their tasks successfully and LEGION was not called upon to give any support. Two German trawlers, the ANDO, 300 tons, and the GROTTO, 200 tons, which were the only enemy ships in the harbour, were sunk by the naval demolition party from H.M.S. RODNEY under the command of Lieutenant C.P.N. Wells-Cole, R.N. By the time SOMALI had arrived at 1100 re-embarkation of troops had already commenced.

37. At Port B, as at Port A, ESKIMO was not called upon to give any support to the landing parties, who completed their tasks successfully, nor was there any enemy shipping present against which she could take action.

38. SOMALI returned to Port X at 1200 to find re-embarkation in progress. The time required for this was increased by the large number of prisoners and volunteers to be embarked in QUEEN EMMA who sailed with 852 persons on board. By 1230, however, the last landing craft had left the shore and at 1255 QUEEN EMMA reported that she was ready to proceed. At 1256 PRINCESS BEATRIX made a similar report from Port B.

39. SOMALI, BEDOUIN, TARTAR, and QUEEN EMMA proceeded to position C at 20 knots. LEGION, ESKIMO and PRINCESS BEATRIX joined company at 1330 and the whole force, in day cruising order, set course at best speed down Vestfjord. Columns of smoke were still rising from the burning oil tanks and plant and a heavy pall lay over the scene of the day's operations.

40. At 1530 as the force was passing Vaeroy, a German reconnaissance aircraft was sighted by BEDOUIN and was heard by the same ship to make a W/T report. BEDOUIN accordingly carried out jamming procedure. The aircraft flew at about 6,000 feet making full use of cloud cover and was engaged by ships' guns as opportunity offered. Although conditions appeared very favourable for a bombing

attack none was made and the aircraft disappeared shortly after I600. In view of this sighting, I made the W/T report of the successful completion of the operation at once, without waiting until the force was clear of the area.

4I. At I700 course was altered to the westward for position P which was reached at 0900 on 5th March, after which course was altered to the southward. Vice Admiral Commanding, I8th Cruiser Squadron, in EDINBURGH, with NIGERIA in company, were sighted at I020 on 5th March and provided escort for the remainder of the passage.

42. It was known on the morning of 5th March that the Germans had announced that a raid had been made and I therefore considered it desirable to signal a brief report of the success of the operation as early as could be done with safety. Accordingly when the force was in position of approximately 64° 00' N.4° 00' W and darkness was approaching W/T silence was broken for this purpose. Unfortunately signalling conditions were very unfavourable and it took much longer than had been anticipated to clear the message.

43. The wounded prisoners from the KREBS were accommodated in the sick bay and my harbour cabin during the return passage. They received the greatest care and skilful attention from my Medical Officer, Surgeon Lieutenant M.G. Low, R.N.V.R., assisted by the sick bay staff, the Flotilla chaplain and the canteen manager. The Army other ranks also assisted. Two of the men were very seriously wounded and owe their lives to the skilled nursing they received. Similar good arrangements for the wounded were made in QUEEN EMMA.

44. The return passage was made without incident and Force "Rebel" arrived at Scapa at I300 on 6th March.

45. After arrival prisoners and volunteers were disembarked from all ships, the wounded being discharged to H.M.H.S. AMARAPOORA.

General Remarks.

46. I was greatly impressed with the efficient handling and station-keeping of the troop carriers, particularly as they were both newly commissioned ships with no previous experience of working in formation. The lowering and hoisting of the landing craft during the operation was carried out in a most efficient manner.

47. Owing to the troop carriers sailing for the Clyde a few hours after our return to Scapa it has not been possible for me to obtain details of the military operation with sufficient accuracy to make any but the most general reference to them in this report. It has, however, been arranged for copies of Brigadier Haydon's report to be forwarded to the Commander-in-Chief, Home Fleet, as soon as it has been prepared.

48. I should like to record with pleasure that throughout the planning and execution of this operation Brigadier Haydon co-operated wholeheartedly and at no time did we have the slightest difficulty in reaching mutually satisfactory conclusions. His presence on board SOMALI, with his staff, was most welcome in every way.

(Signed) C. CASLON,
Captain (D),
Sixth Destroyer Flotilla.

APPENDIX

REPORT ON OPERATION "CLAYMORE"

by Brigadier J.C. Haydon, D.S.O., O.B.E., Commanding Special Service Brigade.
13th March, 1941.

Objects of the operation.

I. (*a*) The Military objects of the operation were to destroy the facilities for producing herring and cod oil in the Ports of Stamsund, Henningsvaer, Svolvaer and Brettesnes, all of which are situated in the Lofoten Islands; to arrest local supporters of the Quisling party; to capture any enemy personnel found in the ports, and to enlist recruits for the Free Norwegian Forces.

(*b*) The Naval objective at the ports was the destruction or capture of enemy ships and of Norwegian vessels found to be working for the Germans.

Forces taking part in the operation.

2. Naval.

(*a*) The 6th Destroyer Flotilla, under the command of Captain C. Caslon, R.N., and composed of:
H.M.S. SOMALI,
H.M.S. BEDOUIN,
H.M.S. TARTAR,
H.M.S. ESKIMO,
H.M.S. LEGION,

formed the Naval escort and were responsible for the safety of the military forces during the approach to and return from the Lofoten Islands and for the provision of close support while the operations on shore were in progress.

(*b*) H.M.S. QUEEN EMMA (Commander C.A. Kershaw, R.N.) carrying the troops destined for Svolvaer and Brettesnes.

(*c*) H.M.S. PRINCESS BEATRIX (Commander T.B. Brunton, R.N.) carrying the troops destined for Stamsund and Henningsvaer.

(*d*) Naval demolition parties carried in H.M.S. QUEEN EMMA and H.M.S. PRINCESS BEATRIX.

3. *Military.* – The Military forces taking part in the raid were:-

(*a*) Operational Headquarters Special Service Brigade in H.M.S. SOMALI.

(*b*) 250 all ranks of No. 4 Commando under the command of Lieut.-Colonel D.S. Lister, M.C. (The Buffs) in H.M.S. QUEEN EMMA.

(*c*) 250 all ranks of No 3 Commando under the command of Major J.F. Durnford-Slater (Royal Artillery) in H.M.S. PRINCESS BEATRIX.

(*d*) One Section No 55 Field Company Royal Engineers (2nd Lieut. H.M. Turner, Royal Engineers).

(*e*) 4 officers and 48 other ranks of the Norwegian Forces, under the command of Captain Martin Linge.

The detachments of Royal Engineers and of Norwegian troops were divided between H.M.S QUEEN EMMA and H.M.S. PRINCESS BEATRIX in accordance with the tasks to be carried out in each port.

Concentration of the force and preparatory work.

4. Operational Headquarters Special Service Brigade, Nos. 3 and 4 Commandos, the Royal Engineers detachment and the Norwegian troops embarked at Gourock in H.M.S. QUEEN EMMA and H.M.S. PRINCESS BEATRIX during the afternoon of Friday, 2Ist February, I94I, and left for Scapa Flow on the evening of that day.

Scapa was reached at I430 hours on the 22nd February and the ships were anchored between H.M.S. NELSON and H.M.S KING GEORGE V.

The troops remained at Scapa until the force sailed for the Lofoten Islands at 000I hours on Saturday, Ist March, I94I. Thus, there intervened a period of almost a week during which all the final arrangements, plans and orders could be prepared, published and explained and during which those who were to operate together during the operation could meet and get to know one another.

There can be no doubt whatsoever regarding the essential nature of this comparatively short time of preparation.

Though the nature of the raid precluded meticulous rehearsals of the tasks allotted to each troop or detachment, the week at Scapa was invaluable from the military point of view, in that it gave both officers and men time to accustom themselves to the ships from which they were to work; to get to know the officers and crews of the landing craft which were to take them inshore, and, in general, to make the personal contacts which are so essential a preliminary to an enterprise of this kind.

5. So far as the Naval and Military Commanders were concerned, the period at Scapa was filled by a series of conferences, at which all details and difficulties were examined and solutions reached.

Several points of major importance emerged during these meetings. The first concerned the problem of supporting fire from the destroyers.

Captain C. Caslon, R.N., the Senior Naval Officer, having studied the charts of the area of operations, reached the conclusion that, owing to navigational difficulties, the escorting destroyers would not be able to lie closer than approximately I mile from each port.

This distance, taking into account the somewhat tortuous nature of the approaches, and the half-lights of early morning, made it unlikely that the destroyers would be in a position to afford support by direct fire or that they would even be able to keep the landing craft in view throughout the passage between the ships and the shore.

These were, of course, important considerations and changed somewhat drastically the military aspect of the operation, under which it had been envisaged that the landing craft would be able to move into each port with the escorting destroyers in the closest attendance and dominating any possible opposition with their guns.

However, in view of the information available concerning the enemy forces which were likely to be encountered, it was decided to accept the disadvantages and difficulties arising from the possible employment of indirect fire and to insert special instructions in the operation order concerning the use of this method of support.

In this connection, it will be appreciated that the lack of gridded maps, the restricted size of each port, the danger areas which would have to be allowed for and the desire to avoid any unnecessary damage to Norwegian property, all tended to complicate the situation and to make it more and more apparent that there would probably be a period in each port during which the troops would have to rely only on their own weapons and on such covering fire as could be given by any detachments which had already been landed.

In these circumstances Commanders were instructed to make their approach with caution and to use the leading craft at each port as a scout so that all would not be subjected to fire at one and the same time.

Further, troops were to be prepared to open fire and mutually support each other from their landing craft should the need arise.

The situations which might have arisen clearly called for the use of S.L.C.s[9] but there were none available.

6. A further decision arrived at after a study of the navigational difficulties, concerned the movement of H.M.S. QUEEN EMMA after the landing craft for Svolvaer had been launched.

It was thought originally that the two A.L.C.s[10] required for Brettesnes could be dropped at the same time as those for Svolvaer and that they would then be able to proceed astern of their escorting destroyer through the narrow channel named on the chart as Holen Skjoldver.

It was decided, however, that it would be both unsound and unwise to risk passing either a destroyer or unescorted landing craft through this passage.

As a result of this decision, H.M.S QUEEN EMMA was instructed that, having dropped the landing craft for Svolvaer, she was to proceed to Brettesnes in company with the escorting destroyer, passing to the south of Skravven.

As this route was appreciably longer than that through Holen Skjoldver and as it was desirable that the concentration of the force after the conclusion of the shore operation should not be delayed, orders were issued that the troops landed at Brettesnes should be ready to re-embark at II30 hours which was I hour earlier than the time limit fixed for the other three ports.

7. The third matter of importance from the military point of view was the possibility which was explained by the Commander-in-Chief, Home Fleet, that the escorting destroyers might be forced to leave the vicinity of the four ports should a naval action be precipitated by the move of the force to the Lofotens.

The period during which the destroyers might be away could not, of course, be forecast with any accuracy but, as a precautionary measure, each man was ordered to take ashore with him rations sufficient for 48 hours.

8. It should be stressed that it was the few days spent at Scapa which gave each Commander ample opportunity to examine in the most complete detail the problems which faced him and to consult naval officers concerned on any points of difficulty arising out of them.

It is also worthy of emphasis that, had the nature of the operation entailed a long approach in darkness for the landing craft, or had the tasks allotted to the various detachments been such as to require exact and repeated rehearsal, this preparatory period of six days would not have been long enough.

In such circumstances, I4 to I8 days might well have been required.

The approach to the Lofoten Islands.

9. The force, which bore the code name "Rebel", left Scapa Flow at 000I hrs. on the Ist March and proceeded first to Skaalefjord in the Faroes where the destroyers were to refuel.

The fjord was reached at I900 hrs. on Ist March, and the weather conditions had been such that it was hoped, with some degree of confidence, that Force "Rebel" had escaped enemy observation.

I0. After a stay of about five hours, the force proceeded on its way routed through various points previously fixed by the Commander-in-Chief, Home Fleet.

II. During the night of Monday, 3rd March, Force "Rebel" entered the Vestfjord and shortly before 0400 hrs on the following morning, the many navigational lights in the neighbourhood of the Lofotens came into view.

That these should have been burning at what appeared to be full brilliance was somewhat surprising but certainly gave good cause for the hope that the arrival of the force had been unheralded and that the complete effects of surprise might be obtained. Such indeed proved to be the case.

I2. The exactness of the timing and the extreme accuracy of the naval approach, both of which were due to the careful arrangements and the untiring supervision of Captain C. Caslon, R.N., and of his Navigating Officer, Lieut-Commander Shaw, R N., cannot be praised too highly

There is no doubt whatsoever that the accomplishment of the military tasks on shore was much facilitated thereby.

The operations on shore.

13. The operations ashore proceeded according to plan and all tasks allotted to the force were carried out. The times of the initial landings at each port varied but troops were ashore at all of them by 0650 hours. By 1300 hours both H.M.S. PRINCESS BEATRIX and H.M.S. QUEEN EMMA had re-embarked all their troops and were ready to sail.

Inter-communications.

14. Owing to the excellence of the intercommunication arrangements made by Lieut. Sir Marshall G.C. Warmington, Bart., R.N., of H.M.S. SOMALI, it was possible to obtain at all times a most clear and accurate picture of the progress of the operations on shore.

The personnel for the various signal detachments were all drawn from the Home Fleet. They were faced with the task of operating wireless sets to which they were not accustomed, and with but little time to practise with them.

The ease with which they overcame this difficulty and the speed and accuracy with which the many signals were passed says much for their individual skill and for the instruction and training they were given by the naval officer to whom I have referred above.

State of the light at the time of the landings.

15. The original intention was to make four simultaneous landings at 0630 hrs. but, after further examination of the meteorological data, it was considered that such early landings would force the A.L.C.s and M.L.C.s[II] to make their difficult approaches in conditions of what may be termed "dangerous" darkness.

The time of landing was therefore put back to 0645 hrs.

In the event the morning of March 4th was exceptionally clear and calm. There was no fog, no sea mist, no rain or snow and what breeze there was blew from a favourable though unusual quarter.

Thus the landing craft approached the shore under rather better light conditions than were required or were desirable.

However, it is difficult to see how such rare conditions can be legislated for except by abandoning the idea of making the landings simultaneously and allowing instead a 30 or 45 minutes period during any part of which they may take place.

The obvious danger of such a procedure is that the defences at the point where the earliest landing is made may be given time to warn other points at which landings are attempted 10 or 20 minutes later.

Effect of low temperatures.

16. Even during the short passage between H.M.S. QUEEN EMMA, H.M.S. PRINCESS BEATRIX and the various ports, it was found that weapons had a distinct tendency to freeze up and become hard to operate.

Should such low temperatures be anticipated again in the future, some special arrangements would have to be made to guard against this danger.

Opposition.

I7. At no point on shore was any opposition encountered, though some of the enemy personnel, notably those at the air station outside Svolvaer who were armed with a machine-gun and other weapons, might well have inflicted casualties and delayed progress. So far as is known, the only shots fired by the enemy were the three or four rounds aimed at H.M.S. SOMALI by the armed trawler KREBS. No casualties were incurred by our troops.

Reception by the inhabitants.

I8. The reports received from the Military Commanders at each port show that in every case our troops were given a welcome, the genuine enthusiasm of which cannot be doubted.

Although it must have been abundantly clear that the demolitions which were being carried through would inevitably have sad effects on the livelihood of many, there always seemed to be the over-riding realisation that they were well worth aiding and abetting so long as they were also the means of retarding and interfering with production urgently required by the enemy.

In many instances, the gifts distributed by our troops were at once matched by presents given to them by the inhabitants. In short, they were welcomed by a people whose natural virility and inherent soundness of character had ridden safely over the many insidious dangers which must follow from months of enemy occupation.

Military action at the four ports.

I9. The following were the Senior Military Officers at each port:-

At Stamsund – Major J.F. Durnford-Slater, R.A.
At Henningsvaer – Captain A.S. Ronald, K.R.R.C.
At Svolvaer – Lieut.-Colonel D.S. Lister, M.C., The Buffs.
At Brettesnes – Major M.E. Kerr, The Rifle Brigade.

20. The characteristics which seem to stand out from the operations as a whole are the excellent and frequent reports rendered by the senior officers at each port; the speed with which the detachments carried out their allotted duties, and the initiative shown by junior commanders in seeking for and carrying through useful and important tasks in addition to those specifically mentioned in the operation orders.

I would particularly bring to your notice Lieut.-Colonel D.S. Lister, M.C., The Buffs, who was in command of the operations at Svolvaer and Brettesnes and Major J.F. Durnford-Slater, Royal Artillery, who commanded the troops at Stamsund and Henningsvaer.

2I. Lieutenant H.M. Turner, Royal Engineers, and his section of No. 55 Field

Company Royal Enginers accomplished excellent work and carried out their tasks in a most skilled and competent manner.

22. Consolidated results of the operation are given in the Annexure.

Assistance rendered by the Norwegian troops.

23. It is not too much to say that the operations on shore could not have been carried through within the time limits laid down in the Operation Orders or with the ease or good relations and understanding that existed had it not been for the enthusiastic help and co-operation of the Norwegian detachment commanded by Captain Martin Linge.

This officer never spared himself for one moment either during the preparatory period or during the raid, itself.

His enthusiasm and personality were infectious and it is hoped that his most valuable services and those of his detachment may be brought to the notice of the Norwegian authorities.

Outline plan for the raid.

24. The outline plan for the Military operations, which dealt with the total force to be employed, the division of the force between the four ports and the main tasks to be accomplished at each, was drawn up in the office of the Director of Combined Operations.

This plan was not altered in any one of its essential features.

Naval assistance and co-operation.

25. Nothing could have been more inspiring than the help and assistance given to the Military force by the Royal Navy.

It will suffice to say that no officer, N.C.O., or man left Scapa Flow without the deep seated and often expressed hope that it would be his privilege to co-operate again with the Royal Navy in the very near future.

26. It is hoped that it will not be considered out of place if in this, a Military Report, some tribute is paid to the Senior Naval Officer with Force "Rebel."

Captain C. Caslon, R.N. (H.M.S. SOMALI) was responsible for carrying through the arrangements which resulted in the force arriving undetected and with absolute accuracy at the appointed destination, and for their safe return to this country.

Throughout the operation his bearing, skill and obvious ability could not but give confidence to all who came in contact with him.

So far as the Military Commanders were concerned there could not have been a more easy person to work with and this comment applies with equal force to the captains of the other destroyers forming the 6th Flotilla.

(Signed) J.C. HAYDON,
Brigadier,
Commanding Special Service Brigade.

ANNEXURE
CONSOLIDATED RESULTS OF OPERATION "CLAYMORE"
4th March, 1941

I. *Shipping destroyed and sunk.*

Sunk by	Ship	Tonnage	Flag
H.M.S. SOMALI	Armed Trawler KREBS	300	German
H.M.S. TARTAR	HAMBURG	9,780	"
	PASAJES	1,996	"
H.M.S. TARTAR (after partial destruction by naval demolition party).	FELIX HEUMANN	2,468	"
H.M.S. BEDOUIN	MIRA	1,152	Norwegian
Naval Demolition Parties	EILENAU	1,404	German
	RISSEN	250	"
	ANDO	300	"
	GROTTO	200	"
R.E. Demolition Parties	BERNHARDT SCHULTZE	1,500	
		19,350 tons	

2. *Factories destroyed.*

Stamsund	Henningsvaer	Svolvaer	Brettesnes
Lofotens Cod Boiling Plant.	Allen & Hanbury[12]	Cuba } Herring	Oil and fish meal factory.
	Johannes Malnes [12]	Silda } oil.	Cod meal factory.
Møller Medicinal Oil	Aarseather Bros.[12]		
Yttervicks Cod Meal	Renneberg[12]		
Blix Cod Oil	Christiansen[12]		
Vagle Cod Oil.	Linon Seleskap[12]		
	Clement Johnson[12]		
	Electric Light Plant		
	Henningsvaer Oil Feeding Stuffs.		

3. *Oil Tanks and approximate total of oil destroyed.*

Stamsund	Henningsvaer	Svolvaer	Brettesnes
Kerosene Tanks. Oil Tanks.	Hendnksen Paraffin Tank. S. Bang Oil Tanks.	Oil Tanks. Oil Tanks at Klofterhl.	Oil Tanks.

Approximate total = 800,000 gallons.

4. Quisling supporters captured   12

5. Enemy subjects captured:
   - (*a*) Naval   7
   - (*b*) Army   3
   - (*c*) Air Force   15
   - (*d*) Merchant Navy   172
   - (*e*) Civilians   14

(f) S.S. Police	2
	= 213
Total Prisoners	<u>225</u>

Footnotes:

¹ *Operation "Claymore" – the destruction of fish oil plants in the Ports of Stamsund, Henninigsvaer, Svolvaer and Brettesnes in the Lofoten Islands, the arrest of local supporters of the Quisling party, the capture of enemy personnel in the ports, the evacuation of recruits for the Free Norwegian Forces, and the destruction or capture of enemy ships and of Norwegian vessels found to be working for the Germans.*

² *D/F beacon – an aid to navigation.*

³ *Zenit flight – a daily meteorological flight flown by the Germans.*

⁴ *Wind force 3 – gentle breeze of 7-10 knots; sea 24 – slight sea, moderate average length swell.*

⁵ *Sea 10 to 20 – smooth to slight sea with no swell.*

⁶ *For positions of Port A (Stamsund), Port B (Henningsvaer), Port X (Svolvaer), and Port Y (Brettesnes), see Plan 2.*

⁷ *V/S – visual signal.*

⁸ *A L C – Assault Landing Craft.*

⁹ *S.L.C. – Support Landing Craft.*

¹⁰ *A.L.C. – Landing craft for landing troops.*

¹¹ *M.L.C. – Landing craft for mechanised vehicles.*

¹² *Boiling Plant.*

ADMIRAL SIR JOHN C. TOVEY'S DESPATCH ON RAID ON MILITARY AND ECONOMIC OBJECTIVES IN THE VICINITY OF VAAGSO ISLAND (NORWAY)

27 DECEMBER 1941

RAID ON MILITARY AND ECONOMIC OBJECTIVES IN THE VICINITY OF VAAGSO ISLAND

The following Despatch was submitted to the Lords Commissioners of the Admiralty on the 7th January, 1942, by Admiral Sir JOHN C. TOVEY, K.C.B., D.S.O., Commander-in-Chief, Home Fleet.

Home Fleet.
7th January, 1942.

Be pleased to lay before Their Lordships the attached report on Operation "Archery."

2. The operation was well conceived, planned and rehearsed with skill and thoroughness, and executed with great efficiency, precision and boldness. Though a minor operation, it affords a fine example of smooth and effective co-operation between the three Services and reflects great credit on Rear-Admiral H.M. Burrough, C.B., Brigadier J.C. Haydon, D.S.O., O.B.E., and all officers, ratings and ranks taking part.

3. The co-operation of the aircraft of Coastal and Bomber Commands was most effective. The operation could not have proceeded without it.

(Signed) JACK C. TOVEY,
Admiral,
Commander-in-Chief.

From: THE NAVAL AND MILITARY COMMANDERS, OPERATION "ARCHERY."

Date: 2nd January, 1942.

To: THE COMMANDER-IN-CHIEF, HOME FLEET.

The following report, by the Naval and Military Commanders, on Operation "Archery" which was carried out on Saturday, 27th December, 1941, is forwarded.

2. The intention of Operation "Archery" was to carry out a raid on military and economic objectives in the vicinity of Vaagso Island with the object of harassing the coastal defences of S.W. Norway and diverting the attention of the enemy Naval and Air Forces from Operation "Anklet."[1]

Planning.

3. The Naval and Military Commanders were appointed on 6th December, 1941, which gave three weeks to plan and rehearse the operation. This is considered to be the absolute minimum time required. At least two full rehearsals should take place to allow timing and communications to be perfected. Weather conditions frequently make rehearsals impossible for days on end and this must be allowed for in the programme.

4. After the preliminary meeting between the Force Commanders and the Air Adviser to the Chief of Combined Operations, the plan was drawn up in London. It is strongly recommended that this procedure be followed in future as the facilities for obtaining the latest intelligence and information of all kinds are so much better than those elsewhere.

Composition of the Force.

5. (*a*) *Naval.*
H.M.S. KENYA (Rear Admiral Commanding, I0th Cruiser Squadron – Naval Commander).
H.M.S. ONSLOW (Captain (D), I7th Destroyer Flotilla).
H.M.S. ORIBI.
H.M.S. OFFA.
H.M.S. CHIDDINGFOLD.
H.M.S. PRINCE CHARLES.
H.M.S. PRINCE LEOPOLD.
H.M. Submarine TUNA.[2]

(*b*) *Military.*
Operational Headquarters, Special Service Brigade.
Detachment of the Special Service Brigade Signal Section.
All ranks of No. 3 Commando.
Two Troops (less one Section) of No. 2 Commando.
An R.A.M.C. detachment from No. 4 Commando.

An R.E. detachment from No. 6 Commando.
Troops of the Royal Norwegian Army.
Officers from the War Office (M.I.9).
A Press Unit of correspondents and photographers.
Total Military Personnel: 5I officers, 525 Other Ranks.

(*c*) *Air Force.*
Ten Hampdens of 50 Squadron (for smoke laying and bombing).
Blenheims   } Fighter
Beaufighters   } protection.
I9 Blenheims of Bomber Command (for bombing diversion).

Rehearsal.

6. The Naval Force, with the exception of ONSLOW and CHIDDINGFOLD, assembled at Scapa Flow by I5th December, when embarkation of the Military was completed. A programme of rehearsals followed.

7. The Force proceeded from Scapa at 2II5/24th December arriving at Sullom Voe at I330/25th December. Heavy weather was encountered on passage and on arrival both PRINCE CHARLES and PRINCE LEOPOLD discovered and reported various defects including compartments forward flooded to a depth of about fourteen feet.

8. In order to allow time to make PRINCE CHARLES and PRINCE LEOPOLD as seaworthy as possible, and in view of the latest meteorological reports it was decided at I6I5 to postpone the operation for 24 hours.

9. All ships had topped up with fuel and all repairs had been completed by I400/26th December. The weather forecast was far more promising and it was therefore decided to sail the Force at I600 that day to carry out Operation "Archery" at dawn, 27th December, I94I.

The Naval Approach.

I0. The passage across the North Sea commenced in bad weather but, as anticipated, the weather rapidly improved as the Force proceeded to the eastward and conditions were perfect on arrival off the Norwegian coast.

II. Position by the landfall, which was made exactly as planned, was confirmed on sighting the mark submarine TUNA in the position ordered. She was passed at 0739, one minute late on planned time.

I2. The Force entered Vaagsfiord[3] on time apparently unobserved and it seems possible that the look-out post at Hovdenoes was not manned. KENYA moved over to the southern side of the fiord while CHIDDINGFOLD led PRINCE CHARLES and PRINCE LEOPOLD to the bay south of Hollevik as planned. ONSLOW closed on KENYA'S starboard quarter and OFFA closed astern of KENYA. ORIBI remained near the entrance of the fiord to cover the Force from the west.

The Bombardment.

I3. Hampden aircraft[4] timed their arrival in the area perfectly, keeping all the attention well up-fiord and drawing the fire of four or five light A.A. guns.

I4. At 0842 PRINCE CHARLES made the signal indicating that Assault Landing Craft were formed up and moving ahead. KENYA was moving ahead slowly and at 0848, just before the line of fire opened, star-shell were fired to burst over Maaloy Island. These were bursting and illuminating the point of aim on the island when, half a minute later, the line of fire opened and the bombardment commenced, ONSLOW and OFFA joining in as soon as clear.

I5. The battery on Rugsundo which had already been bombed by Hampden aircraft opened fire on KENYA at 0856. It was erratic and the rate of fire low, but nevertheless proved a great nuisance throughout our stay. The guns were thought to be smaller than 5.I-inch and were more probably about 4.7-inch. On bursting, the shell gave off a purple smoke.

I6. At 0857¾ the "cease bombardment" signal was made by the Military in the Assault Landing Craft now rapidly approaching their objectives. The Naval bombardment of Maaloy Island thus came to an end and from reports received from the Military who landed on the island, there is no doubt whatsoever that it had been completely successful.

I7. At 0858 KENYA, having changed over to full charges, opened fire on Rugsundo. After 2½ minutes the enemy guns were silenced. The smoke bombs, dropped by the Hampdens near Rugsundo, were by now effective and gave cover to our ships in the fiord.

Smoke Laying by Aircraft.

I8. At 0858½ on a signal from KENYA, seven Hampden aircraft, showing great skill and dash, came in at very low altitudes to drop their smoke bombs. These were placed with great precision on Maaloy Island, and as a result the landing there was unopposed. The bombs were dropped on a front of approximately 250 yards, and as there was practically no wind, gave a screen of ideal density in which visibility was some I5-20 yards.

I9. The smoke bombs dropped at the landing place in South Vaagso were only 50 yards out of the desired position, but one of them most unfortunately struck a landing craft setting it alight and causing some 20 casualties from burns.

20. Despite this serious accident it is considered that these bombs were of great value, for they enabled the troops to be put ashore with few casualties from the automatic weapons which were bringing fire to bear on the landing place, and which might have inflicted even heavier losses had they been given a clear and unimpeded view of their targets.

2I. It must here be noted that the aircraft which dropped the bombs at South Vaagso appeared to be on fire and not properly under control. It was almost certainly the Hampden bomber which later fell into the sea near the entrance to Vaagsfiord. If this was so, then the degree of accuracy achieved in placing of the bombs must have been the result of a very gallant attempt on the part of the crew of the aircraft to carry out in full their allotted task's. PRINCE LEOPOLD proceeded to the rescue, but unfortunately only one of the three members of the crew picked up, survived.

22. One Hampden bomber which overshot the target attacked and silenced positions in the area with machine gun fire

23. It is regretted that one other Hampden failed to return from this operation.

24. Of the three Hampden bombers detailed to attack the Rugsundo battery, one had to return with engine trouble, but the other two carried out an attack, the results of which could not be observed from KENYA but which were apparently very successful.

Military Operations.

25. For the purpose of the operation, the Military Forces set out in paragraph 5(*b*) were organised into the Operational Headquarters which remained throughout in the Flagship KENYA, with the Brigade Commander in close touch with the Naval Commander on the bridge, and the troops who were put ashore in Assault Landing Craft from KENYA, PRINCE CHARLES and PRINCE LEOPOLD and in the ship's boats from ORIBI.

The Forces ashore were divided into five Groups for purposes which will become clear in the course of this report.

General Tasks of each Group (see sketch map attached) [not in fact published – Ed.]

26. The purpose of Group I was to land near Hollevik and clear the Halnoesvik area where a German gun had been reported. Having accomplished this task Group I was to move along the coastal road to South Vaagso and form a reserve for Group 2 unless given other orders.

Group 2, which was to be put ashore immediately south west of South Vaagso, was to attack the town itself and carry out a number of Military and industrial tasks.

Group 3 was to assault the Island of Maaloy.

Group 4 was retained as a floating reserve in the hands of the Military Commander of the Force.

Group 5 was to be landed from a destroyer on the western shore of Ulvesund in order to cut communications between South and North Vaagso and to send a fighting patrol into the latter village.

The Landings.

27. At 0839 PRINCE CHARLES and PRINCE LEOPOLD lowered all landing craft which moved off in formation about three minutes later. In little more than five minutes No. I Group was ashore at Halnoesvik and the landing craft of Nos. 2 and 3 Groups were moving towards the headland just south of Halnoesvik Village.

28. Just before the landing craft came into view of the enemy defences in South Vaagso and Maaloy Island, KENYA opened fire. The Naval bombardment was extremely accurate and most effective, and Lieutenant-Colonel J.F. Durnford-Slater,

who was in command of Group 2 and the Senior Officer proceeding ashore, was able to let the landing craft of Groups 2 and 3 approach to within 100 yards of their landing places before sending up the "cease bombardment"" signal. KENYA signalled the Hampden aircraft who then came in at very low altitudes to drop their smoke bombs. As a result of these bombs Group 3 completed their landing unopposed and the volume of fire brought to bear on Group 2 was considerably reduced.

The Operations Ashore.

29. Groups Nos. 2 and 3 landed almost simultaneously, and from that time onwards the sequence of events was as follows:-

30. Group I cleared the area and village of Halnoesvik very rapidly and signalled the Headquarters Ship for instructions. They were at once ordered to move along the coastal road and to come into reserve at Lieutenant-Colonel J.F. Durnford-Slater's Headquarters which were situated near Group 2's landing place. This signal was made at 0950.

31. Group 3 very quickly gained control of Maaloy Island, where those enemy troops who had not been killed by the Naval bombardment were for the most part demoralised and dazed by its effect, and quickly surrendered. At 0920 Major J.M.T.F. Churchill was able to signal that all guns on the island were in our hands and four minutes later he reported that the whole area was under control. ORIBI, carrying Group 5 and followed by ONSLOW, moved past Maaloy some I0 minutes later, as soon as the smoke had cleared sufficiently for them to do so, and entered Ulvesund.

32. Group 2, from the start, encountered very stiff opposition, both from, German Infantry who fought to the last man in the buildings, in which they were established, and from snipers, armed often with automatic rifles, who took up positions on the hillside west of the town where they were very difficult to locate owing to the excellent natural cover. It must be emphasised that the opposition in South Vaagso was severe in degree and skilful in quality. It appears from the interrogation of prisoners that the garrison had been fortuitously augmented by a detachment who had been moved into the town for Christmas but, however that may be, there is no doubt that the fighting spirit, marksmanship and efficiency of the enemy in this area was of a high order.

33. At I020 Group 5 were landed just south of the village of North Vaagso. They cratered the coast road between North and South Vaagso and were able to capture a number of prisoners who had escaped ashore from ships attacked by ORIBI and ONSLOW. A fighting patrol, which was sent forward into North Vaagso directly the Group had landed, collected the chief Quisling, took over the telephone exchange and, before leaving, wrecked the instruments.

34. In the meanwhile Group 3 had been instructed (0925) to send a party by landing craft to destroy the herring oil factory at Mortenes, and at I0I5 Captain A.S. Ronald landed with his troops in the area of the factory and completed its destruction without meeting opposition.

35. From I000 hours onwards, the situation became confused in South Vaagso, where Group 2 were encountering strong opposition in the northern end of the town.

The destruction of communications with the forward troops rendered control by the Flagship difficult.

36. By l020 hours the whole of Group 4 had been despatched to the assistance of Group 2,and were committed on the left flank.

37. By l030 hours house-to-house fighting in the centre and northern end of the town had become bitter, resulting in severe casualties, especially in officers and senior N.C.O.s. Group I arrived from Halnoesvik and was committed in support of No. 4 Troop in the centre. With the authority of Force H.Q., Group 3 on Maaloy Island contacted Group 2, and on request the latter despatched No. 6 Troop.

38. No. 5 Group at North Vaagso were ordered to move south and close on the rear of the enemy in South Vaagso.

39. No. I Troop, (Group 2) secured the landing place, cleared the southern end of the town, capturing a prominent Quisling, and prepared the main demolitions.

40. At l230 hours Lieutenant-Colonel Durnford-Slater, after personally directing operations in the town, reported to Force Headquarters that resistance was nearly overcome and that demolitions were in progress.

4l. As the majority of the industrial targets had been destroyed and as landing craft were becoming dispersed in ferrying wounded and Norwegian volunteers out to the ships and might take some time to reorganise for withdrawal purposes, the Military Commander, in agreement with the Naval Commander, ordered re-embarkation at l250 hours.

42. The withdrawal of all groups was carried out without opposition. The Firda factory, which was the last of the industrial targets, and the Seternes Lighthouse were demolished before the troops re-embarked.

43. Group 5, who had been delayed in their southward move along the coast road by the shelling of beached merchant shipping in Ulvesund, were ordered to re-embark in ORIBI to the north of South Vaagso.

44. At l408 hours Lieutenant-Colonel Durnford-Slater reported that all troops had left the shore, and returned himself in the last landing craft.

45. The re-embarkation had been completed and all landing craft hoisted by l434.

46. In considering the course of the operation particular attention is drawn to the following factors which both had important bearings on the course of the fighting: in the first place, the hampering effect of the desire to comply strictly with the orders which had been issued to avoid all possible damage to Norwegian property; and in the second place, the conflicting claims of the comparatively short time limit imposed by the whole nature of the operation, and of the restrictions on speed which are inherent in all street fighting but particularly when it is conducted against determined opposition.

47. It here requires mention that the opposition was overcome, and all the demolition tasks completed, often under heavy enemy fire, well within the time limits laid down and that such results could not possibly have been obtained had it not been for the personal leadership of Lieutenant-Colonel J.F. Durnford-Slater, and for the sense of discipline, the initiative and courage that was shown time and again by junior leaders, both officers and N.C.O.s.

Tasks Completed.

48. One hundred and two prisoners were captured, comprising 7 officers (I Army and 6 Merchant Navy), 9I ratings and other ranks (40 Army, I5 Navy and 36 Merchant Seamen), and 4 Norwegian "Quislings". In addition 77 Norwegian volunteers were embarked. It is estimated that at least I50 Germans were killed in South Vaagso and Maaloy by Naval, Army and R.A F. Forces in the course of the operation.

49. The tasks executed on shore were as follows:-

-    (i)   All German Offices were burnt or demolished.
-   (ii)   The W/T Station and mast were destroyed.
- (iii)   The German car and lorry garage was destroyed.
-   (iv)   One German tank of I0 to I5 tons was entirely destroyed.
-    (v)   Four coast defence guns and one anti-aircraft gun on Maaloy Island were blown up.
-   (vi)   The petrol tanks on Maaloy Island were cut by explosives.
- (vii)   The ammunition store on Maaloy Island was demolished.
- (viii)   The German barracks and Headquarters on Maaloy Island were burnt out by the initial Naval bombardment.
-   (ix)   A searchlight and generator were blown up on Maaloy Island.
-    (x)   A beach mine store was destroyed.
-   (xi)   A telephone cable hut was destroyed.
- (xii)   All huts used as billets by German soldiers, both in South Vaagso and Maaloy were burnt down.
- (xiii)   The Ulvesund Hotel, entirely occupied by German soldiers and held as a strong point, was burnt down.
- (xiv)   The mechanism of Seternes Lighthouse was destroyed.
-   (xv)   The road was cratered between North and South Vaagso.
- (xvi)   The telephone exchange at Rodberg was taken over and the apparatus smashed.
- (xvii)   The building and plant of the main canning factory in South Vaagso were entirely destroyed by explosives.
- (xviii) The herring oil factory at Mortenes was entirely destroyed by explosives and fire.
- (xix)   The Firda factory was set on fire and left blazing.
-   (xx)   A smaller canning factory and herring oil factory were set on fire, and the plant damaged by explosives (not yet confirmed).

Naval and Air Operations – 0900-I445.

50. During this period PRINCE CHARLES, PRINCE LEOPOLD and CHIDDINGFOLD had moved across to Slaaken Bay on the south side of the fiord to obtain cover in accordance with the pre-arranged plan.

5I. The first sortie of Blenheims arrived shortly before 0930 while ORIBI and ONSLOW were taking up position to enter Ulvesund but it was not possible to establish reliable R/T[5] communication with them. (Maaloy Island was now in our hands but the smoke was still too thick for the destroyers to pass through Maaloysund.)

52. Two minutes later, at 0932, Rugsundo Battery re-opened fire on KENYA who hotly engaged with "A" and "B" turrets and again silenced the guns which did not re-open fire until I308.

53. By 0930 the smoke screen across the Rugsundo line of fire was thinning and CHIDDINGFOLD was ordered to reinforce with smoke floats and funnel smoke, while moving fast. She did this well and also engaged the battery with a few salvos.

54. At 0945 Maaloysund was sufficiently clear for the destroyers to proceed. ORIBI followed by ONSLOW entered Ulvesund.

55. The first enemy aircraft appeared at I005, when two ME. 109s came in and immediately engaged two of our Blenheims one of which was shot down two minutes later. This Blenheim would possibly not have been lost, and the mortality among German aircraft, later in the day, would probably have been higher, if efficient R/T communication between ship and aircraft could have been established and maintained.

56. Quite apart from the need for efficient communication it was apparent that two R.A.F. officers should be carried in the Headquarters Ship with the sole duties of concentrating on the air situation and directing the fighters. The ideal would be to have officers personally known to the fighter pilots and for these officers to have carried out rehearsals from the Headquarters Ship.

57. KENYA fired occasional salvos at Rugsundo Battery, to check gun range and to discourage any attempt to get their guns functioning again.

58. The second sortie (Beaufighters) arrived at I0I5 and about 25 minutes later was in pursuit of the first two enemy bombers – two JU.88s – to put in an appearance. These two aircraft never got within range of KENYA'S guns. Only intermittent R/T communication could be established with the Beaufighters.

59. At II00 KENYA opened fire, at long range, on two ME. I09s who quickly turned away and disappeared to the south.

60. During this period the position regarding merchant shipping in Ulvesund had not been clarified so it was decided to send in KENYA'S motor dinghy, with Lieutenant J.N. Kempton, R.N., in charge, to investigate and report. After entering Maaloysund this boat was heavily fired upon, caught fire and burnt out. The crew were rescued by a Support Landing Craft.

6I. About noon, a small number of enemy bombers were sighted to the northwards but no attack developed at this stage.

62. During the period since the bombardment of Maaloy Island had been completed. OFFA had been protecting the Force from the west, and shortly after noon reported a merchant ship and Armed Trawler escort proceeding to Vaagsfiord from the north. She was ordered to capture if possible and CHIDDINGFOLD ordered to support her. Unfortunately, in spite of all efforts, the merchant ship – S.S. ANHALT – beached herself and the escort vessel endeavoured to escape.

63. OFFA proceeded to chase and engage the Armed Trawler DONNER, securing several hits. The crew abandoned ship but the vessel continued to steam out to sea at

I0 knots. OFFA proceeded alongside the trawler and finding that she had insufficient fuel for the return passage to the U.K. under a prize crew, destroyed her and then picked up survivors from her crew.

64. During this period CHIDDINGFOLD had closed the merchant ship ANHALT and, using loud hailer, ordered the crew, in German, to bring their boats alongside. They were told that if the order was disobeyed they would be fired on. The boats disregarded the warning and pulled for the shore, only a few yards distant. CHIDDINGFOLD immediately opened fire and sank one boat. The other, although hit, succeeded in escaping inshore while CHIDDINGFOLD was engaged with enemy aircraft.

65. It was at this time, I236, that all ships became engaged with enemy bombers. Several formations, generally consisting of two or three Heinkels, were driven off and their bombs dropped wide. One H.E.III was destroyed.

66. These raids continued until about I300 and shortly afterwards Rugsundo Battery re-opened fire. KENYA immediately replied from "X" and "Y" turrets and with 4-inch. KENYA was hit by one round on the armour belt and a few minutes later a near miss abreast the port torpedo tubes slightly wounded one rating. At I3I7 KENYA received a hit which burst and holed her about ten feet above the water line abreast the bridge. Rugsundo Battery was then finally silenced.

ONSLOW and ORIBI in Ulvesund.

67. Having received the signal that Maaloy Island was in our hands and Maaloysund clear, the destroyers passed through the narrows and entered Ulvesund at 094I. A good deal of light fire was directed at the ships and ORIBI sustained three minor casualties.

68. When clear of the smoke, the German S.S. REGMAR EDZARD FRITZEN, S.S. NORMAR, and Armed Trawler FOHN were observed proceeding so as to beach themselves in the small bay immediately to the north of Brandhaunnes Point. Shots were fired across their bows and their upper decks were swept with Oerlikon fire but they had gained sufficient time to succeed in their project.

69. ORIBI proceeded up Ulvesund and landed Group 5 at I007. Two ME.109s were in the vicinity one of which attacked ORIBI with cannon fire but obtained no hits.

70. ORIBI and ONSLOW then proceeded to destroy the three ships referred to in paragraph 68, the Dutch Schuyt EISNER which had also been abandoned, and another German merchant ship, the ANITA L.M. RUSS, with a tug in company, which at this time had entered Ulvesund apparently unaware that a raid was in progress.

7I. ORIBI after an engagement with two low flying ME. 109s, re-embarked the remainder of Group 5 with their prisoners, while both destroyers gave supporting fire and dealt with snipers who were troublesome during the re-embarkation. On completion of their tasks they rejoined the Force at Vaagsfiord at I356 and then engaged Rugsundo to keep that battery quiet while KENYA was re-embarking her troops. CHIDDINGFOLD also laid a smoke screen to mask it. All troops having been re-embarked the Force commenced to withdraw at I445.

Bombing Diversions.

72. At 1202 13 Blenheims from No. 114 Squadron, each carrying four 250-lb. G.P. bombs and some 4-lb. incendiaries attacked from a height of 250 feet the aerodrome at Herdla.[6] Many hits were observed on the timber runways and an enemy fighter was seen to turn over while taxying. P.R.U.[7] photographs taken immediately after the attack confirmed craters on the aerodrome.

73. It is to be regretted that two Blenheims were lost from this squadron due to a collision after bombing; both aircraft fell into the sea. It is probable that this happened because one of them was hit by flak.

74. Six Blenheims from No. 110 Squadron, each armed with two 500-lb. bombs left Lossiemouth at 0850 to patrol off the Norwegian coast southwards from Obrestad. After keeping together to a point two miles south west of Eigeroe the leader and one other aircraft carried out an apparently successful attack on a single ship of 1,500 tons, while the remaining four proceeded towards a convoy observed four miles further south.

75. None of the four aircraft which turned south to attack the convoy have returned to base, but a number of explosions were seen round the convoy and one ship was observed to be sinking rapidly with her stern well out of the water. There is no evidence to show how these four aircraft became casualties, but one was seen to make a good landing in the sea with the port engine on fire, while another crashed into the sea after being attacked by a fighter.

Fighter Protection.

76. Fighter protection over the Force was provided from 0928 until 1615 by Blenheim and Beaufighter aircraft of 404, 254, 235, 236 and 248 Squadrons operating from Wick and Sumburgh aerodromes. Five sorties were made, and with the exception of the fourth, enemy aircraft were encountered by each sortie and a satisfactory toll taken of them, for the loss of 2 Blenheims and 2 Beaufighters.

The Naval Withdrawal.

77. The destroyers were ordered to proceed out of the fiord and form a screen for the Assault Ships and KENYA, who left last. KENYA stopped off Hovdenoes Point and fired 15 rounds of 6-inch, at point blank range, at the Merchant Ship ANHALT and she was left aground and burning fiercely.

78. A few minutes later, at about 1500, when ships had just cleared the fiord, a formation of Heinkel bombers came in to attack. These aircraft were hotly engaged by KENYA and destroyers with the result that the formation broke up and their sticks of bombs fell wide.

79. After the escort of Beaufighters had had to return to base at 1600 single aircraft were driven off by the Force in the dusk and bright moonlight. When darkness fell a large alteration of course was made and the Force arrived at Scapa, without further incident, at 1600, 28th December, 1941.

(*Signed*) J.C. HAYDON,
Brigadier.
H.M. BURROUGH,
Rear Admiral.

Footnotes

[1] *Operation "Anklet" was a longer term operation in the Lofoten Islands.*

[2] *KENYA acted as H.Q. Ship and carried Brigade Operational H.Q.*
ONSLOW, ORIBI, OFFA and CHIDDINGFOLD – Destroyers.
PRINCE CHARLES and PRINCE LEOPOLD – Infantry Assault Ships, later
known as "Landing Ships, Infantry (Small)".

[3] *Vaagso lies 2½ miles up this fiord, whose entrance is less than half a mile*
wide.

[4] *The aircraft operated from bases on the N.E. coast of Scotland, a distance of*
approximately 300 miles.

[5] *R/.T. = radio telephone.*

[6] *Herdla – the nearest enemy aerodrome, some 80 miles south of Vaagso.*

[7] *P.R.U. – Photographic Reconnaissance Unit.*

ABBREVIATIONS

A&AEE	Aeroplane and Armament Experimental Establishment
A/A	Anti-aircraft
A/S	Anti-submarine
A/T (baffle)	Anti-torpedo
ALC	Assault Landing Craft
ASIS	Armament Supply Issuing Ships
Bn, Bns, Btn	Battalion
CB	Companion of the Order of Bath
CBE	Commander of the Most Excellent Order of the British Empire
Cdr	Commander
CIGS	Chief of the Imperial General Staff
C-in-C	Commander-in-Chief
CMG	Companion of the Most Distinguished Order of Saint Michael and Saint George
D/F	Direction Finder/Direction Finding
DA	Deputy Adjutant
DC	Depth Charge
DSC	Distinguished Service Cross
DSO	Distinguished Service Order
FAA	Fleet Air Arm
GCB	Knight Grand Cross of The Most Honourable Order of the Bath
GCVO	Knight Grand Cross of The Royal Victorian Order
GOC	General Officer Commanding
GOC-in-C	General Officer Commanding-in-Chief
GP bombs	General Purpose bombs
GSO	General Staff Officer
GSO1	General Staff Officer, Grade 1
GSOI	General Staff Officer, Intelligence
GP bombs	General Purpose bombs
HA	Heavy Artillery
HBM	His Britannic Majesty

HDA	Harbour Defence Asdic
HE	High Explosive
HF	High Frequency
HM	His Majesty
HMHS	His Majesty's Hospital Ship
HMS	His Majesty's Ship
HQ	Headquarters
KBE	Knight Commander of the Most Excellent Order of the British Empire
KCB	Knight Commander of the Most Honourable Order of the Bath
KRRC	King's Royal Rifle Corps
LA (battery)	Light Artillery
MC	Military Cross
MLC	Minor Landing Craft
MNBDO	Mobile Naval Base Defence Organisation
MV	Motor Vessel
OBE	Officer of the Most Excellent Order of the British Empire
OR	Other Rank(s)
Pdr/pr	Pounder
PRU	Photographic Reconnaissance Unit
QMG	Quartermaster General
RA	Royal Artillery
RAF	Royal Air Force
RAMC	Royal Army Medical Corps
RDF	Radio Direction Finding (Radar)
RE	Royal Engineers
RM	Royal Marines
RN	Royal Navy
RNR	Royal Naval Reserve
RNVR	Royal Navy Volunteer Reserve
RT, R/T	Receiver-Transmitter/Radio Transmitter/Radio Telephony
S/M	Submarine
SLC	Support Landing Craft
TSR	Torpedo/Spotter/Reconnaissance
V/S	Visual Sighting
W/T	Wireless Telegraphy/Wireless Telephony

INDEX OF PERSONS

Index of Naval, Military and Air Units